MW00773488

FOUND

OF

PERSONALITY

FOUNDATIONS OF PERSONALITY

Combining Elements, Crosses, and Houses
with Jungian Psychological Concepts
in Horoscope Interpretation

Karen Hamaker-Zondag

SAMUEL WEISER, INC.

York Beach, Maine

Revised edition published in one volume in 1994 by
Samuel Weiser, Inc.
Box 612
York Beach, Maine 03910-0612

99 98 97 96 95 94
9 8 7 6 5 4 3 2 1

Library of Congress Cataloging-in-Publication Data
Hamaker-Zondag, Karen.
      [Elementen en kruizen als basis van de horoscoop. English]
      [Aard en Achtergrond van de Huizen. English]
      Foundations of personality : combining elements, crosses, and houses with Jungian
psychological concepts / by Karen Hamaker-Zondag.
            p.   cm.
      Previously published : Elements & crosses as the basis of the horoscope. The houses and
personality development.
      Includes bibliographical references and index.
      1. Astrology and psychology.   2. Horoscopes.   3. Personality—miscellanea.
I. Title.
BF1729.P8H3613   1994
133.5'4—dc20   94-17757
                                                                              CIP
ISBN 0-87728-808-9
EB

This book was previously published as two separate volumes—*Elements & Crosses as the Basis
of the Horoscope* and *The Houses and Personality Development.*

Cover illustration is "Zodiacal Clock, Padua" courtesy of Images Colour Library Limited,
London. Used by permission.

Typeset in Baskerville

Printed in the United States of America

Elements & Crosses
as the Basis of the Horoscope

Karen Hamaker-Zondag

SAMUEL WEISER, INC.

York Beach, Maine

To my colleagues
in the Astrological Foundation *ARCTURUS*

TABLE OF CONTENTS

LIST OF CHARTS

INTRODUCTION

Following the appearance of my book *Astro-Psychology*, many people asked if I would write a handbook elaborating its ideas and showing how they could be carried out in practice. I have gladly fulfilled that request. In this first volume, *Elements and Crosses as the Basis of the Horoscope*, I am introducing a concept that has proven to be an invaluable basis for horoscope interpretation. In the next three volumes of this series, I will continue to expand on this basis.

Many astrological reference books supply the reader with a definition of the planets in the signs, the aspects, etc., and are otherwise quite helpful; yet for all sorts of practical reasons they tend to omit any guidelines for combining the unique personal information symbolized by the horoscope itself. Therefore, it often remains unclear why a certain aspect has a strong effect in one horoscope while in another that same aspect may seem to do very little. Before analyzing a horoscope using information from reference books, we need to build a framework which forms a basis for all the factors that are to be interpreted.

In my opinion, astrological literature has paid too little attention to the construction of such a framework. Because of this lack, we run into a number of contradictions, and it is difficult to ascertain what conditions actually will appear in the person's life. After much investigation and many comparisons with analytical

Sign	Symbol	Day Ruler Night Ruler		Element	Cross
Aries	♈	Mars Pluto	♂ ♇	Fire	Cardinal
Taurus	♉	Venus —	♀	Earth	Fixed
Gemini	♊	Mercury —	☿	Air	Mutable
Cancer	♋	Moon —	☽	Water	Cardinal
Leo	♌	Sun —	☉	Fire	Fixed
Virgo	♍	Mercury —	☿	Earth	Mutable
Libra	♎	Venus —	♀	Air	Cardinal
Scorpio	♏	Pluto Mars	♇ ♂	Water	Fixed
Sagittarius	♐	Jupiter Neptune	♃ ♆	Fire	Mutable
Capricorn	♑	Saturn Uranus	♄ ♅	Earth	Cardinal
Aquarius	♒	Uranus Saturn	♅ ♄	Air	Fixed
Pisces	♓	Neptune Jupiter	♆ ♃	Water	Mutable

psychology, I have seen that the symbolism, background, and function of both the elements and the crosses—separately and in relationship to one another—serve as a basis for interpreting the horoscope. If astrologers are to use this system, the basis must be completely practical in its application. This book is, in fact, a continuation and more profound study of my theoretical *Astro-Psychology*. I have tried to explain things so that one can begin working without having read my first book. Naturally, I assume the reader has some acquaintance with the meanings of the signs and the houses, thereby needless repetition can be avoided. To clarify the symbols and signs used in the charts for my American readers, see the table provided.

I owe many thanks to Maggie Schors, Fred Molenberg, and my husband Hans for their many sensible comments about the original manuscript; the text was written with enthusiasm, and thanks to them it became much more readable.

Amsterdam, June, 1983

CHAPTER ONE

THE BASIS OF THE HOROSCOPE

1. TOTALITY OF THE PSYCHE

A concept central to psychology is that of "psychic totality," which includes both the conscious and unconscious sides of our psyche. Both sides are complementary in proportion; they are opposite and yet complete each other in all respects. Man identifies, however, only with the conscious part of his psyche, the part that says "I," seldom able to realize the important role his personal and collective unconscious plays. Every moment of the day the unconscious forces itself upon him in countless ways, whether convenient or not. Sometimes it manifests as a "Freudian slip" which makes it clear that other factors are alive in him, or perhaps it expresses as an inexplicable but especially helpful brainstorm or suggestion that comes from within.

Immanuel Kant considered the question of whether man had an unconscious, although he used other words for it. In *Anthropology* he wrote:

> ...the area of sensations and sense impressions in man (and also in animals), of which we are not aware (although undoubtedly we can affirm its existence), is unfathomable; this is the area of "obscure" images. With its opposite, the area of "lucid" images, it shares but very few points of contact open to the conscious mind. That so few areas of the great map of our mind, as it were, are

> illumined should awaken wonder in us as to our true
> being. A higher power would only need to cry, "Let there
> be light!", and even without the slightest action on
> anyone's part, *half* a world would be shown to him. ...
> since the area of "obscure" images is the largest in man.[1]

It is obvious that Kant meant the same with his "area of obscure or
dark images" as an analytical psychologist does when he speaks of
man's unconscious. That unconscious can never become completely
conscious; only certain portions of it can become clear to man
during the course of his life. Kant also talked about the fact that our
consciousness can reach no more than half of our psyche—half a
world.

We can discover much about the structure of the unconscious
through the study of people's behavior, associations, and emotions.
Through countless forms of unconscious expression (dreams,
fantasies, slips of the tongue, etc.) we can gradually form an idea of
its structure and operation. We will still be unable to grasp it with
our conscious minds, as the unconscious functions completely
independently and autonomously. Goethe once said:

> ...a human being should not stay too rigidly fixed in a
> condition of unconsciousness or ordinary consciousness;
> he must return to the refuge of his unconscious for there
> lie his roots.[2]

Goethe hereby indicated that there is a difference between the
conscious and the unconscious psyche. The unconscious must be
considered in any psychological approach to astrology if we want to
arrive at a balanced and total view. Consciousness allows man to
experience his world, to comprehend and understand, and—in our
Western culture—to adapt to outer reality, to which this side of the
psyche is geared. The unconscious, on the other hand, is geared to
adapting to inner reality.

---

[1]Kant, Immanuel, Anthropologie, par. 5. Citation from: Psychologische Club Zürich:
Die Kulturelle Bedeutung der Komplexen Psychologie. Festschrift zum 60. Geburtstag von C.G. Jung, Berlin, 1935. Teil I: Toni Wolff: Einführung in die Grundlagen
der Komplexen Psychologie, p. 52.

[2]*Ibid*, p. 54. Goethe made this statement to Riemer on August 5, 1810.

A concept such as *consciousness* can give rise to much confusion if not clearly defined. Nowadays, it begins more and more to mean insight or the broadening of insight, and many people think it is very positive to "live consciously" or "to be conscious." In psychology, however, *consciousness* has a distinct meaning which shows little agreement with what most people ordinarily understand by the term. In the latter case perhaps we can better speak of awareness and reserve the term consciousness for psychology. By consciousness Carl Jung understands the following:

> ...the relation of psychic contents to the ego, in so far as this relation is perceived as such by the ego. Relations to the ego that are not perceived as such are unconscious.[3]

The psyche consists of two complementary spheres that show opposite qualities: consciousness and the unconscious. The ego can share in both spheres; all experiences from both the inner and the outer world must go via the ego in order to be perceived. Consciousness is thereby further described by Jung as "...the function or activity which maintains the relation of psychic contents to the ego."[4] The ego he describes as "...a complex of ideas which constitutes the centre of my field of consciousness and appears to possess a high degree of continuity and identity."[5]

Consciousness has the function of relaying information to the ego, which possesses a particular constancy regarding its readiness to consider certain information important and applicable to itself and other information not so important. The ego may not want to see some things consciousness passes on to it. These incidents or ideas are then repressed and disappear from consciousness into the unconscious. Repressed contents can begin to lead their own life there, penetrating the field of consciousness now and then where they deliver painful 'dents' to the ego or may even contribute to correcting an ego that has become too one-sided.

[3] Jung, C.G., *Psychological Types*, Collected Works, Vol 6, Routledge & Kegan Paul, London, 1977, pp. 421-422.

[4] Jacobi, J., *The Psychology of C.G. Jung*, Routledge & Kegan Paul, London, 1973, p. 16.

[5] *Ibid*, p. 16.

Jolande Jacobi already noticed at an early stage the possible confusions around the concept of consciousness and expressed it as follows:

> ...In common parlance 'consciousness' is often used interchangeably with 'thinking', although this is inadmissible, for there is a consciousness of feeling, will, fear, as well as other life phenomena. Nor should the idea of 'life' be equated with 'consciousness', which unfortunately frequently happens. A person who is asleep is alive and yet not conscious. There are different degrees of consciousness. Perceiving something is an act of consciousness, in which, however, the perceived has not as yet been assimilated; it remains as it were passive compared with a conscious, discriminating, understanding, assimilating attitude.[6]

In his textbook *Bewusstsein*, C.A. Meier has elucidated a clear example of the confusion surrounding the term consciousness. I repeat it here in its entirety so as not to remove it from context:

> ...Here we are faced with a paradox. Awareness would be the product of a synthesis between consciousness and the unconscious. This is reminiscent of an expression which has become current in analytical psychology jargon and which often leads to misunderstandings: people used to be fond of saying that somebody was 'very unconscious', meaning with this that such a person solely acts according to conscious motives. But from an analytical viewpoint this means that he does not include his unconscious backgrounds in the discussion so that it is generally correct to say that this person clearly acts according to conscious motives and therefore should be very aware. The object of analytical psychology is, however, to make man also aware of his unconscious motivations and to postpone any decision making until he achieves this clarity in himself. Not until then would such an individual, according to our terminology, really

---

[6]*Ibid*, p. 16.

deserve the predicate 'aware', in other words not until the moment when he has resolved the conflict made conscious in this way and has taken a decision...[7]

2. CONSCIOUSNESS AND THE FOUR ELEMENTS

Although the contents of the human consciousness are infinite, we can order them so they reveal a clear structure and a typical form. That is, one can distinguish between general behavior and certain forms of behavior that are peculiar to a certain group of individuals.[8] These behavior patterns can be reduced to the way one consciously adapts to reality, the specific manner of approaching and comprehending the world. We can distinguish four different elementary processes of consciousness, which show a remarkable similarity with the four elements of astrological tradition, namely:

Sensation: perceiving as such and seeing what the object is like, for instance—hard, sharp, warm, etc. This corresponds to the element earth.

Thinking: asking *what* the perceived object actually is and how it can be incorporated into the existing frame of reference. This corresponds to the element air.

Feeling: experiencing what the perceived object calls forth in the way of desire or aversion, on the grounds of which it is accepted or rejected. For instance: is it pleasurable or not, is it nice or not? This corresponds to the element water.

Intuition: unconscious knowing or "inferring" where the perceived object comes from or how it will evolve further. Often the object is not consciously perceived, but is instead a sort of "sensing" of the background. Jung called this a form of indirect perception. This function corresponds to the element fire.

[7]Meier, C.A., *Bewusstsein*. Erkenntnistheorie und Bewusstsein. Bewusstwerdung bei C.G. Jung, Walter Verlag, Olten, 1975, p. 16.

[8]Wolff, T., *Studien zu C.G. Jungs Psychologie*, Rhein Verlag, Zürich, 1959, p. 81.

In order to show how different functions approach the same information, Jung once gave the following example:[9]

1. *Sensation*: I see that something is red, that it has a certain sheen and sparkle, a certain form and smell.

2. *Thinking*: I recognize this object as a glass filled with red wine.

3. *Feeling*: I judge the whole; I find it extremely pleasing. For a teetotaller it would be a highly repellent object, however.

4. *Intuition*: I suppose that it is a Pommard 1937 and that it could be a Christmas present from my host's friend X.

Concerning intuition, Jung often emphasized that the accuracy of the intuitive type is less than fifty percent in most cases. Whether the intuition is right or not, the essential point is that the intuitive type approaches the phenomena around him in a certain *manner.* This type will continually look behind things without knowing it or without consciously seeing the object or phenomenon as such, while the sensation type will automatically see what the object or phenomenon looks like and how it presents itself. The four functions of consciousness don't say whether the contents are good or bad; primarily, they express a certain way of approaching things with consciousness.

Together all four functions form a complete view of a situation or a complete consideration of an object. Astrologically, this means the four elements combine to form a whole, a totality that theoretically would make it possible to observe, appraise, see through and experience *all* facets of a given object or phenomenon.

Since each individual's consciousness can only have one superior function, one main orientation, on the basis of the four elements we can distinguish four general types. They always remain general types because so many factors come into play, depending upon each individual horoscope. One can speak of types to a greater or lesser degree. Some people may have a conscious orientation or

---

[9]Meier, C.A., *Bewusstsein*. Lehrbuch der Komplexen Psychologie C.G. Jungs. Band III. Walter Verlag, Olten, 1975, p. 133-134.

superior element made up of a combination of two elements or psychological functions, and one of them will always predominate (see Section 4 in this chapter). These general types are of great importance, as they illustrate how a person relates to the world around him, how he experiences, views, and judges it. The following material introduces the main characteristics of the four elements or the four types of functions: fire, earth, air and water.[10]

THE FIRE OR INTUITIVE TYPE

The fire signs, Aries, Leo and Sagittarius, live mainly in a world hidden behind the material existence. Concepts such as *the future, possibility, discovery* and *dynamic* play a large role in the world of the fire type. Life and all of its material and non-material manifestations are seen from the inside out by the fire type, as he intuitively feels how everything is or could be. For him the world is a story full of fantastic possibilities in which he plays an important role.

The person with a strong fire influence is self-centered and therefore makes an egoistic and insensitive impression, a trait of which he is seldom aware. He lives according to his own morals and is faithful to his own ideas as far as they allow him perspectives and possibilities. Routine work may be unbearable, as it kills his spontaneity and constricts his irrepressible activities. Through his rather open, expectant, and sometimes naive attitude, he is receptive to experience, seeking its meaning and possibility. Through this attitude of consciousness, he can acquire deep insights into hidden connections. Concrete facts and objects play no role for him. In daily life, he can be almost helpless in practical affairs because he is always seeing behind things and not the things themselves.

[10]For a more comprehensive and detailed description of the four types the following books are recommended: von Franz, M.-L., & J. Hillman, *Lectures on Jung's Typology*, Spring Verlag, Zürich, 1971; Greene, Liz, *Relating: An astrological guide to living with others on a small planet*, Samuel Weiser, Inc., York Beach, Me., 1977, Chapter 3; Hamaker-Zondag, K.M., *Astro-Psychology*, Aquarian Press, Wellingborough, 1980. Chapter 4; Jung, C.G., *Psychological Types*, Routledge & Kegan Paul, London, 1971. Chapter 10; Whitmont, E.C., *The Symbolic Quest: Basic Concepts of Analytical Psychology*, Princeton University Press, Princeton, 1969, Chapter 8.

THE EARTH OR SENSATION TYPE

The signs Taurus, Virgo and Capricorn react in an exactly opposite manner than the fire signs. If looking behind appearances was central for fire, here perceiving concrete facts themselves forms the central idea. Everything possible is felt out and tested for its concrete value with the senses. Reality and efficiency are concepts that belong to this type. Things that can't be perceived with the senses simply don't exist for the earth type. Earth will have precious little understanding of the fantasy world of the fire signs, a fantasy world that is just as real for the fire type as the earth itself.

The consciousness of the earth type is geared to concrete experience, a reason why so much value is placed on outward beauty: *beautiful* is something that can be perceived concretely and judged accordingly. The fire sign's search for possibility is something that would only give rise to anxiety in an earth sign: the danger for earth is that he might lose all he's built up in the way of material security for something he can't or doesn't want to imagine. Therefore, out of a need for security, the earth type builds for a future that offers a solid, practical basis; he will aim for it with purpose, energy and a tenacious ability to persevere. Because the earth type seeks a foundation in concrete facts and actualities, he runs the danger of missing the essential relationships between things, which his experience can only coordinate with difficulty, if at all. On the other hand, dedication to the concrete and material gives this type an outstanding feeling for form and proportion.

THE AIR OR THINKING TYPE

What earth neglects—namely the connection between facts—is precisely the strong side of the air signs Gemini, Libra, and Aquarius. In this element, the emphasis is on abstract thought, theory and ideas. Consciousness is directed at the most logical, objective approach and assimilation of the things observed or experienced. The air signs gladly discuss their findings with others, being known for their ability to communicate. Through the logical process of thinking and exchange, the air type is often flexible in speech and action, though this flexibility can become so exaggerated that there may be little stability.

Air examines the behavior of those around him as well as his own for logic; thus the air type runs the danger of being too rational in his motives and can appear to be cool and unfeeling. His attempts to force life into a mold of rigid formulas and motives without taking the value of feelings into account can be self-defeating. An emotional approach to things poses difficulties for him, as his feelings can't be rationalized, nor can they be captured in words. His emotional life is his weakest area.

The consciousness of the air type is aimed at combining objects and ideas as logically as possible; this combination is the frame of reference from which he judges how life should be. On the whole, he has no sense of the realistic value of his thoughts and theories; they form reality for him, *his* reality, just as a fantasy world is reality for a fire type. This is why an air type doesn't need to be practical; practicality is a typical earth quality.

THE WATER OR FEELING TYPE

Where air is least at home, we find the water signs Cancer, Scorpio and Pisces developing their greatest capacities. These signs predominantly perceive and evaluate the world in an emotional way. The logical connection between things, so important to the air signs, doesn't play a direct role. For water types the feeling evoked by a person, object or situation is important. Everything is judged on this basis.

For consciousness, feeling is an almost inexplicable process, even when feeling is the specific means through which one views the world. It gives a certain form of "after the event" consciousness; in other words, the water sign is able to identify (unintentionally) with someone else and become that person to such a degree that he only later learns to establish his own identity on the basis of all that he is *not*.

A deep, sensitive, and emotional involvement in events is characteristic for water signs, even though they don't necessarily show it. Sensitivity can make them so vulnerable that they tend to hide behind an unemotional mask, one reason why a water type doesn't always come across as a warm, sensitive, and empathetic type. The feeling process can take hold of this type to such an extent that the outside world only serves as impulse, bringing the process into motion or sustaining it, so that a warm reaction doesn't need to follow. The element of water can then be "cold" to the touch as well.

Because water consciousness orients itself through the feeling function, it needs constant stimulation from outside. That need often makes water signs demanding, yearning, absorbing, and clinging. Through emotional contact with the outside world, they can literally feel things that can't be explained. They come so close to the core of a situation they sometimes hit the nail on the head. Bringing their conclusions into words is a difficult business for them for that reason.

WEIGHING THE IMPORTANCE OF EACH ELEMENT

Every element has its essential and special way of looking at life experience. None of the elements has more or less value than another and we all have the four. The four elements together form a totality. If we could approach a situation with our thinking, feeling, sensation, and intuitive consciousness, then and only then, could we come to a truly conclusive judgment about that situation. Consciousness, however, is always using one or two functions or elements, with the other elements operating from the unconscious. It is outside the ability of human consciousness to give a perfectly complete and balanced judgment. No matter how objective a person attempts to be, his judgment will always be colored by his own personality. Understanding our own element division can reveal our own *coloration,* the glasses we see through.

Everyone has all the elements in his horoscope: the circle contains the whole zodiac and is always the basis of the horoscope. With each of us, the relationship between the elements is different, in many cases one or two elements are over-emphasized. This is completely in agreement with the experience of psychology which speaks of one superior function, helped perhaps by one or sometimes two important auxiliary functions.

In establishing the division of elements in a horoscope, it is an error to simply sum up the planets found in that element. We would be ignoring the fact that some planets are more important for human consciousness than others. In the division of elements we should not forget that we have connected the elements with a certain attitude of consciousness. Automatically the more important role is played by the personal planets (the Sun, Moon, Mercury, Venus and Mars). Once we have found the one or two most important elements for consciousness, we know that the remaining elements are connected with the unconscious. In the examples on the following pages, we will go into this more thoroughly.

The most personal and individualized points in the horoscope are the Sun, Moon, Mercury and the Ascendant. The sign on the Midheaven and the ruler of the Ascendant are important, though subordinate to the first group, turning the scale only in case of doubt. Venus and Mars can be called purely personal, though in all cases they are less important than the Sun, Moon, Mercury and the Ascendant. Jupiter and Saturn take an in-between position.

The planets beyond Saturn (Uranus, Neptune and Pluto) can clearly be called impersonal. They are located in the same sign for long periods of history and form more a characteristic of that period of time than direct personal traits. They can give a certain color to one's character if they are important in a particular horoscope—for instance, if they are connected to the personal planets. Their content and meaning are impersonal, and for the most part connected with the unconscious part of the human psyche. Their actions are unverifiable, in great part beyond control, and sometimes sudden (Uranus); in short, human will and consciousness have little grasp of their contents.

When we find a horoscope containing an element comprised of three impersonal planets—for instance, Saturn, Uranus, and Neptune (as was the case in 1942-43 when they were all in air)—and another element containing two personal planets—for instance, the Sun and Moon—that second element will be by far the most important for that person's consciousness, coloring his vision of events much more than the element containing the impersonal planets. The element with the impersonal planet will play a role dependent upon its relation to the element in which the Sun and Moon are found.

In the horoscope, the ego is reflected by the Sun. Generally speaking, the ego identifies with a certain psychological function (or astrological element), so the Sun's element is certainly of great importance. That element doesn't necessarily indicate the dominant conscious function, as the definite answer must come from the rest of the horoscope. However, it has been my experience time and again that the Sun plays a special role in any conclusions about the elements.

3. ESTABLISHING THE ELEMENT DIVISIONS

A fixed rule in astrology is that the planets in the *signs* reflect the *potential* of the person, while the planets in the *houses* reflect the *circumstances.* Experience gained through one's circumstances influences character over the course of time. Often this occurs unconsciously: if someone burns his fingers enough times on a heater, he will finally learn not to touch it impulsively, even if he is reckless by nature. Experience, in this case painful, teaches that something in one's attitude or character must be altered to avoid being hurt. The astrological houses offer a range of experience during a person's lifetime, teaching one how to act in an adequate yet individual way in various areas of life, which doesn't need to follow a set standard. The horoscope shows what actually is *in a*

Element	Sign Number	Sign Name	House
FIRE	1 5 9	Aries Leo Sagittarius	1 5 9
EARTH	2 6 10	Taurus Virgo Capricorn	2 6 10
AIR	3 7 11	Gemini Libra Aquarius	3 7 11
WATER	4 8 12	Cancer Scorpio Pisces	4 8 12

Figure 1.1. The elements and the houses.

Elements	Signs	Houses	Total
FIRE	♃ ☋	☋ ☿	4
EARTH	♀ ☉ ♂ ♄ Mc.	☉ ♂ ♄ ⚷	9
AIR	♀ ⚷	♀	3
WATER	⚷ Asc. ☽	☽ ♃ ⚷	6

Figure 1.2. The division of the elements as they appear in the signs and the houses in Fred's chart. (See Chart 1.)

person, not the degree to which this is tolerated by the predominant morality of the time.

Since the houses offer so many possibilities of development, they must be included in any diagram of the elements. The houses reflect not only our circumstances and possibilities for experience, but they also form an essential part of the psyche. When a planet is placed in a certain house, traditional astrology holds that the planet's energy is specifically directed to the area of life symbolized by that house. Consequently, something in one's psyche causes that person to be occupied with these specific matters. In this light, we can hardly deny the ancient law, "As above, so below," which also can be worded "As within, so without." What we contain within us is reflected in our circumstances. As the houses are expressed in specific circumstances, they mirror our inner world, teaching us a great deal about ourselves.[11]

Just as we classify the signs of the zodiac under the elements, we can assign the elements to certain houses, as shown in figure 1.1. The order of the fire *houses* corresponds to that of the fire *signs,* as do the earth *houses* to earth *signs,* etc. Experience has shown that planets in the houses, in so far as they relate to the division of the elements, play an increasingly powerful role as one grows older.

To create a mental picture of the element distribution in any chart, we can separate the elements as shown in figure 1.2. In this

[11] For a comprehensive analysis of this: Hamaker-Zondag, KM., *Astro-Psychology,* Aquarian Press, Wellingborough, 1980, pp. 114-138.

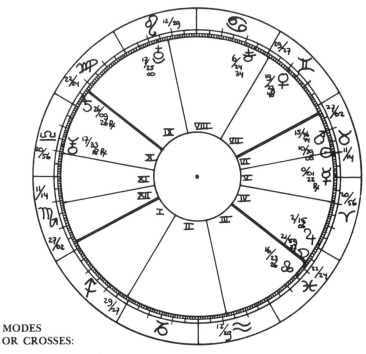

**MODES
OR CROSSES:**

Ⓐ Cardinal:

Ⓒ Fixed:

Ⓒ Mutable:

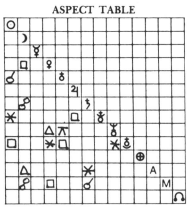

ASPECT TABLE

	O	)	☿	♀	♂	♃	♄	⛢	♆	♇	⊕	A	M	☊
Sun	O													
Moon		)												
Mercury			☿											
Venus			□	♀										
Mars	♂			♂										
Jupiter						♃								
Saturn			♂				♄							
Uranus	⛢				□			⛢						
Neptune			△	⅄					♆					
Pluto	□		⚹	□				⚹	♂					
Part of Fortune											⊕			
Ascendant			△			⚹						A		
Midheaven			♂	□		♂							M	
North Node														☊

ELEMENTS:

illustration we will use the data from Chart 1 on page 14. The four elements are listed so that we can relate them to the zodiacal signs and houses. Next to each element we enter the symbols for the planets posited in the signs of that element. (For example, if Jupiter appears in a fire sign, we put his symbol next to the fire category.) Then we enter the planets posited in *houses* that correspond to the element category. For instance, Mercury may not be in a fire sign (Aries, Leo, Sagittarius) but in this case it is in the 5th house which is a fire sign house in the natural zodiac. We can then determine how many planets affect the various element categories (though it isn't necessary). Entering the planetary symbols on a list such as this provides an immediate view of the distribution of personal and less personal energy.

To determine the element influence by both the planetary sign and house placement, we should always consider the following factors:

a) Although we may determine a total figure on our list, this total can never be used as a quantitative amount in any diagnosis of personality. When you have many planets in one element, if those planets are mostly impersonal, they will not indicate a dominance of that element in consciousness. (The outer planets—Neptune, Uranus and Pluto—cannot be considered to count more strongly than a person's Sun, Moon, and Ascendant, for example.)

b) We work with the concept of ten planets (the Sun and Moon are not planets, but for convenience sake we call them such). Because each planet has two possible categories on our list our total should add up to 20. We can also enter the sign of the Ascendant and the Midheaven (abbreviated as Asc. or A./Mc. or M.) in the "sign" section on our list. We cannot enter them under the "house" section for both positions are always the starting points (or cusps) of the first and tenth houses. Because the Asc. and Mc. are entered only in the sign section, the addition of these two factors brings our total to 22.

Chart 1. This is Fred's chart. He was born May 1, 1951 in Gronigen, Holland at 9:30 pm. The time is from his birth certificate. House system is Placidus. Chart used with permission.

c) Sometimes a planet is located very close to the cusp of the following house, as in the case of the Moon in Chart 1. Such a planet is then considered as belonging to the following house. Although the Moon in our example is located on the cusp of the 4th, we enter it as if it were a part of the fourth house. When looking to determine the energy that forms a personality, any planet that is moving from one house to another will progress to the next house in a very short time after birth. If the cuspal planet is a fast moving one, its influence will probably affect factors of personality described by the next house.

In general, when entering planets in the house section on the list, we can apply the following rules:

a) When a planet is within 4 degrees of the cusp (or starting point) of an *angular* house, it is said to develop its influences in the angular house. The angular houses are the first, fourth, seventh and tenth.

b) If a planet is within 3 degrees of the cusp of any other house, it will be most active in the following house. This rule is applied with a considerably smaller orb (usually about 1 degree) to retrograde planets, such as Neptune in Chart 1. Neptune in our sample chart is within 3 degrees of the cusp of the eleventh house, but because it is retrograde, it remains active in the tenth. Only if it had been located exactly on the cusp would it have been entered in the eleventh house on our list.

Though these rules can be used fairly well in practice, a certain amount of uncertainty is inherent, unless the time of birth is very exact. The slightest deviation in the birth time can alter the house cusps, and therefore alter the sphere of planetary influence as far as the house symbolism is concerned. These rules are valid for determining cuspal influence in the houses only, and should not be used for determining which element a planet is in by sign. For example, if a planet is posited at 29° Leo, its sign cannot be altered. The planet is considered to be in Leo, even though it is very near to the sign of Virgo. If that same planet is at 29° Leo and *also* at the end of the third house, its house position will be entered in the 4th house rather than the third.

4. INTERPRETING THE ELEMENT DIVISION

When we look at *potential* (planets in *signs*) in Fred's horoscope (Chart 1), the strongest category is that of earth. He has Sun, Mercury, and the MC there, followed by the less important Mars. The Sun and Mars repeat themselves in *circumstances* (indicated by planets in *houses*), so the element earth remains strong. The next strongest category is that of water, for it represents the personal nature (Moon and Asc.). The other planet in this element is Uranus, which is not considered a personal one. The Moon is found in a water house as well, so we can also consider this element important.

Mercury is in an earth sign in Chart 1, but it moves to the fire element by house position. However, the fire element holds few personal planets, just as the air element only lays claim to Venus, which repeats itself in air circumstances (houses). It is exceptional when planets repeat the same element by house, and Chart 1 has an above average occurrence of this phenomenon. In conclusion, we can say that the earth element receives the most emphasis on our list. The second most important category is water.

Chart 2 on page 18 (Marilyn Monroe) gives us a completely different picture. As you can see from figure 1.3, without doubt, the element air is most important. Air contains the most personal planets which moreover repeat themselves in air houses. The other three elements are about equal in strength. Water has the most

Elements	Signs	Houses	Total
FIRE	♀ Asc. ♇	♇ ♅	5
EARTH	Mc.	♀	2
AIR	☿ ☉ ☽ ♃	☉ ☿ ♃ ☽	8
WATER	♇ ♄ ♂ ♅	♄ ♂ ♇	7

Figure 1.3. The division of the elements as they appear in the signs and houses in Marilyn Monroe's chart. (See Chart 2.)

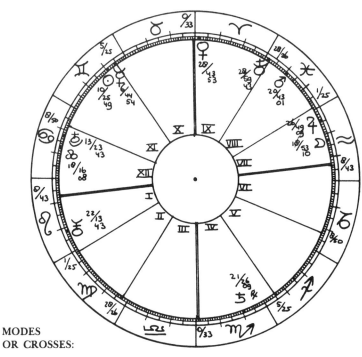

**MODES
OR CROSSES:**

(T) Cardinal: ♀♄/♅☽♃♀

(9) Fixed: MC Asc ♅☽♃/♂♀☉

(6) Mutable: ☿☉♂♄/♄♅

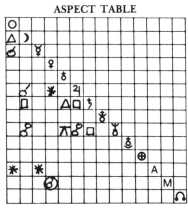

ASPECT TABLE

	Sun	Moon	Mercury	Venus	Mars	Jupiter	Saturn	Uranus	Neptune	Pluto	P.o.F	Asc	MC	N.Node
Sun	○													
Moon	△	☽												
Mercury	☌		☿											
Venus				♀										
Mars					☍									
Jupiter		☌	✳			♃								
Saturn	□			△	□	♄								
Uranus							☍	♅						
Neptune		☍			⊼	☍	□		♆					
Pluto									☌					
Part of Fortune										⊕				
Ascendant	✳		✳								A			
Midheaven			☉									M		
North Node													☊	

ELEMENTS:

Fire: (5)
♀♄
Asc /♄♅

Earth: (2)
MC
♀

Air: (6)
☿☉☽
♃ ♃☽○

Water: (7)
♄☽☉
♄ ♄♅♄

planets, but those are primarily impersonal planets, applying to a whole generation. Venus and the Ascendant are located in fire signs, but Venus is conjunct the Midheaven (and earth circumstance) while there is little further evidence of earth to be found. One element is important for consciousness without a second element ever crystallizing.

In these two examples, it seems fairly simple to name the most important element. There are, however, countless horoscopes where the division is much more difficult. The distribution is so broad that the astrologer can barely make a choice. For instance, someone with the Sun in Aries (fire), the Moon in Taurus (earth), Mercury in Pisces (water), and a Libra Ascendant (air) in potential has the four most important personal indicators in four different elements. The location of these planets in the houses will give a more definite indication. Regardless of which function or element ultimately manifests as most important, *one* important personal content always remains strongly connected with the unconscious of the person in question. Naturally this has specific results for the character structure.

I shall clarify this principle somewhat in a short explanation of the psychology of the four functions of consciousness as far as they are important in astrology. Instead of the expression "function of consciousness" we can use "element" in the strictest astrological sense of the word. We distinguish four different functions of consciousness: thinking, feeling, sensation, and intuition, as we have already described. These four functions can be divided into two pairs—thinking and feeling, which form a judgment about a situation; and sensation and intuition, which perceive a situation. We can call the first pair (thinking and feeling, thus air and water) "judging." Jung called these functions "rational," a word that can be confusing. The judging or rational function is much more occupied with judging an object or situation on the basis of

---

Chart 2. Marilyn Monroe. She was born June 1, 1926 in Los Angeles, California at 9:09 am. Data from Jam Kampherbeek, Holland. House system is Placidus. (Kampherbeek is well known in Holland for the reliability of his data for he collects birth information and doesn't correct charts for his own purposes.)

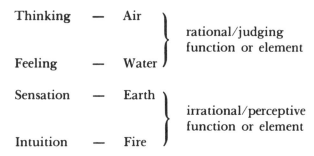

Figure 1.4. The elements and functions divide into pairs.

meaning (thinking) or value (feeling) than it is with the actual object or situation in itself.

The other two functions are called perceptive or irrational. (The term irrational as used here is descriptive only and has absolutely no judgmental value!) Sensation (earth) and intuition (fire) restrict themselves much more to the object itself. Sensation perceives how something appears—its form; intuition inwardly perceives where an object came from and how it can develop. In other words, intuition sees the relationship between things in a context independent of time rather than seeing the things themselves. Thereby, it perceives the changing of the form. The pairs look like figure 1.4.

Within the pairs division we can introduce another important division. The functions belonging to a group are always completely opposite each other in the specific and essential view of the world of events implied in these functions. The sensation type is always busy determining the perceptible concreteness of the moment and therefore must ignore all possible past and future changes of form. Otherwise, this type might become distracted by the relationship to other possible, but intangible, objects or situations. If this was done, the individual would no longer be a sensation type. The intuitive type does just the opposite. They both perceive, yet their focus is so contradictory that we can speak of polar opposites. (Therefore, one's awareness of one's own function hardly plays a role.)[12]

---

[12]A survey of the theory of functions is found in the books listed in footnote 10 by Toni Wolff, C.A. Meier, E.C. Whitmont and M.-L. von Franz.

Two important polarities are found in the division of functions of consciousness. Feeling and thinking (water and air) stand just as diametrically opposite each other as sensation and intuition (earth and fire). In astrological terms, this means that the elements air and water show great tension toward each other because they are psychological opposites, just as are earth and fire. When two important elements belonging to such a dualistic pair become prominent in a certain horoscope, a primary tension will develop. Since the elements are opposites and incompatible, only one function can develop in consciousness while the other necessarily remains associated with the unconscious. There is more inner harmony, or at least less elementary tension, present in horoscopes when two elements appear that are not opposite each other.

In Fred's horoscope, we saw a strong earth-water potential. Earth and water are not in polarity so there isn't a pronounced inner tension on this point. Marilyn Monroe's horoscope, on the other hand, has a strong air potential with water having the next greatest strength. Though the water planets can be called impersonal, they could still cause difficulty since they contrast with the element of consciousness (air).

In conclusion, when we have divided the elements in a horoscope and have determined the most important element, we can soon see if there are deep characterological tensions coming from the major opposing elements or whether these elements are in harmony. The elemental determination of tension is very important for the framework in which we will later analyze the aspects. We can clarify this point by looking at figure 1.5. (See page 22.)

The contrasting elements are always in opposition in a sense, while both elements flanking another element can get along with that element. For instance, water opposes air, but can get along better with earth or fire. See figure 1.6 on page 23. Naturally, when water has to choose between earth and fire, it will choose earth; because like water, it is more introverted, while fire is very exuberant and outgoing. Yet fire will never experience the same tension with water as air does because fire actually understands water better than air (the opposite of water) does. Fire can join the world of water, which is a dream world of fantasy and possibility, without too much logic and theory, without violating its own nature. On the other hand, air, which is opposite water, has little understanding of this attitude, because for air, logic and theory play the main role.

In my practical experience, conflicts in a horoscope arising from non-opposing elements (for instance, a square between Gemini-air and Virgo-earth) are less tense than elements that *are* opposing; for instance, a square between Virgo (earth) and Sagittarius (fire). In evaluating aspects and other important data, the elements play a very important role in the background: the division of elements is one of the basic factors in a horoscope. Inner elementary tension, by the way, should not be given a negative value, because it is just this underlying tension which gives us the impetus to go forward! Determining the amount of tension is the first step in interpreting the division of elements.

The strongest function of consciousness (the strongest element) is what children use to adapt and react to the world. The strongest element must then clearly be present in potential; in other words, with important planets in the signs of that element. In youth, the planets are mainly effective in potential. As we grow older, the houses play a greater role and the totality can begin to work. In both sample horoscopes, the element strongest in potential was also represented by the corresponding houses being strongly occupied, showing influence later in life. (In other words, the air signs might be strongest, but with strong placements in the air houses as well.) When the strength of an element increases in such a way, the attitude developed unconsciously in youth, in agreement with

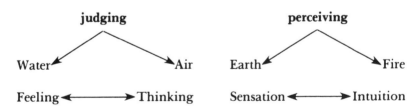

Figure 1.5. The diagram shows the tension that occurs within the framework presented in figure 1.4. As you can see, *judging* is related to *thinking* (air) and *feeling* (water). Yet, feeling and thinking are of a different polarity. The same situation is illustrated as *perceiving* causes a polarity to take place between *sensation* (earth) and *intuition* (fire).

potential, will remain predominant through life in one's views and reactions.

In psychology, the continually developing function of consciousness most important for our view of the world is called the superior function. Analogous to this is the superior function in astrology. Thus, in Fred's horoscope that element is earth, both in potential (sign) and circumstance (house), while in Marilyn

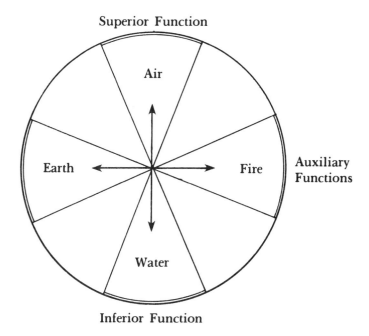

Figure 1.6. The gray areas between the functions illustrates how the functions mix. The area between air and earth, for example, provides the air-earth type. In this figure you can see that there is never a mixture of conflicting elements because they cannot share the gray middle area. When one function is conscious, the contradictory function is always in the unconscious. Planets in the unconscious element will always react from the unconscious part of the psyche. The remaining two elements can help the conscious function, but these need to be developed, as they belong half to the conscious and half to the unconscious.

Monroe's horoscope the superior element is air. The elements earth and air respectively had already developed when they were young. Such a development takes the form of a progressive differentiation; in other words, the superior function distinguishes itself more and more from the other functions because we can work with it more easily and clearly. The element then works so naturally that we are not even aware that we are acting typically for that element. An air type, for instance, will automatically approach everything through thinking.

In contrast to the obviously developed superior function, there is another function or element connected with the unconscious area of the psyche and therefore outside the mastery of the will and the conscious mind. This function we call inferior; astrologically, it is represented by an element opposite in direction to the superior element. If fire is the superior element, then earth is the inferior. If air is the superior element, then water is the inferior, etc. In Fred's horoscope, the earth element is superior; it follows then that the fire element is connected with the unconscious. The planets located in fire signs therefore work in his horoscope out of the unconscious: Jupiter in Aries and Pluto in Leo.

Being associated with the unconscious, Pluto symbolizes a part of the human psyche that by its very nature cannot be controlled by the conscious mind. Yet it is important to know that Pluto is part of the inferior or unconscious element, since Pluto can express itself in the psyche in various ways; for instance, a desire for power or show of power, mental showdowns, contests, and the like. If Pluto is located in an inferior element, that person will have great difficulty becoming conscious of those traits in himself. Moreover, it is characteristic of unconscious contents that they can break through into consciousness at the most inconvenient moments and cause disturbances. This calm and sensitive earth-water type can suddenly show a tough, fighting spirit and stubbornly stand his own ground, to the amazement of those who don't know him intimately.

In this context, it is also important to know that the psyche always strives for balance and that the unconscious has a compensating function in regard to the conscious mind. In practice, the stronger the consciousness and the stronger one's self-image, the stronger the unconscious will counteract these functions. The degree to which these counteractions act as a jamming station depends on the readiness of the conscious mind to digest or integrate such impulses. When we have two strongly occupied opposing elements in a horoscope, as one develops into a superior element the other will necessarily become the inferior element. In such a case, if the inferior element is just as strongly occupied, the unconscious counteractions are powerful and keep the conscious side under pressure.

In Marilyn Monroe's horoscope, we see the air element located opposite a strongly occupied but impersonal water element. Yet, the influence that evolves within the water element forms a powerful opposition for consciousness in different ways. When such a polarity becomes too strong, then compulsive actions due to the inferior element can appear, entirely escaping the person's awareness. With a strong air-water polarity, and air the superior element, one would perceive his world from a rational structure. Because of his strong water element he would also be fascinated by the illogical, the emotional and the most sentimental. Bouts of emotionalism, the irrational feeling that there is something missing in all that rationality, or sentimentally being in love, are all ways the water element can show itself. It gnaws on the foundation of the structure one identifies with (in this case the element air) and leaves behind a feeling of doubt and uncertainty.

We often see such a person attempting to reinforce the conscious structure. He begins to wonder why things are going a certain way, tries to contain the world within more rigid thought patterns, and becomes even less flexible as a result. This increasing rigidity of consciousness evokes even stronger unconscious reactions. The conscious mind is overwhelmed more forcefully with incomprehensible feelings, until a crisis helps achieve a state of balance between the unconscious and the conscious. This balance often doesn't happen until the complete inadequacy of the structure in all its facets is experienced and accepted. Persons with such a division of functions don't actually steer their lives with their conscious minds, but in reality live through their inferior functions. In the case of Marilyn Monroe this is the element water. Hence the following remarks of C.A. Meier:

> ...the function which is inferior per definition often is
> much more noticeable than the differentiated. Especially

in a thinking type an uncertain and precarious emotional life can strike us much sooner than his thinking, which is beyond reproach.[13]

In many cases, strangely enough, the fire element gets upset about material things, whereas earth, specifically oriented to concrete life, doesn't see anything wrong. Such a situation occurs when the fire element is strongly occupied (containing the Sun and the Moon, for instance), but the earth element influences the personal contents (for instance, Mercury and Ascendant in earth). When fire is superior, the element earth is directed toward security, and can unleash powerful counteractions from the unconscious—especially when fire has a great need for freedom and wild adventures. A businessman with this element division can plan the most fantastic schemes from behind his desk, but when it comes to actualizing them, he must play for security if he doesn't want sleepless nights.

Another example of a fire type with earth contradictions is the statement, "I would like to work part-time so I could have more free time for myself, but then I'd have to have at least $50,000 in reserve in my bank account!" An astrologer could explain this statement by referring to the earth content of the horoscope, without bringing in the conscious-unconscious division. By leaving out the principal characteristics of the superior and inferior functions, one only recognizes the existence of factors colored by a certain element, while the functioning of these factors within the psyche remains completely unclear. One can't determine in this way the origin of compulsive actions which can only be associated with unconscious impulses. The conscious mind, controlled by the will, doesn't need to be compulsive; when we are up against the incomprehensible, uncontrollable unconscious, we *do* feel this need.

In addition, the polarity between the superior and the inferior function gives a much greater depth to the development of a person's motives. Now we can discern how much a person really wants certain things and on which points he is so sensitive that he will lose control at the slightest excuse. Moreover, what Toni Wolff says is all too true.

[13]Meier, C.A., *Bewusstsein*, p. 138.

...the problem of the opposition of the types is often...the real though unconscious cause of a neurosis, and this problematical question is therefore also the problem that plays the greatest role in such cases at the beginning of psychological analysis.[14]

So far we have discussed the horoscopes of adults who already have worked out part of their circumstances and to whom we can relate the total horoscope. A child lives up to his potential (planets in the signs) much more than he does according to circumstances (planets in the houses). His protected environment guards against extremes in circumstance, with a few exceptions. A great difference between potential and circumstance could contribute to a certain amount of tension. For instance, a fire planet in an earth house demands greater adjustment to the demands of circumstance than that same planet in an air or water house.

Tension can arise within the element division in many ways:

a) Two opposing elements appear most important in the element division as a whole. If one of these elements becomes superior, the other can only express itself through the language of the unconscious.

b) The total division can seem harmonious, but that doesn't necessarily imply stability. The various planets making up this totality can be forced to express themselves in strange territory; for instance, the Sun in an air sign that is expressed through a water house. This polarity between potential and circumstance can give rise to ultimately developing another function into our chief function, whereby the actual potential becomes suppressed. Upbringing and other circumstances can play a great role here, though this doesn't necessarily lead to something as radical as a change of superior function.

c) A certain element can be completely lacking, both in potential and circumstance. Not having the contents of that element nor feeling the need to direct energy in those areas of life indicated by that element doesn't hinder the person. Whether life will run

[14]Wolff, T., See footnote 1, p. 64.

smoothly or not in those areas depends upon the rest of the horoscope (aspects, relations between the houses, etc.). I would like to emphasize that a missing element doesn't necessarily mean that one feels hindered, as normal function is possible. (In some cases the environment can be more troubled by the missing element than the person himself!)

d) A certain element can be represented in potential (sign) without having any way of expressing itself in circumstance (house). In such a case, the contents (planets) have a more difficult time coming into their own right. The need for expression becomes more acute as more personal contents are involved: for instance, having the Sun, Mercury, and Ascendant in earth signs, with earth houses empty. Then there is a stronger possibility of developing into another function type for which a distinct potential exists.

e) A certain element is not present in potential (by sign) but appears in circumstance (by house). In such a case, the experiences of life can bring about changes in character, even though that may not happen easily. Having no planets in air signs, but having planets in air houses means, for instance, that social traits are not very strong in potential, but they can be refined through contacts with friends, acquaintances, or a partner. (Take the rest of the horoscope into consideration, of course.)

f) Some horoscopes show such a broad element distribution that the astrologer can barely make a choice. That means the person in question may have difficulty developing the superior function. For instance, someone with Sun in Aries, Moon in Taurus, Mercury in Pisces and a Libra Ascendant won't have an easy youth, due to the inner contradictions. Four important personal contents in four different elements mean that one important personal content will always act from the unconscious, as I mentioned at the beginning of this section. (In such cases, I have often found that the element in which the Sun is located becomes important, or in any case plays an important role.)

5. SUPERIOR AND INFERIOR ELEMENT: POSSIBILITIES AND DIFFICULTIES

In the last section we discussed the relationship between the inferior and superior functions. We assumed that one element will clearly crystallize, but in practice, this is not always the case. When two non-opposing elements both play an important role in consciousness, each containing personal contents, this can produce a mixed type that has characteristics from both. Eventually, the balance usually falls to one element and the second element then plays an important auxiliary function. Of course, this cannot be the case with opposing elements such as air-water and fire-earth! There can never be a mixed type formed from two elements in which one is inferior by definition and operates from the unconscious. The division of the elements with its emphasis on the personal planets primarily says something about our *consciousness*. We show this schematically in figure 1.7. Imagine that earth is the superior function. Then by necessity fire is located in the unconscious. The two remaining elements—air and water—can develop as auxiliary functions.

Fred's horoscope has the element division shown in figure 1.7. Earth is superior, fire inferior. Being strongly occupied, the element water soon becomes auxiliary and remains subordinate to the

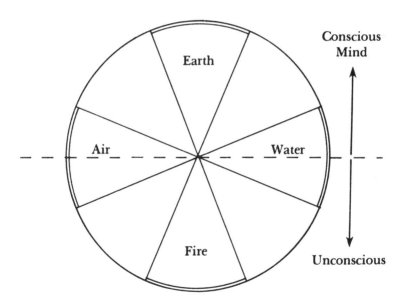

Figure 1.7. The element division in Fred's horoscope. Here Earth is the superior function while Fire becomes inferior. The Air and Water facets of self develop as auxiliary functions.

element earth in expression, but the water characteristics can be seen in Fred's conscious mentality and his behavior. We can call him an earth-water type, with an emphasis on earth.

In Marilyn Monroe's horoscope (see page 18), it isn't as easy to select a second element since she was predominantly an air type with strong unconscious emotional reactions from the element water. Auxiliary functions could only be formed by the elements fire and earth, neither of these being contrary to air, her superior function.

Though much has been written about the constructive side of the inferior function, there still seems to be an aversion or fear in many people regarding the concerns of that element, as though it were something we shouldn't actually possess. It is difficult for us to imagine that a function posing so many problems for our consciousness can also be constructive, can even be our salvation in certain difficult psychological situations. One of the clearest descriptions of the inferior element's function, or (psychologically speaking) the inferior function itself, is to be found in *Lectures on Jung's Typology* by Marie-Louise von Franz and James Hillman. M.-L. von Franz sketches for us the following role of the inferior function.[15]

> ...The inferior function is the door through which all the figures of the unconscious come into consciousness. Our conscious realm is like a room with four doors, and the fourth door by which the Shadow[16], the Animus[17] or the Anima and the personification of the Self[18] come in.

---

[15]von Franz, M.-L., "The inferior function," p. 54, in von Franz, M.-L., & J. Hillman, *Lectures on Jung's Typology*, Spring Verlag, Zürich, 1971.

[16]Seen individually, the "shadow" represents the "personal darkness," the meanings of our psyche during our lifetime that are not admitted or are rejected or repressed. Seen collectively, the shadow represents the general dark side in the human being, the structural tendency towards darkness and inferiority, that every person has within him. Becoming conscious of our inferior function often causes a confrontation with the shadow connected with it. See Jacobi, J., *The Psychology of C.G. Jung*, Routledge & Kegan Paul, London, 1973, pp. 109-114.

[17]The concepts *Anima* and *Animus* may become more clear when we consider Jung's example: every Adam has within him his Eve (anima) and every Eve her own Adam (animus). Each person seeks to encounter someone who resembles the inner Adam or Eve in order to remain psychologically in balance. From: Lievegoed, B.M., *De Levensloope van de mens*, Rotterdam, 1978, p. 90.

They do not enter as often through the other doors, which is in a way self-evident: the inferior function is so close to the unconscious and remains so barbaric and inferior and undeveloped that it is naturally the weak spot in consciousness through which the figures of the unconscious can break in. In consciousness it is experienced as a weak spot, as that disagreeable thing which will never leave one in peace and always causes trouble. Every time one feels he has acquired a certain inner balance, a firm standpoint, something happens from within or without to throw it over again. This force always comes through the fourth door, which cannot be shut. The other three doors of the inner room can be closed. But on the fourth door the lock does not work, and there, when one is least prepared for it, the unexpected will come in again. Thank God, one might add, for otherwise the whole life process would petrify and stagnate in a wrong kind of consciousness. The inferior function is the ever-bleeding wound of the conscious personality, but through it the unconscious can always come in and so enlarge consciousness and bring forth a new attitude.

As long as one has not developed the other functions, the two auxiliary functions, they too will be open doors. In a person who has only developed one superior function, the two auxiliary functions will operate in the same way as the inferior function and will appear in personifications of the Shadow, the Animus and the Anima. When one has succeeded in developing three functions, in locking three of the inner doors, the problem of the fourth door still remains, for that is the one that is apparently meant not to be locked. There one has to succumb, one has to suffer defeat in order to develop further...

---

[18]The Self is the center of our psychic totality, just as the *I* is the center of our consciousness. The Self contains both the conscious and the unconscious parts of the psyche. See Jacobi, J., *The Psychology of C.G. Jung*, Routledge & Kegan Paul, London, 1973, p. 107.

This doesn't sound very pleasant to the conscious mind, yet the conscious mind is but a part of our total psyche. Even people who know Jung's typology don't necessarily know which type they actually are. This fact confronts us with the paradox that the conscious mind isn't necessarily as conscious as it seems, according to Edward C. Whitmont.[19] He also says that a person belongs to a certain type when the function of that type is the most developed and differentiated. Whether he is conscious of this or not is another question, as one's orientation often begins in childhood without conscious choice. Whitmont also states:

> ...It cannot be stressed enough that the inferior function is inferior because of insufficient development rather than deficient capacity. A feeling type is perfectly capable of thinking; he just will not bother to do it. Consequently he habitually and automatically takes notice only of his feelings. The thinking type is capable of feeling but it happens in spite of him, more often than not. He does not do the feeling, it does *him*, in the form of unconscious emotion...[20]

Whitmont's last point, as we stated earlier, is one of the characteristics of the inferior function, and therefore our consciousness has no grasp on it and cannot steer it. The conscious mind only experiences the inferior element's way of expression in arbitrary moments—often when it is inconvenient! The inferior element has still more characteristic features and ways of manifesting itself which can be listed as follows:

a) The inferior function, in contrast with the conscious mind, is relatively undeveloped, thus reacting in an elementary manner. This manner of acting is called "archaic."

b) The reactions of the inferior function are slow and can hardly be speeded up, even after much practice. The inferior function demands our time, something in short supply in our Western

---

[19]Whitmont, E.C., *The Symbolic Quest: Basic Concepts of Analytical Psychology*, Princeton University Press, Princeton, 1969, p. 153.

[20]*Ibid*, p. 154-155.

culture. M.-L. von Franz[21] gave the example of a girlfriend with an inferior earth function. Shopping with her for a blouse was an ordeal; the whole store had to be turned upside down and still her friend could not make a choice. Her inferior function (sensation) works very slowly, as all inferior functions do. That is why we become annoyed with that part of our psyche. The slow reaction of the inferior element is helpful in some regard, however; through that slowness the unconscious has a chance to penetrate the conscious mind and do its work. A confrontation can take place. All the time the girlfriend was busy buying a blouse—an earth function—her superior fire function was temporarily switched off, even though it would grab the reins again soon enough. All kinds of contents in herself, of which she was unaware, could enter her consciousness through the process of buying a blouse. This gives her the possibility of recognizing certain dormant character traits and/or faculties, even though recognition may come later when one reflects upon the experience.

That same slowness of the inferior function also means that we would rather avoid that element or function, for we are accustomed to the much quicker reactions of the superior function. Therefore, the inferior function is not called in right away. The quicker superior function continually takes the lead when reacting to information, even though the situation may require an entirely different approach than that function is suited for. For instance, ask a thinking type what he is feeling, as M.-L. von Franz suggests, and he will answer with a mental idea or a conventional silencer. If you really press the point he will become embarrassed, not having any idea what he actually feels. He can think for hours about that!

c) As we saw earlier, the consciousness cannot use the inferior function as a foundation. It comes and goes at its own pleasure; the power of our will does not reach the area of our inferior element. To refer again to the feeling type; naturally he can think—often thinking long and deeply—and can achieve quite a bit on this level. But despite all the knowledge he possesses, and the fact that he can think adequately, at critical moments he may not be able to

---

[21]See footnote 15, p. 8.

command his mental function and might, for instance, fail an examination he otherwise could have passed easily.

d) The inferior element shows the area where we are vulnerable. This Achilles heel manifests itself through those things to which we are vulnerable, and which we find hard to bear, thus causing us to react in an emotional way. The inferior element eludes our grasp, giving us the feeling of not being able to control or protect that side of ourselves, and therefore it can be very tricky or prone to overcompensation. When our inferior element comes into play, the least incident can unbalance us and we react in a childish, oversensitive or insecure way. We can even unconsciously and unwillingly terrorize our surroundings: others walk around on tiptoe, afraid of another irrational outburst and finding it absolutely impossible to talk to us at the time.

e) The inferior element connects our conscious and unconscious, which is of great importance for maintaining or repairing psychic balance. Through the unconscious, we adapt to our own psychic totality, just as through the superior function our conscious-ness adapts to the outside world. The compensating function of the unconscious is the motor which maintains our conscious life. To this end, the unconscious has its own language and its own mechanism. Once these mechanisms appear strange to the conscious mind, we will examine the unconscious more closely.

6. MECHANISMS OF THE UNCONSCIOUS

Dreams, daydreams and fantasies are the most important mechan-isms we can use to become aware of our unconscious. Dreams may suggest what is going on in the unconscious of the individual, even when consciousness has no knowledge of this, but also when something has already penetrated through to consciousness. For example, in our daydreams we may continually play the role of an unconquerable figure for whom nothing is impossible and who always makes things turn out all right. This can be an unconscious compensation for an attitude and pattern in life that is much less impressive. Feelings of inadequacy, failure, lack of ability, and anxieties from our daily lives can call forth counterparts in our dream world, without our being directly aware of these anxieties or even remembering what we were daydreaming about. It happens without any effort from our conscious mind, and compensates for the outer situation. Becoming conscious of the contents of our dreams, daydreams and fantasies can help us become aware of our outer situation so we can do something about it, within our ability.

If we do not pay attention to dream indications, the unconscious has other ways of manifesting itself, ranging from seemingly minor slips of the tongue or forgetfulness, to the development of serious neuroses. Though the conscious mind experiences this as highly unpleasant, the resulting tension will press upon consciousness in order that the disturbed balance between the conscious and unconscious be restored, allowing the psyche to balance itself.

The forms of expression used by the unconscious are very specific: the unconscious speaks a language of images, as in our dreams. Like the irrational part of the "primitive" spirit, it precedes, lies beyond, or transcends reason. Expression through imagery is one of the most specific characteristics of the unconscious. Mental contents and processes can be represented in imagery, for instance, as figures and events. Thoughts and feelings appear in the guise of persons who speak them or act them out. Moods can be expressed by images of landscape, instincts by animals, etc. At some level, each individual knows his own specific images. One person will feel a deep melancholy seeing a leaf fall from a tree, while another person may not even *see* the leaf fall, but in turn will experience the same sort of melancholy gazing at a seascape.

The forms of unconscious expression always penetrate consciousness without being influenced or changed by it. These manifestations, therefore, are pure and original, undifferentiated to a great extent. Our consciousness takes in the everyday course of events. We learn to use a function or element better and better, as it refines its expression through use. In contrast, the inferior function residing in the unconscious stays in an undeveloped condition; we cannot or will not deal with it. On its own, it sometimes breaks through into consciousness. The possibility of developing or refining itself in this way is slight, so this element remains active in its original state. Therefore, the inferior function is called primitive, because it is simple, undeveloped and original. The word primitive is loaded with negative prejudice in our time and the word "archaic" reflects its meaning more objectively.

In someone with the thinking function as the main expression of consciousness, the feeling function (water element) will express itself in an archaic manner. Though he can set everything he sees and hears into neat, orderly rows in his thought world, sometimes such deep and elusive feelings well up that he feels completely overwhelmed. Sometimes he lets himself be swept away by them, even into sentimentality. He cannot steer his feelings nor understand why the calm, balanced thinker can suddenly come under the spell of emotions and feelings. We can cite the well-known example of the professor in the film *The Blue Angel.* During the day, he was a rigid, straight professor and a disciplinarian with his students, while at night he was the helpless victim of a nightclub performer. She could inflame him by setting loose his inferior feeling function. She only misused him, and the manner in which he allowed himself to be completely bowled over into a world of dreams existing for him alone clearly shows the archaic and in some ways childish character of his feeling function.

When a certain element can be singled out as being the inferior element, such as fire in Fred's horoscope and water in Marilyn Monroe's, then the planets located in these elements will express themselves in an archaic way, not influenced by consciousness. This does not mean these planets will express themselves in a negative manner. It is true that these planets are connected with the counteractions of our unconscious and the conscious mind isn't always thankful later. Nonetheless, these planets can give us a helping hand through their activity whenever our consciousness runs away with us. Often, these planets correct us and show that we hold ourselves too rigidly within the bounds of our conscious mind, which is still limited and rather one-sided.

A strongly intuitive (fire) type with Venus in earth can be capable of a permanent relationship, despite his search for possibilities, freedom, and basic truths. The earth element compels him to search for security in the area of love. The partner helps this otherwise fiery individual stand more firmly, with two feet on the ground. Inwardly, the fire type will have some difficulty with this restriction of his freedom. Still, in connection with the unconscious, his earth Venus produces both an inner tension and eventually a greater inner balance, no matter how contrary that may sound. How far these conscious and unconscious contents collide with or fulfill each other depends upon the individual's self-awareness, and that in turn depends on how much he can accept himself with all his imperfections and possibilities.

It is striking how many people fall in love with their opposite type, though we would say at first glance that they do not belong together at all. Yet, such radically different attitudes of consciousness do not have to lead to a split; on the contrary, such relationships are often very creative because one represents the unconscious of the other. The "language" spoken by their contrasting superior elements is so at variance, however, that when the people involved do not see this difference, conflicts can result.

It will be evident by now that the division of elements is of great importance for the foundation of the horoscope; also that the tension between opposite elements in the human psyche as well as between people is not necessarily negative. This tension may give rise to creativity. It cannot be denied that tension within a horoscope coming from the division of elements may cause frustration, yet I would rather call this creative frustration: the driving motive behind all of our actions comes from this very division.

7. EXAMPLES OF ELEMENT DIVISION INTERPRETATION

When we begin the interpretation of a horoscope, the element division gives us a first impression. It is a general scheme that can be used as a reference for a more refined interpretation. Taking Fred's horoscope on page 14 as an example, we have found that earth plays the main role, followed by water. On this basis, we can say the following about his hosorcope:

Fred's consciousness is directed towards a concrete perception of facts and phenomena and their practical and material value. His views are based on a sober, everyday reality. In such a reality, everything has a concrete and tangible form, inspiring a sense of security, and he will feel completely comfortable with himself. In the concrete and material realm, he can express himself very well. His feeling for form and proportion is well-developed so he can be creative in this respect without much effort. Besides having a practical, patient nature he has a fairly directed way of spending his energy, going about his work and hobbies in an efficient and diligent manner. He has a feeling for work situations, conditions, and relations, and this is strengthened by his well developed water element that fulfills his superior earth element in many respects.

Because of the combination of earth and water, he needs a feeling of loyalty and union in order to develop his earth characteristics: perseverance, solidarity and reliability. Due to the passive nature of both elements, this man unmistakably needs stimulation from his surroundings, family, friends, or wife to motivate him. Although he is perfectly contented by himself, due to the strong water element, his self-image is largely derived from what he can mean to other people. His attitude is predominantly turned inward, and consequently we can say that he is rather reserved. His inner life is strongly developed, making him vulnerable and overly sensitive. Because his consciousness is primarily directed to the perceptible world, supplemented by a feeling evaluation of what he sees and experiences, the abstract and theoretical belong to his weaker side. It is sometimes difficult for him to place facts and phenomena in a broader frame of reference, though he will have a good view of the facts as such.

Since his superior element is earth, the fire in his horoscope will produce counteractions now and then. Concepts such as *change* and *possibility* are central to fire and, seen in the light of his underdeveloped fire planets, Fred will have difficulty with change and a skeptical attitude toward new developments. Possibly he is anxious about change, and will approach any new possibility negatively, as for instance: "I won't succeed in than anyway, or, what *can't* go wrong!"

The here and now, the concrete and tangible, form the reality to which he limits himself. As a result, he will focus on concrete pleasures, not so much raw sensuality but more the enjoyment of having extra money for good clothes, luxury items, furnishings for his house, good food, in short, everything pleasurable or comfortable. A fire type—disregarding the rest of the horoscope!—can live for years in a bare, unpainted room without even noticing.

Looking again at Fred's horoscope, it will now be clear that the trine aspect between the Moon in Pisces and his Scorpio Ascendant is very important for his consciousness, as this aspect is formed by two water signs, the element playing such an important role for his consciousness. In contrast, the conflict arising from fire to earth through the Pluto in Leo square the Sun and Mars in Taurus can be more detrimental than we might assume from the conventional interpretation of the aspects. In this horoscope, earth is the main element, which means that these signs squaring each other are at the same time opposing each other as superior and inferior element. If they had been two auxiliary functions there might still have been a fire-earth conflict, but for Fred's consciousness this would have been less acute.

As another example, the opposition between Saturn in Virgo and Moon in Pisces is also very important for Fred's consciousness. Again the aspect is formed from the superior element (earth), but now with an auxiliary element (water). In contrast, the trine aspect between Venus in Gemini and Neptune in Libra will work from the unconscious parts of the psyche since the element air, where this aspect is found, is not one of Fred's conscious functions. With an earth-water combination, the fire and air elements will work from the unconscious. The air element can still develop in a later stage, since it has an auxiliary function and is not in conflict with the superior element. In this way, according to the effect of the aspects, we can bring about a differentiation, a first step toward a more selective approach to reading the aspects.

The conclusions about Marilyn Monroe's horoscope are similar. Her chart appears on page 18. Here again, one element plays the main role—in this case, air. As a result, water is fated to become an inferior element. Marilyn's conscious attitude was a rational and theoretical approach to facts and events; relating people, facts, and abstract thoughts to one another took a primary place. The generally harmonious and mediating behavior of an air type can give the impression of "trimming one's sail to the wind." Her intellectual capacities joined with her flexibility of thought, word and gesture, and she was able to communicate, to make contacts, and handle herself easily in social situations.

She continually tried to arrange everything into neat little cubicles in her own mental world picture, adjusting her own theories and beliefs accordingly. Through this, she ran the risk, despite her obvious social skills, of alienating people around her. With this strong an air emphasis, there is also a good possibility that she would create an unreal, abstract dream world in which everything has its place, without feeling compelled to try out these theories in reality. Any person with this element breakdown could build a personal world that is so mental in nature that she would make a definitely cool or perhaps emotionless impression on others.

At this point the unconscious element, water, could either come to her aid or undermine her. The planets Pluto, Saturn, Mars and Uranus, located in water signs, played an important role. Her emotional life was unable to develop because of her rationally-oriented consciousness. It created a strong pull and exerted an intense pressure on her consciousness, emerging now and then into her consciousness with sudden explosions. Earlier we stated that the psyche continually strives for balance. The presence of air in this horoscope is so dominant that the counteractions from the unconscious water element would have to be just as powerful.

The inferior element always works suddenly; it rears its head at the most unexpected moments. This lack of control is reinforced by the location of Uranus in a water sign. Saturn was also located in a water sign (Scorpio), which often indicates a slowed reaction from the unconscious, which, once it has broken through, can persist for a long time. Moreover, Saturn, indicating feelings of responsibility and a sense of perseverance, cannot be easily directed in the inaccessible unconscious. She could run into difficulty through her perseverance in affairs bound to fail or by taking responsibility either too seriously, or not seriously enough. Once she was emotionally committed to something, she went all out for it. The location of a planet in an unconscious element, therefore, does not have a necessarily negative meaning.

Mars in a woman's horoscope usually indicates the image she carries of her husband or male partner (called the *Animus* in Jungian psychology). Marilyn's Mars in Pisces could cause all kinds of difficulties from the inferior element unless she was extremely cautious in her love affairs and sexuality. In fact, she needed to be careful in every aspect of her emotional life, having the inclination, just as the professor in *The Blue Angel*, to give in to drives in herself which she couldn't fully understand.

The strong duality between the element air, so filled with personal planets, and the element water, strongly occupied by impersonal planets, created a strong tension in her character which manifested itself as an adaption primarily to the outer life and a lack of adaptation to the inner. The fire element, indicated by the Leo

Ascendant, served as a refuge; she could surrender herself more and more to new possibilities, she could wander further with her thoughts, just like a fire sign would and she could create a fantasy future no one else could enter.[22]

The element tension in Marilyn Monroe's horoscope is greater than Fred's, even though air is strong both in potential (signs) and in circumstance (houses), something that appears so promising at first glance. On one hand, Marilyn applied all her communicative, connective and intellectual capacities with success, but the overly strong emphasis on air in this non-conflicting way automatically put the counter-element of water under a disproportionate amount of pressure. Here it was not the conscious mind that was in conflict, but rather the unconscious that was disharmonious with the conscious mind. To some degree this is always true, yet in this case an unusual amount of tension was involved. The rest of the contents of the horoscope should be viewed in this light.

Finally, one more example: Peter. See Chart 3 on page 42. This horoscope has the element division shown in figure 1.8. Peter's horoscope stands out because of its broad distribution. The Aries Sun and the Leo Ascendant are in fire, and the Taurus Moon and M.C. as personal contents are in the opposite element of earth. In air, we find Venus in Aquarius and Mars in Gemini, in water we

Element	Signs	Houses	Total
FIRE	☉ ♄, Asc.	—	3
EARTH	☽ Mc. ♄	☽ ♄ ♂ ♀	7
AIR	♂ ♄ ♀ ♃	♄ ♃ ♄	7
WATER	♄ ♀	♀ ☉ ♄	5

Figure 1.8. The element division for Peter, Chart 3.

[22]An astrologer would never be able to predict from the horoscope alone the degree to which this will happen in the person's life, but he could certainly indicate the danger and know that it plays a certain role.

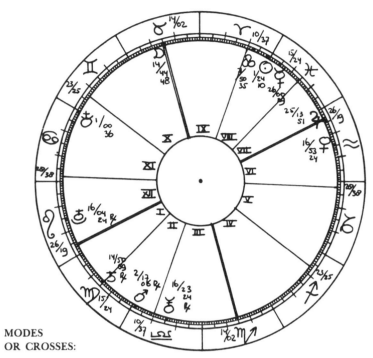

MODES
OR CROSSES:

⑥ Cardinal: ☉♂♀⚷ / ♃☽

⑪ Fixed: ☽MC⚷Asc♀♃ / ♄♅♇☉☋

⑤ Mutable: ♄☿ / ♅♀⚷

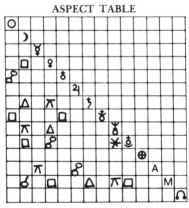

ASPECT TABLE

	☉	☽	☿	♀	♂	♃	♄	♅	♆	♇	⊕	A	M	☊
Sun	☉													
Moon		☽												
Mercury			☿											
Venus	□		♀											
Mars	⚼			⚹										
Jupiter					♃									
Saturn	△		⚼			⚸								
Uranus	□			□			⚹							
Neptune	⚼	△					⚷	⚼						
Pluto	□		⚼					✶	⚹					
Part of Fortune										⊕				
Ascendant		⚼		⚼							A			
Midheaven	⚸		□		△		⚼□			M				
North Node													☊	

ELEMENTS:

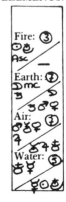

Fire: ③
☉♂
Asc
—

Earth: ⑦
☽MC
♄
♂♀♀

Air: ①
♂⚷♀
♃
⚷♀♄

Water: ⑤
♅☿
☿☉♂

find Mercury in Pisces, a placement not to be underestimated. In short, there is something in every element, and at first glance it seems difficult to make out what is dominant. Experience has taught me that in such a case the Sun, the Ascendant, and Mercury are especially important. The Sun plays an important role, particularly in childhood. In Peter's horoscope the Sun is in fire, not conflicting with Mercury in Pisces, following the division of elements. In practice, Peter does seem to view the world from the fire element. With the passage of years, however, some change has gradually taken place. In the horoscope this is indicated by the rather strong fire potential in personal contents (signs) contrasted with the complete lack of fire circumstances (houses). Though air and earth signs are most strongly represented numerically, this does not mean these elements are the most important for consciousness. Earth is important because the Moon is located in it, both by sign (Taurus) and circumstance (being in the tenth house), while Venus and Mars also appear in earth houses. Water, on the other hand, has a lower numerical value, but we find Mercury there in both sign and house. The Sun is in the eighth house. Thereby, water has a good relationship with the element of consciousness, fire, while earth is contradictory to fire. This assures that fire and water will play an important role, certainly in the first part of life. See Chart 3.

Strong counter-reactions come from earth and to a lesser degree from air, making his base shaky. There is a chance that Peter will take a different course than would be indicated by the Sun: there are no fire house placements while earth as a whole is very strong. This implies a couple of possibilities. First, he can escape into the function reflected by the water element to reduce the tension between fire and earth, and slowly make that into his superior function (unconsciously of course). A second possibility is that at a certain point in his life, he makes a temporary or permanent reversal and lets the element earth become the superior function. It may sound somewhat simple, changing from one function to the other, but in practice this often involves a number of crises, where one is

---

Chart 3. Peter was born on March 22, 1950 at Lisse, Holland, at 3:30 pm. The data is supplied from his birth certificate. House system is Placidus. Chart used with permission.

forced to see one's shortcomings through neurotic symptoms. With such a broad distribution where the elements of both the Sun and Ascendant are unable to give form to circumstance, it is possible that the element is exchanged in one's lifetime, with turbulent results. Fire and earth always remain a polarity, and his Sun will show itself from an angle which, astrologically, is directly contradictory to the one presented by his Moon.

Air is least occupied by sign (potential) and even less occupied by house (circumstance). From this, we may conclude that logical, abstract thinking is not Peter's strongest side; he probably will not have much need for it. His emotional life (water element), on the other hand, will play a continually greater role for him, perhaps helping him develop into an entirely different person in the course of his life.

In Peter's horoscope, the square aspect between Venus in Aquarius and the Moon in Taurus (as well as the other Venus and Moon aspects) will initially be active in his unconscious. Considering the ever-developing emotional content, this is apparently contradictory since the Moon and Venus have always been considered planets that rule (or symbolize) the emotions. To prevent any confusion, we should bear in mind the following difference: the division of the elements shows which element is characteristic for the *manner* in which one approaches the world. The planets are energies and indicate more the *contents* of that energy than a manner of approach. For instance, someone with water as superior element sees everything around him through his emotional faculty, yet that does not necessarily imply that he is warm and sensitive. This is decided by the planets. Returning to Peter's horoscope, though we can say fire will be of importance in his youth, it does not follow that it will remain so at a later age. On the contrary, the distribution shows a number of tensions that can manifest themselves during crises and cause sudden reversals. Fire remains his strongest element in *potential*; this implies that he will never be able to refine nor differentiate any new main function as well as he does his actual superior function.

The division of the elements in itself is a very important feature of the horoscope which will be clearer when we relate it to the division of the crosses. We will deal with this more thoroughly in the following chapter and see how they can be combined in Chapter Three.

CHAPTER TWO

THE CROSSES:
ACTIVITY AND DIRECTION OF PSYCHIC ENERGY

1. THE CONCEPT OF ENERGY IN PSYCHOLOGY

The introduction of the concept *energy* into psychology and astrology makes it possible for us to see separate psychic phenomena in a functional relationship to each other. It makes it possible to distinguish processes within a nearly inextricable dynamic reaction as if we were dealing with static data.

The concept *psychic energy* has been consciously borrowed from physics, and its place in psychology was analogous in the beginning. In certain respects, the general laws of physics can be applied to psychic energy, although psychological investigations have repeatedly shown deviations from the traditonal meaning and processes of physics. As a result, the concept *psychic energy* has gradually begun to lead an independent existence. Mainly, these deviations are due to the fact that we are not dealing with lifeless material but with the intricate human psyche, in which a complex of factors influence the progress of the psychic processes.[1]

One of the most important correspondences is that energy can only flow when inequalities or differences within the psyche cause a kind of *fall.* Just as water keeps moving as the river flows from high to low, so the psychic current depends upon differences in *charge* between psychic contents. We cannot grasp physical energy itself, we only know it through its manner of manifestation. Similarly, we

---

[1]Wolff, T., *Studien zu C.G. Jungs Psychologie*, Rhein Verlag, Zurich, 1959, p. 174.

can only observe psychic energy through its specific patterns of expression and reaction. Studying these can give deeper insight into the way psychic energy moves.

The psyche functions as an independent totality, adapting both to outward conditions and to inner structural specifics of the individual. Just as moral, ethical, social and cultural values can change radically in a short period, so can inner values change as one grows older. Every phase of life brings with it special psychological circumstances, needs, and wants. This interaction of the psyche with the continually changing inner and outer values makes the psyche one large dynamic system.[2] Psychic energy keeps everything going in this system, whether the individual likes the way this takes place or not.

In the preceding chapter we saw the importance of the division of the psyche into conscious and unconscious sections. Jung went a step further and divided the unconscious as follows:

The personal unconscious (the top level of the unconscious): stored there are all the contents which can be made conscious or which once were conscious. These are the things we have forgotten, repressed, and didn't want to recall, as well as our own complexes and hidden talents, which lie dormant in this part of the unconscious.

The collective unconscious (the deeper levels of the unconscious): these levels never have and never will become conscious. What is contained here is the universally human, without any personal tinge. All inherited reaction patterns, all primitive human contents are present in this level. This part of the human psyche connects an individual with every other human being and is the source of motifs shared the world over. The collective unconscious is sometimes also called the objective psyche in Jungian psychology. No longer being

---

[2]For more information concerning phases of life see: Hamaker-Zondag, K.M., *Astro-Psychology*, Aquarian Press, Wellingborough, 1980, Chapter 8; Lievegoed, B., De Levensloop van de mens. Ontwikkeling en Ontwikkelingsmogelijkheden in Verschillende Levensfasen, Rotterdam, 1978; Jung, C. G., "The Stages of Life," *Modern Man in Search of a Soul*, Routledge & Kegan Paul, London, 1933, pp. 109-131.

Publisher's note to the 1994 edition: *Astro-Psychology* was first published by Aquarian Press in England. It is now available as *Psychological Astrology: A Synthesis of Jungian Psychology and Astrology*. York Beach, ME: Samuel Weiser, 1990.

connected with personal and thus subjective values, it reacts and works completely from the collective unconscious and universal human values.[3]

The psyche is always striving for balance, and psychic energy plays a key role in this. Whenever our consciousness receives too strong an emphasis, mechanisms of repression are overly activated, and the unconscious initiates compensating actions, completely beyond the control of the individual's will. When psychic energy has been concentrated too long in consciousness, characteristics dormant in the unconscious haven't had a chance for expression. This results in an inadequate ability to react in certain situations, and thus an inner need arises to bring this potential ability to the surface. The great difference in charge between consciousness and the unconscious results in a transfer of psychic energy to the unconscious. This happens, for instance, when someone continually uses his superior element at times when his inferior element would be better equipped to handle the situation. As the conscious constantly draws attention to itself, and the unconscious subsequently receives little or no energy or attention, a difference in charge gradually occurs. This continues until the deficiency of the inferior element is so great that it begins to draw energy back to itself. The connection between the conscious and the unconscious is formed by our inferior function.[4]

When the superior element is air, we tend to see everything from a mental viewpoint. We react to our surroundings with our minds, we communicate words rather than feelings. If air is the superior element, water is the inferior function, and will stay in the unconscious. Air will not handle emotional circumstances as easily as water would, so this individual may try to be logical or mental in an emotional situation. Too much energy is being put into the superior function, giving no energy to the unconscious water element. This may cause environmental problems, because the individual is not reacting to circumstances in a way that others will understand. Some may say this person is "cool." Or you may find

---

[3] For the most comprehensive information about the collective unconscious see Jung, C.G., *The Archetypes and the Collective Unconscious*, Collected Works, Vol. 9, Part 1, Routledge & Kegan Paul, London, 1975.

[4] Wolff, T., *Studien zu C. G. Jungs Psychologie*, Rhein Verlag, Zurich, 1959, p. 190.

this person talking at moments when tenderness is required. This causes psychic problems within the self, for sooner or later the unconscious will take the needed energy to itself, and the superior function will have to cope with unconscious pressures.

The example above shows the process of expression of psychic energy within time, in a series of events. However, if we examine the movement of psychic energy in the light of the psyche's totality, we can distinguish certain coordinated and simultaneous processes. The conscious-unconscious division of the psyche is the basis of *synchronic compensation*: *i.e.,* the phenomenon that, as certain conscious contents are lacking, there is a simultaneous increase in unconscious activity. (If the unconscious gets the upper hand, the conscious is functioning inadequately at the same time.)

One can speak of a division of powers within the whole. Through Freudian slips of the pen or tongue, our conscious notices an increase in independent unconscious activity and is eventually able to correct it. This correcting is a conscious *interference* to slow down the natural movement of psychic energy. Without interference, psychic energy would flow from where it is present to where there is a lack. A natural movement from full consciousness to the emptier unconscious would then take place. There is no law dictating that energy must first flow back into the unconscious until a static balance is achieved. On the contrary, Toni Wolff says, "...It is inherent to the creative nature of the psyche that intereference with the plain course of nature forms its structure."[5] This indicates that humans possess the possibility of influencing psychic processes in certain directions.

There are two different processes in the course of psychic energy:

> A horizontal or *diachronic*[6] process that takes place in time and which is connected with a chronological order of events, and

> A vertical or *synchronic*[7] process that relates to the transfer of psychic energy, i.e. the amount and the

[5]*Ibid*, p. 188.

[6]Diachronic means of or pertaining to the time of the earth's existence.

[7]Synchronic means a process in the spatial sense: more than one thing is happening at different levels at the same time.

direction of flow at any given moment between consciousness and the unconscious.

The direction and division of psychic energy at a certain
moment in the synchronic process is accompanied by a certain
attitude of consciousness. This attitude evokes reactions from both
the unconscious and the outside world. The nature of the unconscious implies that its reactions escape the conscious mind, yet,
mixed with the actions of consciousness, these reactions in turn
evoke counteractions from the outside world. These counteractions
are experienced as important incidents or events. These events in
turn have repercussions and influence the attitude of consciousness.
The flow of energy that consciousness demands is changed,
bringing another alteration in the unconscious and its reactions.
From events occurring chronologically in time, we can learn about
the nature and the extent of the interaction between the diachronic
process (horizontal in time) and the synchronic process (the vertical
transfer of energy in a more spatial sense) and therefore about the
relative amount of energy involved. Psychic energy is a time-space-
continuum, whereby independent events relate to each other within
the division between consciousness and the unconscious. Psychic
energy explains not so much the material form of expression as the
mutual relationship between psychic contents.

To give examples, everyone has said at times, "I used to be
interested in that, but now I've completely lost interest." Or, "I used
to feel more intensely or perceive things more sharply, but now I'm
indifferent." And applied in a more spatial sense, "I would really
like to do certain things, but in spite of my will power, I don't seem
to be able to bring up enough energy." This shows a first condition:
energy can neither originate from nothingness nor return to
nothingness; the total amount of energy in a closed system always
remains constant. In psychology, this condition means that energy
has withdrawn from a former investment and has now activated
another content, which may as yet be unknown to us.

In the second case, in spite of his will power, the person
in question can achieve nothing. Energy is not at the disposal of
consciousness, implying that this energy must be present somewhere
in the unconscious. Often we notice this by a more vivid dream life
or, where there are repressions and other psychic imbalances, we see
such symptoms as nervousness, restlessness, emotional irritability,

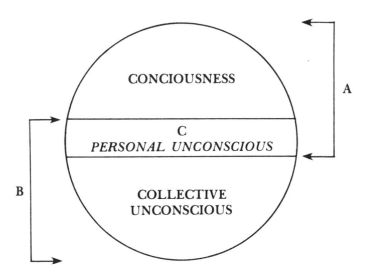

Figure 2.1. The personal unconscious holds the middle ground. The upper sextion (A) indicates the area belonging to consciousness, as seen in terms of psychic energy. The lower portion of the figure (B) indicates the area out of which unconscious reactions emerge which can "correct" consciousness. In the middle ground (C) the personal unconscious rests. This is the part of the unconscious that can be made conscious by the development of consciousness within the individual.

---

exaggerated activity, incomprehensible and inexplicable fears, depression and other similar phenomena.[8] The energy which is withdrawn from consciousness gives a greater intensity to unconscious contents, through which these contents intrude upon consciousness and cause disturbances. Keep in mind that symptoms and disturbances are also mechanisms to balance the psyche, and that the flowing of psychic energy does this. Psychic energy follows its own natural course here; flowing to a deficiency which needs to be filled. In terms of physics, this flow would only come to a standstill when there is equal energy everywhere and the deficiency is made good. Psychologically, however, the possibility exists of

[8]*Ibid*, p. 183.

channeling or partly turning aside the current through intervention from our consciousness. The creative power of the psyche lies in this: blind processes of nature don't always have to be blindly followed.

In regard to energy, the total psyche is seen as a closed system, in which the conscious and the unconscious interact with each other. The *personal* unconscious is considered part of the conscious system as far as energy is concerned, because its contents are psychologically connected with the ego or the *I* and therefore can be taken up into consciousness.[9] Figure 2.1. will illustrate this concept.

During the formation of the personality in childhood, for instance, a great deal of psychic energy is directed toward composing the ego. The child acts entirely in and from the unconscious, primarily from the collective unconscious. Since the child has had little time to gather and forget experience, the personal unconscious is still very small. The conscious and unconscious systems are hardly divided in a young child. At a given moment, the natural flow of psychic energy is subjected to a certain inexplicable interference whereby it begins to form an ego or *I*. A distinction begins to appear between the conscious and the unconscious parts of the psyche; consciousness then differentiates itself more and more in terms of functions and becomes a relatively closed system. The part of the psyche adjacent to the deeper levels of our unconscious becomes largely separated as a more conscious attitude is assumed. Differences in energy between the conscious and the unconscious system give rise to inner conflicts that express themselves in various ways at each age.

The young child shows a definite ambiguity: should he follow his own natural impulses, so strongly active in him, or should he adapt socially so that his ever-forming conscious self receives praise? In the adolescent, the disparity in energy expresses itself in the so-called *Sturm und Drang* period,[10] while the more mature individual experiences tension as he lives through inner pairs of contrasts (or, better, complementary functions) which demand a solution. Gradually these contrasts in consciousness decrease and a connection

---

[9]*Ibid*, p. 189.

[10]A term denoting the restlessness of adolescence and the insecurity felt during that period. It's a time for proving yourself a real "man" or "woman."

between consciousness and the unconscious can be established. This connection can be positive or negative; it can be maintained either through a stable but rigid attitude of consciousness, where changes are no longer allowed, or it can be maintained through the creation of a dynamic balance, where consciousness still adapts to change without so quickly losing its inner balance.

The connection between consciousness and the unconscious is established by the inferior function, or, astrologically speaking, by the inferior element, whose undeveloped condition draws energy to itself. The gradual adaptive attempts of the inferior element result more in the development of the entire personality than in a differentiation of consciousness. In regard to this point, Toni Wolff says, "...the firmly anchored consciousness becomes a function of the unlocked conscious awareness."[11] Psychic energy is sometimes called life energy because the flowing of energy always means that the psyche remains dynamic. This energy includes adaptation to both the outside world and its own inner world—the unconscious. The direction followed by psychic energy within the individual is closely connected with the astrological crosses, which I dealt with in *Astro-Psychology*. Before we go into specific astrological effects, it is necessary to look closer at the directions of the movement of psychic energy.

2. THE PROGRESSIVE AND REGRESSIVE DIRECTION OF ENERGY[12]

Our life is a process of continual adaptation. We are constantly dealing with both external circumstances that we cannot deny and with internal, often unconscious, factors that likewise cannot be ignored. We can speak of a continuing duality in our consciousness: every day we encounter something new in life which demands a decision based on a conscious or sometimes completely unconscious choice. Our path in life is a reflection of all of our choices. When we

---

[11]*Ibid*, p. 191.

[12]In this section, the following books have been used as reference: Wolff, T., *Studien zu C.G. Jungs Psychologie*, Teil III: Der Psychologische Energiebegriff, Rhein Verlag, Zurich, 1959, pp. 172-213; and Jung, C.G., *The Structure and Dynamics of the Psyche*, Collected Works, Vol 8, Routledge & Kegan Paul, London, 1977, pp. 3-67.

try to imagine what goes on in each person's consciousness it could be pictured as a "battle" taking place between two differing factions. Two extreme possibilities of choice (conscious or not) are asking for a decision. Once the choice has been made, the contents of "yes" remain important for our consciousness, while the contents of "no" disappear to the unconscious to join the countless other contents hidden there.

There are two ways we can adapt ourselves and influence our process of choice. The first way is to adapt ourselves as much as possible to the conscious demands of life, meeting the demands of the surroundings. When our psychic energy works this way, we speak of a *progressive direction*.[13] The progressive direction requires directedness of consciousness and attitude, but includes the risk of one-sidedness. It can easily happen that a particular attitude no longer provides the adaptation required by the surroundings, because changes in these surroundings demand another attitude.

For example, someone who naturally displays an attitude of feeling in his adaptation to the demands of reality may find himself in a situation that can only be resolved through thinking. In that case, the feeling response collapses and the progression of psychic energy (also called life energy or libido) also stops. The outward process of adaptation goes on strike! Psychic energy must then redirect itself and the goal becomes adaptation to inner needs. This is the second direction of psychic energy, the inward direction, or *regressive direction*.[14]

The progressive direction of the libido means that our superior function gradually beomes further developed and differentiated. This function, dealt with at length in the last chapter, determines the way in which we approach the world about us and therefore it deals with things outside ourselves. In the example just given, we can assume water formed the superior element and air the inferior. When insufficient energy is retained in consciousness, (in this case the element water), the process of regression automatically sets in.

[13]This is a psychological term and does not refer to astrological progressions or directions.

[14]Regressive direction is a psychological term, not to be confused with astrological *directions*.

The energy flows back into the unconscious and activates the inferior function there.

One thing should be remembered: the progressive movement is always characterized by the leading role played by the conscious system, whereby the inferior function, with its slight change, supplies just enough tension to accentuate the superior function until too much is repressed or one's approach becomes inadequate. Because the course of the energy can no longer aid the development of the superior function, congestion takes place. This congestion is accompanied by an intensification of the background contents of the psyche and by a continuing inadequacy of conscious adaptation. A fall appears between the conscious and unconscious systems whereby energy begins to flow back toward the unconscious— regression. The stronger the progression, the longer it lasts and the stronger the emphasis on outward adaptation. The more powerful then will be the regression, which is directed at adapting to the "forgotten" demands of the inner self. In *outward* adaptation (progression), subjective factors are all too often dismissed, since in such an adaptation there is always compromise with the divergent contents of one's own self. In regression, all these subjective factors come to the surface.

In contrast to the conscious directedness of the progressive movement, regression is not consciously directed, but is the natural course of psychic energy caused by the development of a "fall" or differences in charge. Therefore, regression is much less concerned with the superior function of consciousness than with the inferior element and its demands. In the first chapter, we learned that the inferior function is directly contrary to the superior conscious function, and because of the nature of this relationship, the inferior function often contains very "disturbing" contents for our conscious adaptation. Perhaps this is one of the reasons why so many people don't appreciate the regressive movement of psychic energy as much as the seemingly pleasant progressive movement. Yet we need both movements equally if we are to grow into integrated human beings.

For example, when fire is the superior function, earth will be the inferior. Earth has many characteristics that disturb fire. Earth loves security, fire adores the insecurity of future possibilities. Earth likes the here and now because it is sure. Fire always wants something new, thinking about what is ahead. If fire is superior, earth will be in the unconscious. When a breakthrough from the unconscious allows earth contents to intrude into consciousness, these contents hinder fire's free expression. Suddenly, the fire types may become very insecure, looking to enhance personal security. These are the people who suddenly want to find out where to obtain the highest interest on their savings, only to forget about the whole idea a few days later. A sudden wish from the unconscious took over the normal pattern. One fire type said to me, "I want to be more free than I am, so I think I will only work part time and I will have more time to do what I like." But his inferior element added, "But first I want to have at least $30,000 so that I won't have to worry about being poor." Obviously the earth contents have intruded on the fire, and the compulsion caused by the earth element has caused this person to continue working full time. This type of energy can be temporary, or in horoscopes with difficult divisions, the energy can last longer.

Carl Jung tried to explain the direction of psychic energy more clearly using the example of a river that flows from a mountain to a valley. Everything flows smoothly until it meets an obstruction, for instance, a dam blocks its course to the valley. If the obstruction is high enough, the water can be dammed up behind the barrier until the water level is high enough to continue flowing. This can occur in different ways. For instance, the current can follow its course in its own natural bed, or the water can be led into a channel, in which electrical energy is produced through means of a paddle wheel generator. In any case, the water flows outwards again, in the direction of the valley.

In terms of psychic energy, this can be expressed as follows: the river originally had a progressive direction, toward the outside world. Confronted with the dam, the river was forced to eddy in circles for a time, an action contrary to the prior direction of current. This eddying can be compared to the regressive movement. Once this has gone on long enough (the water level has become high enough), the progressive direction can be resumed. Sometimes it is even possible to make use of the apparent and temporary standstill (the damming of the water) to produce new energy (electricity can be generated, for instance), though this doesn't necessarily have to happen.

In the theory of psychic energy, progression is a means to come to regression, while, conversely, regression is a means to return to progression. Therefore, adaptation to the outer world (progression) eventually results in clearer perception of the needs of the inner world, because adaptation to this inner world becomes increasingly necessary (regression). Regression brings us more into balance, so we can readapt more effectively to the demands of our surroundings (progression). We can go along with one of these directions of current for a shorter or longer period, but it is the rhythmical alternation between both energy directions that gives us "vitality."

We shouldn't confuse progression with development, since an uninterrupted flow of life doesn't always include development and differentiation. Many forms of animal and plant life have existed from ancient times without further differentiation. In the same way, the psychic life of man can be progressive without there being any evolution to speak of, just as his psychic life can be regressive without showing involution.

Just as progression isn't synonymous with development, regression isn't necessarily a step backwards, although it can be at times. This doesn't necessarily imply degeneration. More often it is just one step in a total process of development, even though the individual may not be aware that he is undergoing any such development. Perhaps he feels himself to be caught in a compulsive situation, a situation corresponding in some ways to childhood. (The inferior function has been activated, after all!) Regression becomes degeneration if the individual tries to hold onto this condition and to identify with the unconscious contents that have emerged.

We should not confuse progression and regression with the terms *extroversion* and *introversion*. Extroversion and introversion can be both progressive and regressive. In other words, someone with a rather stable psychological attitude, who is also extroverted (oriented to the outer world) can be busy for a long time adapting to his own inner world, while outwardly showing little of this process. His attitude can thus remain extroverted, although his psychic energy is completely directed towards his unconscious.

3. The Three Crosses

In my book *Astro-Psychology*, I described the connection between the three crosses in astrology and the direction of psychic energy current or libido.[15] In this section, we will work out this theoretical background in practice.

If the examples that follow sometimes seem extreme or black and white, this is done as a means of putting the essential points into clear perspective. In practice, there are many different factors in a horoscope that can weaken or strengthen the total picture. To judge more fully, we must continually take the whole framework of the cross division into consideration. We will deal with this framework in the following section.

THE CARDINAL CROSS

In traditional astrology, *the cardinal cross* (Aries, Cancer, Libra and Capricorn) is attributed an outward orientation. Values are derived from the surroundings and adaptation to external circumstances plays a main role. Each of the four signs adapts in a completely unique way, corresponding to the four elements.

The outgoing, driving force corresponds to the previously described *progressive* direction of psychic energy. The process of adaptation to external circumstances is central to that direction as well. This doesn't mean that regression never occurs within these four signs. On the contrary, every person goes through progressive and regressive periods in the course of his life. However, the similarity between the cardinal signs and progressive energy lies in a primary focus on the outer world, without needing to make the division into extroversion or introversion. For cardinal people, adaptation to the demands of the outer world will continually take precedence over adaptation to the inner world.

For Aries, this implies a very impetuous attitude, including a desire to conquer, absorb, and fit everything into the mainstream of human experience. At first glance, this hardly resembles adaptation, since Aries sees everything from his own vantage point. However, adaptation to external circumstances in the sense of progressive energy doesn't necessarily imply a flexible social attitude. It is very possible to conform to outward matters and situations, adapting one's psychic direction to the external world, without becoming a

[15]Hamaker-Zondag, K.M., *Astro-Psychology*, Ch. 3.

socially adapted individual! The Aries individual is mainly directed to things outside himself, with which he can occupy himself and towards which he can direct his psychic energy. The situations Aries encounters can make him or break him.

The Cancer individual also conforms to outer norms; it is important for this water sign to know what people think so that he can act accordingly, and his own feelings are quickly adjusted to what is proper. This is a completely different way of expressing progressive energy than we saw with Aries. However, both signs direct energy outwards, just as do Libra and Capricorn.

Libra, like Cancer, derives its values from the surroundings, but being specifically oriented towards social intercourse, it also participates in forming these social values. Flexibility, harmony and balance in relationships are central for this sign, so that here we also see adaptation to the demands of the surroundings, although in a rather mental way.

Capricorn derives its values from the surroundings very concretely. He therefore prefers to undertake purposeful, practical, and preferably prominent work, whereby he attempts to lead everything into channels according to fixed patterns. Capricorn is a maker of laws and regulations, to which he also submits himself. This sign, despite an often quiet, introverted manner, is also strongly involved in what happens around it, and adapts in its own earth sign way.

The cardinal cross, which represents progressive energy, very definitely needs exchange and cooperation with its surroundings, no matter how this is expressed. The signs Aries and Capricorn relate most things directly to themselves; the signs Cancer and Libra relate a great deal to other people as well, which indirectly reflects back upon themselves.

THE FIXED CROSS

The *fixed cross* (Taurus, Leo, Scorpio, and Aquarius) most closely corresponds with regressive energy. Again, this doesn't mean that people with fixed signs strong in their horoscopes constantly live in a regressive manner; rather, they are mainly directed toward adapting to the inner self and inner felt values. In complete correspondence with the laws of the psyche, they will normally experience periods of progression as well. Their main unconscious concern is to straighten out their own unconscious contents, no matter what the world may think. Naturally, this doesn't always happen without crises. This cross is not called the Cross of Christ or the cross of crisis for nothing.

Having an adaptation process predominantly directed to the demands of the unconscious, these fixed signs will be confronted with their own unconscious, in which the inferior element plays the main role. Directly contrary to our conscious attitude, it is the least developed element and largely uncontrolled in its activity. Since the psychic energy of the fixed signs is primarily directed toward unfolding and exploring the unconscious, conscious energy is invested in the inferior element. Therefore, it can make itself strongly felt. Moreover, a fixed sign has an absolute need to continually bring to the surface that which is contrary to its conscious self, in order to realize an inner balance, often a lengthy and difficult process. As the inferior element becomes more important, the characteristics belonging to that element seem to form part of the conscious element. The following section will clarify the intense inner polarity in reference to the four signs themselves.

A Taurus can stay with something for an extremely long time and deal with it very conscientiously. Even though a business has long been declared a lost cause, Taurus will still work faithfully for it, because he still sees something in it. "To see perspective in something" is a typical characteristic of fire, the inferior element for Taurus. Being directed toward inner adaptation, he will take fire characteristics into his conscious attitude, but they still retain their inferior character. Consciously he can't work with them, yet they play an important role for him. They may even be the source of his feeling of loyalty. In practice, this can have both positive and negative results. On one hand, he runs the risk of wasting his energy on lost causes, stubbornly staying too long. On the other hand, Taurus can help an organization or group through a difficult period by continuing to work as though nothing were wrong. His daily life is therefore a combination of a superior earth element (sensation) and an inferior fire element (intuition) which his regressive tendency regularly brings to the surface.

Leo, a fire sign, shows the reverse picture. Parts of the unconscious inferior earth element are often revealed in the Leo attitude. Leo's need for luxury, mentioned in every classical astrology text, can be seen as an expression of this earth element coming to the surface. Of its own accord, a fire sign doesn't care much about material things—the concrete or material is their weakest point. Yet, for a fire sign, Leo is very attached to the material and concrete: the element earth in his unconscious, activated through his regressive tendency, is playing a role in his consciousness. The inferior function often forms that part of our psyche that we try to silence through overcompensation because it creates uncertainty. Leo's sometimes exaggerated display of luxury and material beauty can easily express uncertainty about the material world. Through his material emphasis, he can derive a certain feeling of security.

Scorpio also digs into the unconscious—and in fact is known for this. This water sign, experienced by the world as very emotional, is nonetheless constantly ordering and analyzing everything it experiences. This is a typical air characteristic, but air is the inferior element for a water sign. Here again, the unconscious function is re-activated by the predominantly regressive energy of the fixed sign. Scorpio's digging into the unconscious is thus a combination of a feeling evaluation and an experiencing of events, on the one hand, and a constant endeavor to analyze and explain things mentally, on the other. In accordance with the compulsive nature of the inferior function, Scorpio's analytic approach sometimes seems to predominate—at least to the outside world.

The last fixed sign, Aquarius, is generally known as having a people-oriented approach and a need to exchange ideas and thoughts. Yet this is only an apparent adaptation to the outer world in that he is interested in the world but he holds on as long as possible to his own world view and framework of ideas, and his view is largely derived from his own inner self. Aquarius adheres longest to theories or images of the world which have an emotional value for him; in other words, to those things which connect him with his inferior unconscious water element. Anyone who has thoroughly studied the signs has probably noticed how much Aquarius becomes involved in emotional situations and, more than any other sign, holds on (consciously) or remains attached (unconsciously) to them. Although as an air sign Aquarius will naturally try to rationalize everything, often things only have meaning when they touch his feelings and therefore release something in him that he *can't* rationalize. With his tendency to direct energy mainly towards his own inner self, he won't pass up any chance to experience something completely. He is searching for the essence of all things, in an attempt to fit everything into his mental picture of the world. Aquarius' talent for psychology derives largely from this combination of superior thinking (air) and unconcious inferior feeling (water).

THE MUTABLE CROSS

The third cross in astrology, containing the mutable signs Gemini, Virgo, Sagittarius and Pisces, doesn't always show itself clearly. Some astrologers find it weak in its manner of expression.[16] Others find it a synthesis of the preceding two crosses, while still others call this cross pre-eminently changeable, flexible and accommodating.[17]

Psychologically, the mutable cross has no fixed direction for its energy: it is neither regressive nor progressive, and can express itself in both forms. The mutable cross temporarily follows a regressive or progressive direction in turn, yet neither direction is predominant. Therefore, this cross plays a unique role in the psyche, which we can best illustrate once more by Carl Jung's example of the river. The progressive direction corresponds with the natural downward flow of the river from the mountain to the valley, while the regressive energy direction corresponds with the temporary effect of the water being dammed by a barrier in the river. Once the lake that is formed has collected enough water, the water can be led away (for instance, in a canal), so that the progressive direction again prevails. The mutable cross plays a dual role in this process: on one hand, this cross is able to turn progressive energy into regressive energy through laying a dam, and, on the other hand, the mutable cross is able to release the dammed up energy by forming a channel so progression can start again.

[16]Kündig, H., *Das Horoskop*, Die Berechnung, Darstellung und Erklärung. Ansata Verlag, Zürich, 1950, pp. 171-172.

[17]For various approaches to the crosses see: Jansky, R.C., *Selected Topics in Astrology*, Van Nuys, Ca., 1974, p. 28; Hone, M.E., *The Modern Textbook of Astrology*, Fowler, London, 1970, p. 42; Libra, C. Aq., *Astrologie, haar Techniek Ken Ethiek*, Amersfoort, 1923, p. 42; Arroyo, S., *Astrology, Psychology, and the Four Elements*, CRCS, Reno, 1975, pp. 87-170.

This dualistic function is one possible explanation for the outwardly elusive quality of the mutable. On one hand, the mutable cross can work in an extremely stimulating and adaptable way, and on the other, it is just as capable of bringing in all sorts of obstructions, and thus achieving the opposite. We will constantly find this mutable cross on the junction or turning-point of psychic energy, as in figure 2.2.

Mutable energy is always revolving in the transition from the conscious to the unconscious, being alternately active in one or the other. In certain respects, mutable energy is a synthesis of the progressive and regressive direction, as it includes both. The very fact that the energy keeps revolving around the middle allows the possibility of maintaining both the progressive and regressive directions of energy in balance.

This is probably why wisdom and harmony were traditionally attributed to this cross, although this concept does not mean people born in mutable signs are paragons of wisdom. Rather, the mutable cross is a means for the psyche to dissolve, integrate, and change so

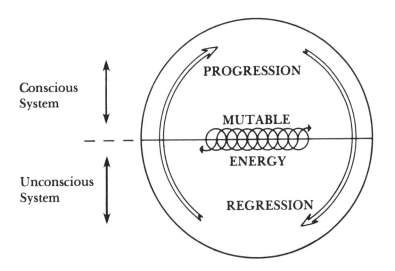

Figure 2.2. The mutable cross illustrates the constant interplay of action between the conscious and unconscious facets of the expression of the energy of the psyche.

that part of the ego disappears or loses some of its value for the whole psyche; only then can one experience things as they really are, without the self being in the way. That *can* lead to wisdom and harmony, but it also includes the danger of becoming estranged from oneself, due to preoccupation with this middle area of the psyche. Once a mutable type has landed in this no man's land, only through contact with strongly progressive or regressive types will he be able to re-experience the depths of his own personality. Otherwise, he must find a way to activate his own regressive and progressive possibilities. The mutable cross, therefore, symbolizes a transition between the progressive and the regressive psychic energy, while at the same time it includes both. This is an apparent duality that is expressed in the dualistic character of the mutable signs as well.

Of the two means of expression for the mutable cross, namely setting up a psychic obstruction (creating a dam) or setting the psychic progression in motion once more (laying a drainage canal), the latter is most apparent. Energy flows outward and is more directly experienced by the person himself and his surroundings. The formation of a dam in the psychic energy current, however, is equally a feature of the mutable cross. The goal is to correct excessive actions of the psyche by reversing the direction of psychic energy and bringing about harmony or balance once more. The formation of a dam, in order that the lake may fill up, also means simultaneously that this same mutable energy will begin forming the new drainage canal. (In extreme cases, the water will never reach any significant level.) This mechanism also characterizes the outward service orientation of the mutable type, as the function of serving corresponds with the meaning of service traditionally attributed to this cross.

This attitude of service is also expressed in another area. When a horoscope is either markedly progressive (cardinal) or regressive (fixed), the mutable cross will be subordinate to the main tendency up to a certain point, while continuing to express unmistakably an essential part of its mutable character. In such a case, we can see a great degree of compliance with the other directions of energy, while the mutable cross retains its own transitional function. For example, a Sagittarius (mutable) may have most of his planets, and even the Ascendant, in fixed signs, and may therefore look rather fixed and oriented toward inner adaptation. When you observe this person closely, however, you may see that he is still mutable, expressing this energy in a subtle way, and he will be more flexible than may be apparent on first sight.

In contrast, a person having strong mutable signs and houses will show a different picture. Psychic energy continually circles around the transition area between consciousness and the unconscious; the conscious system and the unconscious contents predominate in turn. It is difficult for this person or those around him to have a clear image of what he really is as a person. In many cases, self-evaluation doesn't interest him anyhow, unless other contents of his horoscope contradict. It isn't a question he worries about. Having both regressive and progressive directions, he can revert to extremes without wanting to become fixed in either extreme. In that sense, the mutable cross is then literally mutable.

The risk of becoming stuck is inherent in the mutability of this cross, something that is often ignored. This type takes life as it comes, so that adaptation within that narrow border of the psyche often appears more important than assimilation. There is danger that the mutable type will continue to build dams or drainage canals for himself and other people, without ever straightening out his own conscious or unconscious self. When the regressive current doesn't develop any further, the new progressive direction is not as intense as it would have been with a greater depth of regression. The stronger the regressive movement is within the psyche, the clearer the resulting progression will be. This is one possible explanation for Kündig's description of the mutable cross as having little intensity. With the very strong mutable types, this continual inner attempt to create balance can result in a lack of actual, outward balance. The person ignores actual problems or fools himself into thinking that the problem is solved almost as soon as it is recognized, when in reality one has just begun to tackle the problem.

On the other hand, the mutable signs can be very flexible in their approach to life, each in its own way, naturally. Being in a position of transition means that mutable signs can obstruct themselves considerably without noticing it (the dam under construction) but they can also make it easy for themselves by going on as usual despite all their problems (the canal under construction).

The fact that mutable energy has no clear direction, is active only in a limited area, and therefore is difficult to discern, may be one reason why this form of psychic energy is never really described as a separate case in analytical psychology. In the following material, the dangers that can arise from the duality of the mutable cross will receive some emphasis, since, in my opinion, very little has been said in astrology about this. This has nothing to do with a negative evaluation of the mutable signs. On the contrary, it is only for the sake of clarity that they are represented somewhat in caricature.

Gemini, the first mutable sign, is well known for his attitude of "trimming his sails to every wind." The amount of information this sign is able to collect and relate borders on the incredible. Yet he seldom builds a coherent view of the world; everything is left to the circumstances of the moment. Gemini is the happy-go-lucky merrymaker, but he lacks self-knowledge and this can estrange him strongly from himself. As overcompensation, Gemini can pry into the emotional life of others—the natural hunger for information remains—with the result that he can become quite shameless, becoming a walking gossip column filled with the latest news. This is exactly the opposite of the essentially cheerful, vivacious nature of Gemini who prefers to dig canals so that the water can flow again, yet the sign can become a dam for both himself and others.

Virgo, the second mutable sign, is known for its analytical ability which largely serves the idea that everything must be pure. Virgo is a pure sign, and for that reason chastity is usually connected astrologically with this sign. Virgo's constant dissection and consideration of things can result in a complete estrangement from himself: no connections are made, one's own self is looked at very critically and the whole disintegrates into small pieces. When there are no compensating tendencies in the horoscope, Virgo may change into the very opposite of its true nature through this mutable energy. It may seek the pure and pristine in what is not pure and pristine at all. Hence, chastity may lapse into bouts of excessive sexual activity, in the hope this immersion will provide a synthesis which cannot be arrived at through consciousness. The contrast between the inborn moderation of its own nature and the exuberant immoderation of the other side is both bridged and made sharper by Virgo's mutable energy. The mutability makes it possible to unite both sides in one person, but if this synthesis is ignored, it is still possible for Virgo to survive this duality without too much psychic damage. It may not even be much of a hindrance for Virgo.

Sagittarius, the third mutable sign, prefers to spread the information it has found and synthesized. Oriented toward teaching others and needing to investigate and judge everything, he is constantly examining everything around him. Yet he tends to overlook himself. In his mutable fire ardor to put all his discoveries into the right terms, comprehensible for everyone, he risks getting stuck in transmitting information, while his eyes and ears are closed to information that could revise these opinions. His message can then become superficial, rigid dogma, and his life an expression of that dogma, while the human being himself lacks expression. Mutability then appears to be stuck, and the individual may seem to be more obstinate than those born into the fixed signs. The willingness of the mutable cross to adapt is no longer evident. Sagittarius then seems to have become constricted in the opposite of his true nature, by the same energy that could help him to break through his rigidity.

Pisces, the last mutable sign, combines mutability with a feeling (water) approach. This element is still capable of recognizing certain realities, but the mutable cross makes sure that some "extras" are added to these values. Pisces easily fits everything into his feeling world, but the ease with which this occurs means that not everything is tested for value or for its degree of reality. Often the process of assimilation takes place only later. An increasing number of unreal factors can begin to form reality for Pisces and, finally, to predominate. Therefore the danger of coming to live in a self-created dream world is always present. No longer able to experience his own self as such in this dream world, he begins to play an imaginary role and can become estranged from himself. Because all energy is focused on creating ideals and dreams for a non-existent reality, his rich inner life is robbed of its creative power. Once more, it is the mutable energy which can help Pisces out of this situation or help him remain completely untroubled by it, even though those around him may think differently.

A definite directed movement was evident with progressive (cardinal) energy, and an undirected yet clearly distinguishable movement with regressive (fixed) energy. Mutable energy, however, only shows movement without any fixed direction. To say that mutable energy runs the risk of stagnating sounds paradoxical, yet it is not. In this case, the energy has retreated into a very narrow area on the borderline between consciousness and the unconscious. The drainage canal is being dug as soon as the dam begins to be constructed. The progressive and regressive fluctuation is minimal and mutability is nearly at a standstill. Life concentrates itself in a narrow, impersonal border area and can no longer identify with what is above or below. The resulting immovability and lack of flexibility have nothing in common with the tenacity attributed to the fixed cross. The fixed cross can ultimately arrive at a more flexible attitude because of a tenacious delving into its own unconscious. In this respect, the cardinal cross can be said to be somewhere between the mutable and the fixed cross. For instance, someone with a cardinal Sun and all other planets in fixed signs, will show strong regressive tendencies, despite his Sun sign's more progressive direction.

As mentioned earlier, in judging the direction of energy, it isn't correct to consider only the Sun sign, no matter how important the Sun might be in the horoscope. For a clear overall picture it is necessary to make a diagram of the crosses—something we will discuss in the following section.

4. How To Determine Cross Divisions

We first make a classification into potential and circumstances (that is, signs and houses) for the division of the crosses, just as we did with the element division of the horoscope. We check the cardinal cross planets first by listing all the planets found in Aries, Cancer, Libra and Capricorn. Next we look at the first, fourth, seventh, and tenth houses. The fixed cross includes Taurus, Leo, Scorpio and Aquarius, and the fixed houses are the second, fifth, eighth and eleventh. The mutable cross includes Gemini, Virgo, Sagittarius, and Pisces, along with the third, sixth, ninth and twelfth houses.

After each cross we note which planets are found there (in the sign column). Note the sign of the Ascendant and the Midheaven as well. We repeat this for the houses, so that we have a picture of how potential relates to experience and circumstances. As with the element division, we can sum up all the contents, but this total doesn't necessarily tell us anything about the real strength of the cross. Before we can make a judgement we must make a distinction

Crosses	Signs	Houses	Total
CARDINAL	♃ ♄ ♅	☽ ♃ ♀ ♄ ♅	8
FIXED	☿ ☉ ♂ ♇ Asc.	☿ ♄	7
MUTABLE	♀ Mc. ♄ ☽	☉ ♂ ♇	7

Figure 2.3. An illustration of the crosses as they appear in Fred's horoscope. See Chart 1 on page 14.

between personal and impersonal planets, as we did in the previous section.

We can make the same sort of list that we did in Chapter 1. The division of the crosses in Fred's horoscope (Chart 1 on page 14) is shown in figure 2.3. Figure 2.4 illustrates Marilyn Monroe's horoscope (see Chart 2 on page 18).

In figure 2.4. you will see that we have applied the rule that when a planet is located close to the cusp of the following house, it comes into expression in the following house (as discussed in Chapter 1, Section 3). In Marilyn's chart, Venus is located within four degrees of an angular house, near the Midheaven (or the cusp of the tenth house) and isn't retrograde. Venus remains in the sign of Aries, but in regard to houses Venus is counted as being in effect in the tenth house.

Crosses	Signs	Houses	Total
CARDINAL	♀ ♇	♅ ♄ ☽ ♃ ♀	7
FIXED	Mc. Asc. ♅ ♄ ☽ ♃	♂ ☿ ☉	9
MUTABLE	☉ ♀ ♂ ♅	♄ ♇	6

Figure 2.4. The cardinal, fixed and mutable planets and houses in Marilyn Monroe's chart. See Chart 2 on page 18. As you will notice, the planets are not entered in the order of the planetary motion in the zodiac, but as they appear in the chart.

5. CROSS DIVISION INTERPRETATION

In the first part of one's life, potential (sign) plays a greater role than circumstance (house). Therefore we need to look first at the planets in the signs, and only then can we examine any shifts that might occur through the planet being located in a house belonging to another cross.

In Fred's chart (page 14), three of the most important personal contents, symbolized by Sun, Mercury, and the Ascendant, are located in fixed signs. In potential, therefore, one can speak of a regressive movement of energy, which demands that consciousness adapt to its .own inner norms. The mutable signs contain some important personal contents as well: the Moon, Venus and Midheaven. Though this mutable energy can give support to the regressive movement in many respects, Fred will show fewer traits from the fixed cross and more progression (mutability) as he grows older. The fixed cross plays a much smaller role in his circumstances (houses) than it does in potential (sign), even though Mercury in Taurus repeats itself by being in a fixed house (the fifth). The Sun and Mars in fixed signs must express themselves in mutable houses, while the Moon and Venus, located in mutable signs, bring their mutable energy to bear on the cardinal houses that show a progressive movement of energy. (We are restricting ourselves to personal planets.) In all respects, Fred shows a gradual shift in his center of gravity: fixed to mutable, mutable to cardinal. This means that a more balanced division of energy can take place as Fred grows older, and also that the mutable cross, which necessarily marks the position of transition, will become increasingly important. The fixed sign ability to persevere, the driving force behind the will to experience and assimilate, is helped by the ability of the mutable cross energy to make things relative. Moreover, the increasing importance of the cardinal energy helps make the values of the surroundings seem less pressing at the same time that there is a growing willingness to meet certain outer demands halfway. One advantage of this division is that the division of psychic energy becomes relatively balanced. One disadvantage can be that, because of this relative balance, the need of the fixed cross to digest things and conform solely to itself no longer can be fulfilled. And despite a growing balance, he will occasionally feel unsatisfied, especially since this horoscope shows such a strong occupation of the fixed signs.

In Fred's case, the shifts can occur gradually, without too many shocks. By shifts, we mean the transfer of the way a planet (content) expresses itself (determined by the cross it's in) into circumstances (determined by another cross) as indicated by the house. A shift from fixed to cardinal or vice versa (regression and progression) can cause the greatest problems if the horoscope shows no support for the transition.

The second horoscope (Marilyn Monroe in Chart 2 on page 18) shows problematical shifts. The potential is mutable (Sun and Mercury) with a fixed undertone (Midheaven, Ascendant and the Moon). That fixed cross becomes increasingly important because the Sun and Mercury are in fixed houses, whil the mutable houses contain no personal planets. Many of the planets in fixed signs shift to cardinal houses, so tension arises between a regressive direction in fixed sign planets which must express themselves in progression. By itself, that wouldn't necessarily be serious; however, in this division, something personal is lacking in the transitional (mutable) cross, at least in house position. See figure 2.4. In potential, Marilyn was able to maintain a balance between progression and regression, though the relation between potential and circumstance threatened to become more strained as she grew older. Her ability to change to a regressive movement when problems appeared, as well as to withdraw from a regressive situation by finding new channels, had difficulty expressing itself through her life circumstances. Her planets in mutable signs found themselves moreover in fixed houses,

Crosses	Signs	Houses	Total
CARDINAL	☉ ♄ ♂ ♅	♃ ☽	6
FIXED	☽ Mc. ♋ Asc. ♀ ♃	♄ ♂ ☿ ☉ ♅	11
MUTABLE	♄ ☿	♅ ♀ ♌	5

Figure 2.5. The cardinal, fixed and mutable planets and houses in Peter's chart. See Chart 3 on page 42 in order to follow along with the entries made here.

except for Uranus. In contrast, her feminine contents, the Moon and Venus, expressed through cardinal houses. In fact, her cross division is very different than Fred's horoscope: there we saw an increasing balance, while, here, we see a growing duality. This second horoscope, therefore, offers the possibility of experiencing life very intensely, but it also includes the danger of extreme states of mind.

The third and last example, Peter's horoscope (Chart 3 on page 42), shows us a broad picture. The Sun is in a cardinal sign, the Moon, Midheaven and Ascendant are in fixed signs, and Mercury is in a mutable. With the distribution shown in figure 2.5, it is difficult to give a clear opinion about which cross is most decisive in sign. The Sun becomes more decisive in such a distribution, but at the same time more vulnerable. Within this cross division, the cardinal cross comes first, with some reservations, which means that the progressive energy direction is important, although the houses also help determine that this direction is maintained.

The Moon presented as fixed in potential (sign), actually appears in a cardinal house, but the most striking thing is the strong shift of planets from cardinal and mutable signs to fixed houses. In many cases, this would be an indication that despite the initial progressive movement, regression will play an increasingly important role, especially since the mutable Mercury must be active in a fixed house. By such a broad sign distribution, the houses become decisive in meaning at a much earlier age. In Peter's horoscope, we can already see during his first Moon-Saturn cycle,[18] an increasing tendency to measure himself by his own values, even though, as an Aries, he is strongly oriented to the outer world.

Up to a certain point, Venus in a mutable house (the sixth) gives the possibility of forming a bridge between one energy direction and another, because Venus belongs to the personal planets. Characteristically, Peter feels most at ease and in harmony with himself when he activates his own Venus, both in love relationships with women and in his artistic occupations: he is a musician. (Such a personal planet in a bridging position was completely lacking in Marilyn Monroe's horoscope. In her case, only the eruptive planets, Uranus and Pluto, were located in

[18]For a complete discussion of Moon-Saturn cycle, please see my book *Astro-Psychology*.

mutable houses, which offers hardly any hold for conscious experience and assimilation of circumstances.)

The crosses really only take on meaning when we connect them with the elements of the horoscope, while the element division gains new dimension through the crosses. The interpretation of only a single element or only one cross remains extremely limited. The combination of both of these basic factors in the horoscope will serve as a general frame of reference to analyze the horoscope further. In the following chapter, we will combine elements and crosses.

Chapter Three

Elements and Crosses:
Foundation for Structure of Personality

1. The Difference Between Element and Cross

Before we discuss the combined effect of the elements and the crosses, it may be useful to note once more the difference between these two astrological concepts. The elements indicate the way one views and experiences the world, whereby we can distinguish four basic possibilities: thinking (air), feeling (water), intuition (fire) and sensation (earth). *One* of these functions predominates in consciousness, becoming the superior function, which determines the attitude of consciousness. The inferior function is located in the unconscious, opposite the main function of consciousness. The two remaining functions or elements can develop into auxiliary functions of consciousness.

Therefore, the element primarily says something about a person's view of the world, the attitude of consciousness, and the way he experiences and judges everything he meets. These ways of experiencing and these attitudes of consciousness still do not tell us how someone *adapts* to events and circumstances, nor about the processes of assimilation and adaptation. The crosses provide information about these psychic processes while the elements give us information about the contents of the horoscope. They show the basis upon which a person constructs his world view and the element from which one might expect counteractions to come. The crosses, on the other hand, give us *no* information about contents, but rather information about the *processes* which regulate both the relation between the elements themselves and between the person and his environment.

Combining the four elements with the three crosses is bound to fail if we are unable to distinguish the crosses from the specific attitudes of consciousness which we have attributed to the elements. We can best illustrate this elementary difference with an example. When four different elements look at a white tea cup, the earth element will perceive it concretely: it is white, it has a handle and a specific form. The air element is able to distinguish it as a tea cup and allots it a place in the series of phenomena air encounters. Water feels whether it finds the tea cup beautiful and whether it is pleasant to drink from, and on the basis of this, water gives the cup a certain value. The fire element, on the other hand, has had its imagination set loose by seeing the cup, and perceives all the things one might do with the cup. Fire sees the invisible connection, as it were, between the cup and everything else that can be related to it.

When the element earth, on the basis of its concrete, sensory perception, says it is a beautiful cup, earth is saying that the cup's proportion, color, and other external factors are pleasing. When the fire element agrees that the cup is beautiful, on the other hand, it is speaking from an entirely different world. Very possibly the fire type can't even describe what the cup looks like and finds it beautiful because of the unconscious stimulation fire receives when all the possibilities of the cup come to him. This can lead to misunderstanding; both elements speak their own language from their own world and often don't understand that other worlds exist, or at least can't identify with the other element's way of experiencing things. Enormous confusion in language can occur on account of the elements' differences in perspective, even though they use the same words.

Such verbal confusions may also take place within the inner self of every individual; consciousness and the unconscious are compensating each other through all sorts of actions and counteractions. The elements which diametrically disagree with each other are fire-earth and air-water. When a verbal misunderstanding occurs between the superior and the inferior element, some mediation must take place. The psychic energy current makes this connection, which is symbolized astrologically by the crosses. For an understanding of how this can happen, Jung describes the behavior of psychic energy in relation to the four functions of consciousness as a process of adaptation that requires a directed conscious function. This function would be characterized by an inner consistency and some logical coherence. Astrologically this is the element. Because the process of adaptation is directed, everything unsuitable must be excluded in order to maintain the integrity of direction. Jung says that unsuitable elements are inhibited and may escape attention. There is only *one* consciously directed function of adaptation and this astrologically is the superior element. If someone has a thinking orientation that person can't orient himself by feeling, because thinking and feeling are two different functions. Feeling would have to be excluded if the logical laws of thinking are to be satisfied as thought-process cannot be disturbed by the feeling function. In this case libido is withdrawn from the feeling process, and this function becomes relatively unconscious. The inferior functions are activated by regression and when they reach consciousness, they may appear in some incompatible form that is disguised and covered up with the slime of the deep. The stoppage of libido (psychic energy) may be due to a failure of the conscious attitude, and valuable seeds lie in the unconscious contents waiting to be activated by regression. They include elements of functions excluded by the conscious attitude.[1]

A number of important points emerge from this. We see that the verbal confusion between the conscious attitude and unconscious contents can be resolved through the current of psychic energy. Psychic energy (derived from the astrological crosses) connects the four elements in the psyche. The crosses themselves are not connected with the contents of the unconscious or the conscious self, but the results of the current of psychic energy *can* bring about changes in the contents of both areas of the psyche.

We can consider the flowing of psychic energy as a means to straighten out both ourselves and our relation to the world. After a process of assimilation and settling (the regression), progression will start once more: adaptation to the outside world. In the complete process of progression and regression, mutable energy marks both transitional positions.

---

[1] Jung, Carl, G., On Psychic Energy, *The Structure and Dynamics of the Psyche*, Collected Works Vol. 8., Routledge & Kegan Paul, London, 1977, pp. 35-36.

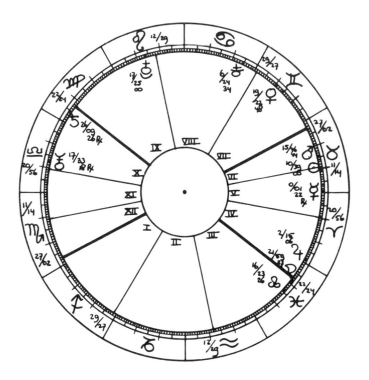

Elements	Signs	Houses	Total
FIRE	♃ ♇	♇ ☿	4
EARTH	♀ ☉ ♂ ♄ Mc.	☉ ♂ ♄ ♇	9
AIR	♀ ♇	♀	3
WATER	♇ Asc. ☽	☽ ♃ ♇	6

Crosses	Signs	Houses	Total
CARDINAL	♃ ♇ ♇	☽ ♃ ♀ ♄ ♇	8
FIXED	♀ ☉ ♂ ♇ Asc.	☿ ♇	7
MUTABLE	♀ Mc. ♄ ☽	☉ ♂ ♇	7

2. ELEMENTS AND CROSSES INTERPRETED TOGETHER

Now that we understand that the astrological elements represent our psychological view of the world and the astrological crosses symbolize the way we assimilate all these impressions, we can consider Chart 1 again. The arrangement of the elements were discussed in Chapter 1 and the arrangement of the crosses in Chapter 2. Consequently, we can now consider how both factors can be brought into synthesis. Fred's chart and the breakdown of his elements and crosses are presented again in figure 3.1.

Fred's superior function is earth, which means that his way of viewing, evaluating, and experiencing everything around him is practical, concrete, and factual. Because of a strong fixed cross by sign, the assimilation process will be slow-working and profound, whether he wants it to be or not. The emphasis on the fixed cross will bring to the surface of the psyche his inferior element of fire, and secondly the element air, so that the planets in those elements will play a strong, if archaic, role for his consciousness. During the first half of his life he may have difficulty with this. Confronted with his inferior element and being afflicted with such a slow-working process of assimilation in potential (the fixed signs), he will plunge into his own depths time and time again. There is no law that says he will be bothered by this, but it may cause feelings of insecurity. These feeling can propel him in two directions: he may cling to what security he does have (in agreement with his Sun in Taurus), or, if his inferior fire element comes to the surface, he may start looking more for possibilities and solutions.

In the first half of our lives, in many cases, we are still busy experiencing all the extremes in ourselves; afterwards, we tend to level off and prefer the middle road. Therefore, Fred will probably feel both tendencies in himself in the first half of his life: clinging to certainties as well as searching intensely for possibilities to experience. The certainties will predominate because of their relation with the conscious superior function. As he grows older, mutable energy will become more important, indicating a growing need to make things relative. This is accompanied by the cardinal cross becoming more important, so assimilation gradually becomes

Figure 3.1. Fred's chart. For this discussion, the element and cross totals are also included.

less regressive, and Fred will also begin to pay more attention to his surroundings. He will become increasingly aware of the demands of his surroundings and will satisfy these demands to some degree, although the potential always remains stronger. He will continue to conform primarily to his own inner values, although they become less compulsive. This is both a positive and a negative development, as I indicated in the chapter on the crosses, depending upon how we see it. In any case, Fred will become more open to the world, but his potential to adapt to his own self is so strong that inner conflicts arise. The elements of fire and air will play an important role in any inner conflict, both as factors to cause disturbances and as factors to smooth things out.

When we diagnose the basic construction of the horoscope, the tensions, inhibitions, and possibilities of the psyche will emerge clearly. When you see strong elementary tension in the horoscope (for instance, when such polar elements as air and water are each strongly occupied), that tension will play a decisive role in the character. Yet we must never conclude that this causes a person to be terribly unhappy. Elementary tension has nothing to do with whether a person feels contented or unhappy, but indicates how consciousness orients itself, how experiences will be assimilated, and where we can expect compensating reactions to originate. Such counteractions can contain both painful and pleasurable experiences.

Much depends upon our attitude towards our total psyche. For instance, a horoscope with air strongly occupied but with the Moon in a water sign, can actually enjoy a supersentimental or melancholy mood now and then. The person doesn't necessarily experience any pain because of this, even though the Moon is active from the unconscious inferior function. On the contrary, experiencing such moods through the Moon in a water sign can even help maintain inner balance, although the Moon's location in the inferior element strengthens this element tension. Tension can work in a very creative way and has nothing to do, I repeat, with whether or not one feels good. These feelings are primarily indicated by the location of the planets and their relationships with each other.

Therefore, the strong tension shown in Chart 2 doesn't mean that Marilyn Monroe felt very unhappy, although her element tension gave a sort of hungry feeling that is difficult to put into words. It comes down to a dissatisfaction with things as they are, arising from a vague awareness that there must be *more,* and that there is still so much that is unfulfilled, though one rarely knows *what.* For convenience, see figure 3.2 on page 80, as we have combined Chart 2 and figure 1.3 from Chapter 1 with figure 2.4 from Chapter 2 so the reader can follow the discussion easily.

The distribution in Marilyn's horoscope indicates a great deal of tension in potential, both in regard to the crosses and the elements. This element tension gave her the unsatisfied feeling we mentioned, which she could experience as unpleasant; but this same tension gave her something very stimulating—the driving force behind her desire for still more. The strong duality between the superior air element, through which she logically experienced and approached the world, and the inferior water element—occupied by impersonal planets—would be obvious to both herself and her surroundings.

The strong occupation of the fixed and mutable crosses indicates that the inner self (her unconscious) would make its demands. The fixed cross means one continually tries to adapt to inner demands—to that which is inexplicable and irrational—for these demands emerge from the unconscious and press on one's consciousness. Since the fixed and mutable crosses were equal in potential, the compulsion to adapt to her own inner self would be eased because the mutable cross offered the possibility of withdrawing into herself and reappearing when it was necessary. The mutable cross barely appears in circumstances (house position), indicating a danger that she could be less flexible about changing from one inner situation to another than her potential promised. The cardinal houses, in contrast, receive more emphasis, which means that once she was headed in a certain psychic direction, she could stay put longer. The fixed houses also receive a strong emphasis. All of this together means that her mutability lost importance as she grew older and as experience began to play a greater role in her life. At the same time, the growing emphasis on the cardinal and fixed houses means that the psychic energy, which maintains contact between consciousness and the unconscious, became just as dualistic as the division of the elements indicates. A strong emphasis on cardinality gives a strong need to satisfy the demands of the outside world, whereas a strong fixed cross gives priority to the needs of one's own inner world. In her case, consciousness and the unconscious were sharply opposite each

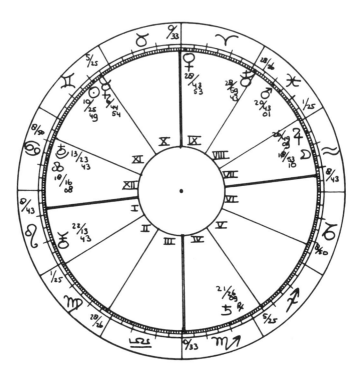

Elements	Signs	Houses	Total
FIRE	♀ Asc. ♇	♇ ♅	5
EARTH	Mc.	♀	2
AIR	☿ ☉ ☽ ♃	☉ ☿ ♃ ☽	8
WATER	♆ ♄ ♂ ♅	♄ ♂ ♆	7

Crosses	Signs	Houses	Total
CARDINAL	♀ ♆	♆ ♄ ☽ ♃ ♀	7
FIXED	Mc. Asc. ♇ ♄ ☽ ♃	♂ ☿ ☉	9
MUTABLE	☉ ☿ ♂ ♅	♅ ♆	6

other. Psychic energy, symbolized by the crosses, strengthened her conscious air attitude through the cardinal cross, while an equally strong fixed cross (already strong in sign) gave the opposite need: namely, to integrate the element of water from the unconscious, whereby air would have to retreat somewhat. With such a strong duality on all fronts, we see a horoscope full of turmoil, with possibilities ranging from instability to great creativity. In actuality, both instability and creativity came to the surface at times.

To what extent are we able to speak of an easy or a difficult horoscope here? In my opinion, it is impossible to give an answer to this question without objective standards or criteria. Any answer would be a value judgment, relative both to ourselves and to the way we see the world. The element and cross division in Marilyn's horoscope definitely shows a tense picture, but these same tensions often lead to creativity and great deeds, owing to that unfulfilled feeling which flows through everything as a silent undercurrent.

How the element tension takes concrete form becomes evident when the rest of the horoscope is considered. The greatest care must be exercised in interpretation. Anything indicating further duality between psychic contents must be scrutinized carefully, since this duality shows so clearly through Marilyn's element and cross division. For the more advanced student, it is perhaps significant to point out that neither Uranus nor Pluto make a major aspect in Marilyn's horoscope. When a planet doesn't make any major aspect, it may indicate that the psychic content the planet symbolizes can work in an uncontrolled and uncoordinated way, whereby the planet can unexpectedly exhibit traits of either its most difficult or its best side. The lack of aspects means there is no argument or stress, but also no stimulus from other planets. The unaspected planet represents a psychic content that can work autonomously within the total psyche. Marilyn's horoscope has two such autonomous planets, Uranus and Pluto, both of which are in water signs. Water is precisely the unconscious element whose counteractions her consciousness must try to keep within bounds. Planets located in that inferior element give us further indications about the source of counteractions. The planets Uranus and Pluto, which are by nature

Figure 3.2. Marilyn Monroe. For this discussion the element and cross totals are also included.

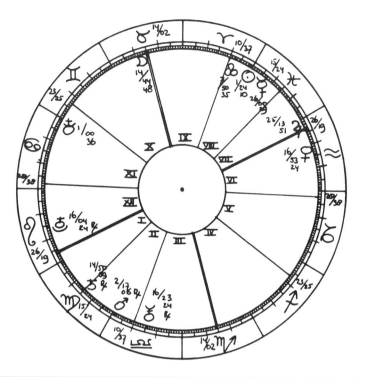

Element	Signs	Houses	Total
FIRE	☉ ♌ Asc.	—	3
EARTH	☽ Mc. ♄	☽ ♄ ♂ ♀	7
AIR	♂ ♅ ♀ ♃	♅ ♃ ♇	7
WATER	♇ ☿	☿ ☉ ♌	5

Crosses	Signs	Houses	Total
CARDINAL	☉ ♌ ♂ ♅	♃ ☽	6
FIXED	☽ Mc. ♇ Asc. ♀ ♃	♄ ♂ ☿ ☉ ♌	11
MUTABLE	♄ ☿	♅ ♀ ♇	5

all but unpredictable for consciousness, are active here from the unconscious inferior element, and moreover are *unaspected*. With such an accumulation of factors, we can say that Marilyn's horoscope tended to become unbalanced. This horoscope shows how important the division of elements and crosses can be for any further interpretation. If, for instance, Uranus and Pluto had been located in air without major aspect, their autonomous actions would not have been so directly threatening to consciousness as they were in Marilyn's case.

The third horoscope, Peter in Chart 3, shows us an example where element is strong enough to be separated out. Figure 3.3 includes Chart 3 and figure 1.8 from Chapter 1, as well as figure 2.5 from Chapter 2, so the reader has easy access to Peter's information now under discussion. The cross division shows considerably fewer difficulties than Marilyn's. In this horoscope, there is also a considerable element tension, in this case from the broad element distribution combined with the fact that the most essential planet—his Aries Sun—is located in an element that doesn't get a chance to express itself in house position. The element opposite the Sun—earth—receives a greater house emphasis. Water, with the personal planet Mercury located in Pisces, also receives the Sun by house position (the eighth house), so that the element of water will increase in importance as Peter grows older. Water has a strongly occupied air element as its opposite. Naturally, every horoscope shows tension. There is no ideal division, just as there are no ideal human beings, but the degree to which a division shows tension can be discerned by looking at a horoscope.

As we said earlier, Peter has the possibility of making a complete change, so that his consciousness would no longer be determined by the potentially strong fire element, but could express a fire/water or even an earth/water combination. The crosses must give us further clarification here. The fixed cross, strongly represented in both potential and circumstances, surpasses the cardinal cross, and surpasses the mutable cross to an even greater degree. This has already caused insistent inner demands in his younger years, as well as when he grows older, so that he feels strongly compelled to

Figure 3.3. Peter's chart. For this discussion the element and cross totals are included.

satisfy these demands and adapt to his unconscious. This means that earth, the probable inferior element in his horoscope, will continually be brought to the surface through psychic energy. Despite the fact that he is an Aries, the combination of the fixed cross and the earth element will help him to display a remarkable amount of tenacity. The possibility, already shown in potential, of making a psychic changeover is confirmed by the cross division. Through the fixed cross, he is so strongly confronted with his own unconscious contents and faculties, that by blending conscious and unconscious elements, a changeover can easily take place, for he would follow the way of least inner resistance. The development of the element division is further completed by the cross division. From this development, we can conclude which points in the horoscope will be of importance before or after the possible change.

As long as Peter experiences life from his element of consciousness—fire—he will be better able to express himself via his Leo Ascendant than via his Taurus Midheaven. As soon as he tends toward earth, because of his element division, his Midheaven will appear more clearly, but at the same time his Ascendant, located in the opposite element, will offer much less support.

Because the possibility of changing the superior element seems to exist within this horoscope, it is also possible to discuss the trend Peter will follow. Despite the carelessness and rashness of the fire element, especially indicated by his Aries Sun, he will develop from a spontaneous individual, jumping from one subject to another, into a person oriented toward a social position in which security and praise (Taurus Moon on the Midheaven) will play a large role. This would be his way of changing from Ascendant to the Midheaven. Of course, in Western culture it is natural that position in society becomes more important as we grow older. We are speaking less, however, about this natural social process than about the fact that Peter's inner experience will eventually express itself in a manner indicated by the Midheaven rather than the Ascendant, which he has followed up until this time. His career would come to mean everything to him, and he would identify with it to such a degree that any change in it or its termination could bring about a huge identity crisis. If he maintains fire as the superior element, the Leo Ascendant would remain important; consequently an end to his career might have a much less radical consequence.

3. A NEW EXAMPLE

In order to show once more the total process of deriving and interpreting the elements and crosses, we will use a new horoscope as an example. Before we can list the elements, look at Paul's horoscope (Chart 4) on page 86. The element division (figure 3.4) and the division of the crosses (figure 3.5) are both on page 87.

Before we begin interpretation, we need to make a few remarks. In this horoscope, we apply the rule pertaining to planets within orb of a house cusp (see Chapter 1, Section 3). The Sun is located at 18° 56′ Cancer, while the ninth house begins at 19° 38′ Cancer. The Sun is located within three degrees of the cusp of the ninth house, so that according to the rule referred to in Chapter 1, the Sun is counted as being in the ninth house. The Sun will be listed in a fire house (in circumstances), which is also a mutable house according to the crosses. If we forgot this rule, we would then derive a completely different element and cross division, even more crucial in the Sun's case since it pertains to such an essential part of the horoscope.

The Midheaven, located at 29° 23′ Leo, *remains* in Leo and does not move to the next sign. A planet close to a house *cusp* may be entered in the following house under certain conditions, but this never applies to a planet, the Midheaven or Ascendant when it is on the cusp of another sign. The Midheaven in this chart is located in the last degree of Leo, so Leo is still decisive. We cannot say that the Midheaven is actually located in Virgo.

When we begin to examine the division of the elements more carefully, the strong occupation of the element water by sign strikes us right away. In no other element are there so many personal planets. By house position, the personal planets Mars and Mercury are again found in water, while the Sun is located in fire, an element already fairly well represented by sign. Earth plays a small role, while the element air, on the other hand, is more important, for it contains Moon both by potential (sign) and circumstance (house).

The total picture indicates someone who views and experiences the world through his feeling function: everything he meets in life is judged through his own feeling standards. Central to this is how he experiences himself, whether agreeable or disagreeable, good or bad, beautiful or ugly, etc. He has an intense emotional involvement with his surroundings, although this doesn't necessarily always

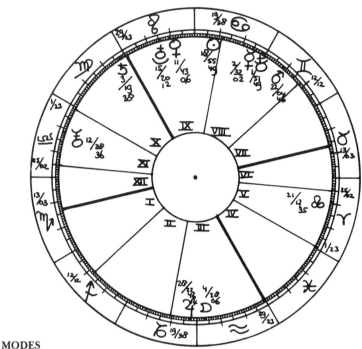

MODES
OR CROSSES:

Cardinal:

Fixed:

Mutable:

ASPECT TABLE

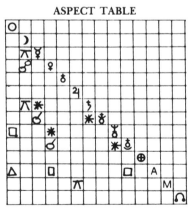

	Sun	Moon	Mercury	Venus	Mars	Jupiter	Saturn	Uranus	Neptune	Pluto	Part of Fortune	Ascendant	Midheaven	North Node
Sun	○													
Moon		☽												
Mercury		☌	☿											
Venus		☍		♀										
Mars					♂									
Jupiter						♃								
Saturn		☌	✳				♄							
Uranus		☌					✳	♅						
Neptune	□		✳					♆	♆					
Pluto		☌						✳	♇					
Part of Fortune										⊕				
Ascendant	△		□					□			A			
Midheaven				☌								M		
North Node													☊	

ELEMENTS:

Fire: 6

Earth: 3

Air: 6

Water: 7

show in his attitude. This is simply the way he sees life and experiences it. He seeks his way through the multiplicity of phenomena with the aid of his feeling function, water.

Since his Moon remains in air, the element contradictory to his superior water element, he will experience a strong tension between his conscious attitude (the Sun) and his unconscious reactions (the Moon). Whenever he is completely involved in further differentiation of his superior feeling function, his Moon will emerge from the unconscious air element, evoking a strong need to arrange everything on a thinking basis. He will prefer to group experiences according to the laws of logic, but this is a weak point since air is clearly his inferior element, working out of his unconscious in a

Elements	Signs	Houses	Total
FIRE	♀ ♅ Mc.	☉ ♀ ♅	6
EARTH	♄ ♃	♄	3
AIR	♂ ♇ ☽	♃ ☽ ♅	6
WATER	♆ ☉ ☿ Asc.	♂ ♅ ☿	7

Figure 3.4. The elements in Paul's chart.

Crosses	Sign	Houses	Total
CARDINAL	♆ ☿ ☉ ♅ ♃	♄	6
FIXED	♀ ♅ Mc. Asc. ☽	☿ ♅ ♂ ♇	9
MUTABLE	♂ ♄	♃ ☽ ☉ ♀ ♅	7

Figure 3.5. The crosses as expressed in Paul's chart.

Chart 4. Paul's horoscope. He was born in Oosterhout, Holland on July 11, 1949 at 3:30 pm. This birth data is from the birth certificate. House system is Placidus. Chart used with permission.

little-differentiated manner. This doesn't mean that Paul is unable to put order into his experiences. The Moon indicates, among other things, the behavior patterns we unconsciously feel best and most comfortable in pursuing. Because his need for ordering experience is so strong, constant practice in this area will help him draw many significant conclusions. Yet he will find that relying on his feeling ability is much easier and gives him the same results as when he keeps plodding along, deliberately weighing logical factors.

At this point, the cross division becomes important. The strong emphasis which both the cardinal and fixed cross receive by sign gives Paul a fairly good balance between his adaptation to demands from the outside world and demands from his own inner self. In this adaptation, the Moon is active from the fixed sign Aquarius. Therefore, in potential, he will feel the need to direct himself to the Moon's demands. Because the Moon shifts to a mutable house in circumstances, Paul will be increasingly able to use the personal contents of the Moon (unconsciously) as a means of restoring or maintaining balance. The Moon becomes an instrument for him to direct his psychic energy temporarily inwards or outwards. Since we are dealing with a combination of factors in this horoscope, we must consider several things:

a) The superior element is water, which means that air is inferior.

b) Planets located in the inferior air element are active from the unconscious, mostly expressing themselves in the form of counter-actions directed at consciousness. Of the greatest importance here is the fact that the Moon is active within that inferior element.

c) The Moon, as such, indicates how we unconsciously behave in order to feel at ease or to experience a certain form of security. Since this mechanism is active from the inferior air element in this horoscope, the Moon will try to satisfy its own demands even more compulsively. This means Paul will try to understand and explain (as logically as possible) what he is actually perceiving and experiencing through his superior feeling function.

d) In potential, the fixed cross as well as the cardinal cross are strongly occupied, with a focus on the Moon. Therefore, in the first part of his life, Paul will very likely obey the inner compulsive demands of his unconscious Moon. This adaptation will come more naturally to him as he grows older, since the Moon is located in a mutable house in circumstances.

e) The mutable cross receives by far the most house emphasis (circumstances) while the cardinal cross hardly appears. The strong cardinal sign potential, which makes outside impulses the most important for Paul, therefore shifts over to mutable and fixed houses. When we consider all these factors, we come to a conclusion. One of the strongest factors of the unconscious, the Moon, shifts into the mutable cross and begins to play a role in the psyche's process of inner and outer adaptation. Nevertheless, through its location in the inferior element the Moon will maintain a strong connection with the unconscious and with regressive energy. The cardinal cross all but disappears in circumstances, causing the mutable energy to proceed more in the direction of the fixed cross, reemphasizing the fixed potential of the Aquarian Moon.

We have especially concentrated on the Moon to show that one of the greatest values of the element and cross division is the possibility it offers as an indication of certain tension-arousing points in the horoscope. Despite its location in the unconscious, the Moon definitely plays a key role here. In any further interpretation, we must pay special attention to the Moon and its aspects, particularly since the Moon is the dispositor of Paul's Sun in Cancer and therefore of the three planets located in that sign! In spite of the rather placid distribution of the other elements, the Moon is able to dominate consciousness (at least temporarily) and the element of water, so that there appears to be a temporary shift of conscious functions.

The fire element offers the possibility of forming a bridge between air and water in this horoscope. The potential is already sufficient for that purpose, with Venus, Pluto and the Midheaven in fire signs, though it is primarily the house positions that make this balance possible. If he takes advantage of the opportunities offered by his horoscope, on the basis of the element and cross division, Paul probably lives completely through his feelings, while he assumes that he evaluates everything very abstractly and logically. His need for logic, however, is a driving force behind his search for values which he will primarily evaluate emotionally. Despite his logic, it won't be thinking alone that helps him recognize inconsistency, but rather a clear feeling that something might be wrong. This is the combination of water as superior function and fire as auxiliary function of consciousness. His initial need to direct himself to the outer world (the cardinal cross) gradually shifts towards adaptation to whatever he experiences as necessary. Inner values will be decisive more and more frequently (the fixed signs and houses), while the psychic energy processes will become more flexible as he grows older.

The concrete and material will not play a significant role in Paul's life, because the element earth does very little in this horoscope. This doesn't mean Paul will live like a hermit; it only indicates that the material, perceptible, form of things as such won't interest him. It will only play a role within his need for feeling evaluation (water). Furthermore, as the fire element develops further, the earth element will recede into more unconscious levels, being contradictory to the fire element. Its counteractions from the unconscious can contribute to inner balance and help him stand with two feet on the ground through confrontations. This becomes a beneficial counterpart to the strong theorizing need of the Aquarian Moon and the fire element's lack of roots in the earth.

4. PHASES OF LIFE IN THE FRAMEWORK OF CROSS AND ELEMENT

In previous sections, we have repeatedly seen how the division of the elements and crosses develops within the individual psyche. This development is closely connected with age. Naturally, the exact age when changes will take place in an individual can never be given precisely, but there are definite phases of life recognized by both psychology and astrology where much is going on inwardly. Puberty and the change of life in mdidle age are well-known phases with characteristic developments that everyone goes through.

When interpreting a horoscope, we definitely need to take these ages into account. If we are to interpret a horoscope having strong air sign occupation, for instance, we can hardly speak of a well-developed thinking function if the horoscope is that of a small child! We can say that the child will gradually orient himself on the basis of the thinking function. Thinking will be rather simple and uncontrolled in the beginning, but, as the child grows older, many original and archaic traits disappear as a result of increasing differentiation. It could well be the case that there is a strong air potential (planets in the air signs) yet few planets in air houses (circumstances). Sooner or later the child would discover that his thinking faculty, well-developed as it may be, isn't always sufficient. Other functions or other elements would play a more important role than if there had been planets located in air houses. This problem would make itself felt at some time in his life, with all the possibilities and difficulties it offers.

One of the most important periods in a person's life is the crisis of middle age, which generally takes place between age forty-two and forty-five. Astrologically speaking, transiting Saturn, transiting Uranus, and the secondary progressed Moon each form an opposition with their own natal position.[2] The structure and contents of life are then ready for great changes. C.A. Meier says the following about this crisis:

> ...sooner or later, but normally speaking around the middle of life, the wheel of functions begins to turn. What has received the main emphasis up until then gradually becomes less important, and what was despised, then appears to full advantage...[3]

When the unconscious contents belonging to the inferior function can no longer be repressed they demand our attention, creating a crisis. Astrologically, we can say the following: in the first half of life it is primarily the potential—the planets in the signs—that is decisive for the individual. This is particularly important during childhood, especially in puberty, when the formation of the ego is important. Astrologically, during this phase the emphasis falls on the Sun. The influence of the planets in the houses generally becomes noticeable during this period. Little by little, the individual accumulates more experience, learns how to assimilate and comprehend more, and involuntarily his circumstances will be incorporated into this inner process of learning and adaptation.

In most cases, the influence of the planets in the houses seems to become more intense in the late twenties. At that time both the

---

[2]See *Astro-Psychology* for details.

[3]Meier, C.A., *Bewusstsein*. Erkenntnistheorie und Bewusstsein. Bewusstwerdung bei C.G. Jung, Walter Verlag, Olten, 1975, p. 140.

secondary progressed Moon, and transiting Saturn, have made one complete circle through the zodiac, returning to their place in the birth horoscope. Astrologically we call this the first Moon-Saturn return.[4] From this period on, one is more clearly and consciously confronted with circumstances through experiences. In the end, this comes down to a constant confrontation with the self. A person may learn a great deal about unknown factors which are actually part of his own unconscious, if he is prepared to pay attention to how he spontaneously reacts to things that come his way. This phase culminates around the middle of life. Both potential and circumstances (sign and house) are very strongly in evidence, and in regard to the elements in the horoscope, begin to fuse at that time. Potential can never completely be suppressed, but becomes more subtle in many cases.

When we are looking at the horoscope of someone just graduating from school, we should discuss it more on an element level, emphasizing the possible tendencies for development. Someone who is middle-aged already has a certain record, and we must take into account that tendencies have largely materialized; one can speak of a furthering differentiation in which the unconscious counteractions have already played a greater role. For instance, if the person has an earth emphasis, we can be confident that the fire contents have hardly come into play. The fire contents will make themselves more clearly felt at middle age, and therefore changes in consciousness may come about. These changes are all the more likely if the strongest element by sign comes off worse by house. It is then possible that the person will develop a strong auxiliary function or even turn this into a superior function. A person can even become exactly the opposite type, with the understanding that the inferior function, in becoming superior, will partially differentiate itself but will never completely lose the traits it originally possessed in the unconscious. It is also very possible that someone has lived for a long time with a function that doesn't suit him. In that case, a shift to a function that *does* suit him may take place in the middle of life. This kind of radical shift especially can take place in an unbalanced element division.

---

[4] For literature about the phases of life, see footnote 2 in Chapter 2. Astrologically, see Robertson, M., *Critical Ages in Adult Life: The Transit of Saturn*, American Federation of Astrologers, Inc. 1976.

The crosses play an important role here as well. The world outside will continue to play an important role for someone with a strong cardinal cross, for instance. In that case, consciousness is directed toward adapting to outer demands. Inner demands are denied, neglected, or hardly felt. When the transition years arrive and the unconscious increases its demands, a person with a strong cardinal cross (in potential and circumstances) can be severely troubled although he may prefer not to show this to the outside world!

This midlife crisis plays a much slighter role for someone with many planets emphasized in the fixed element. All his life, even if unconsciously, he will have been absorbed in the demands of his inner world. From an early age, he probably has been confronted with himself, and he is somewhat accustomed to the intrusion of his unconscious upon consciousness. For him, a different sort of shift will take place in the middle of life. Naturally, this must be examined in connection to the elements.

The mutable cross can go in various directions in the mid-life crisis. Because this cross has to do with transitional situations (from progresson to regression and vice versa), awarenesss of the actual direction of psychic energy may elude a person with a strong mutable cross. Perhaps because of this, the person may not even be aware that he has landed in a crisis, although he may be able to realize it afterwards. When the mutable cross is especially strong in a horoscope, without any appreciable occupation of the cardinal and fixed signs, then the transition of elements will probably take place smoothly, though the actual experiencing of the change occurs later. In the most positive form, the person with mutables strong by sign and house can remain neutral towards himself and others, thus not making the times more difficult than they already are.

When interpreting a horoscope, we must continually consider the phase of life being experienced. The exact division of the elements and the crosses then indicates:

a) The direct potential: planets in the signs.

b) The degree to which one can give form to this potential in the circumstances: planets in the houses.

c) The manner of assimilation: the cross division in potential.

d) The degree to which one experiences the opposition between consciousness and the unconscious: the division of the element pairs;

e) The degree to which this changes as one grows older: the element division concerning the houses in regard to the signs.

f) The degree to which the occupation of the signs and houses can cause tension by the element division.

g) How the assimilation process initially takes place: the cross division in potential, and:

h) How the assimilation process crystallizes, becomes more refined and develops further: the crosses in circumstances.

i) How the assimilation process and functions of consciousness (the crosses and the elements, respectively) can support or oppose each other in the course of one's life.

The instinctive process is still foremost in childhood. During that time, consciousness becomes further crystallized through learning, until preliminary completion takes place around the age of thirty. Only at the time of the midlife crisis can elements and crosses be interpreted in their totality for consciousness; in other words, potential and experience only begins to blend at that time, through which a new personality can begin to develop. Naturally, there are exceptions to the rule. When, because of horoscope structure, someone has dealt with certain progressions related to the psyche at a very young age, and these have been accompanied by profound and drastic experiences, there will be a quickening of the general processes of life, even though the general human tendency still exists.

The division of crosses and elements in the individual horoscope must be closely examined, in the light of personality structure, phase of life, and experience. When we have considered all that, with the help of the division alone, we can discern the problems of someone going through midlife crisis. In the same manner, we can often recognize the major problems of other phases of life. In any case, we must continue to take into account the general psychic significance of the phase, evaluating the role of the elements and the crosses against this background.[5]

---

[5] For literature about the phases of life, see footnote 2 in Chapter 2. Astrologically, see Robertson, M., *Critical Ages in Adult Life: The Transit of Saturn*, American Federation of Astrologers, Inc. 1976.

CHAPTER FOUR

PERSONAL PLANETS
WITHIN THE ELEMENT AND CROSS DIVISION

1. THE CASTLE

While making the element and cross divisions, we learned that the very personal contents—the Sun, Moon, Mercury, and Ascendant—play an important role, since a large part of everybody's framework is directly connected with these components of the psyche. The Ascendant, Sun, Moon, and other planets each play an independent role within the element and cross divisions in addition. Therefore, it is important to know to what extent the contents (or planets) agree with or differ from the basic framework. Countless processes are going on in a horoscope, and it is not always easy to see what is happening internally from anyone's outward behavior and appearance. A person can seem to be in harmony yet have considerable inner conflict. Similarly, a person may seem to have many problems, while inwardly being hardly troubled by anything. The horoscope can reveal much concerning the difference between appearance and reality. The following example may illustrate the relationship between what someone shows the outside world and what lies hidden according to the horoscope.

Let us imagine the horoscope as a huge, unknown castle that we are approaching. In the distance, as we ride up to the building, we first see a large tower with a flag on top. This represents the M.C. (the Midheaven or the beginning of the tenth house). This point in the horoscope indicates the ego-image: that with which we identify ourselves—our flag, in other words—and the status in society connected with this image. The closer our approach to the castle, the more we notice the outside of the building, until we find ourselves standing right before it, on the point of entering. We can only enter the castle by means of a drawbridge and the portal, which can be compared to the entrance and exit of the horoscope—the Ascendant. The drawbridge gives us our first impression of the castle, just as we receive an impression of a new acquaintance through the Ascendant (and thereby the whole first house). This drawbridge may have all sorts of iron fixtures, snags, clasps, trapdoors, and the like, creating an unpleasant impression or seemingly wanting to keep us at a distance. However, the whole castle isn't necessarily furnished in that manner. No matter how much the drawbridge forms part of the castle, it is but one of its many components. Behind this frightening drawbridge, very possibly we will find a most charming and romantic little castle where we could feel quite at home. If we discover this to be so, then we will view the drawbridge (the Ascendant) with very different eyes. Nevertheless, we may be startled at the sight of it.

Astrologically, the Ascendant reflects a person's natural way of acting, his habitual external behavior, and his way of responding to new impulses and impressions. By the Ascendant, we mean not only the cusp of the first house, but also the planets forming angles to it. If the Ascendant has many difficult aspects, the person may seem to be rather difficult, even though a good deal of balance and harmony may be present in the rest of the horoscope. It is equally possible that the Ascendant receives only harmonious aspects, so that the person, despite great conflicts in the rest of the chart, seems to have few conflicts. Our first acquaintance with the Ascendant may be extremely deceptive, if we make a judgement on this basis alone. Yet, we must not forget that the drawbridge fulfills a very essential role for the castle, and this is true for the Ascendant with regard to the rest of the horoscope as well. The Ascendant definitely represents a certain character trait, but it is not the only one. The planets, the aspects, the relation between the houses, and so forth, determine what the rest of the castle looks like. It may turn out to be a castle containing many tastefully and pleasantly furnished rooms, or it may, for instance, consist of very separate sections. Since the planets in the inferior element can bring hidden and gnawing contents to light, we also may learn the cellar in our castle is full of mice and rats. Just as we explore the castle from within, we learn to know the horoscope from within. Then we see how compatible the Ascendant and Midheaven really are with the person, and to what extent the flag covers the cargo.

From this comparison, it may be seen that our first impression will agree more with the person's character if the Ascendant corresponds with the element and cross division of the horoscope than if the Ascendant deviates from the rest of the picture. Someone having a strongly occupied earth element and a strong fixed cross, for instance, will not seem as he actually is if his Ascendant is Gemini (air). The volatility and lightheartedness of this Ascendant would conceal the calmer and steadier character, so the outwardly directed Gemini Ascendant would be misleading. The fixed cross would indicate a person who primarily abides by his own standards. Yet the Ascendant (his natural and direct way of acting) will give his character mutability as a beneficial counterpart to strong regressive tendencies. On the other hand, this can pose a problem, since he seems to unite two characters in one person through this duality. One part continually needs to digest and assimilate experience, while the other part throws itself once more into all kinds of things that are not wholly assimilated (Gemini!), so quickly that the first can't cope with it.

The Ascendant plays a very unique role within the horoscope. It reflects the psychic content that determines how we manifest ourselves outwardly. It is an important part of our character, sometimes so natural that when people call attention to the traits we will have trouble recognizing them. Only when we have carefully observed ourselves for awhile will Ascendant characteristics become clear to us. The inward reaction pattern indicated by the Ascendant is also reflected in reactions to immediate physical circumstances. The Ascendant therefore shows both our direct reaction to intangible things such as experiences and events, and our way of reacting to tangible circumstances such as climate.

2. THE SUN IN THE DIVISION OF TYPES

Opinions vary as to the role played by the Sun in the horoscope. Some consider the Sun equal in importance to the other contents of the horoscope, while others give it a special place since it is the most direct reflection of our essence and our ego. Sooner or later the Sun will make itself felt, no matter how concealed it is. It is concealed in a house where it can't express itself clearly, such as the twelfth, or if it is unaspected. The person is then barely able to express his own nature and essence in his circumstances, while feeling these contents strongly within himself.

In my opinion, the Sun plays a very important role in the horoscope. Sooner or later, it is the point to which we unconsciously wish to return when we have strayed from the path it indicates. One can speak about straying from the path of the Sun in the case of those who orient themselves to the element contradictory to their superior element (often that is the element in which the Sun is located). In psychology, the problem of this 'disturbed type' is represented by M.-L. von Franz as follows:

> ...Some people have trouble in finding out their own type, which very often is due to the fact that they are distorted types. This is not a very frequent occurrence, but it does happen in cases where someone would naturally have become a feeling type or an intuitive, but was forced by the surrounding atmosphere to develop another function. Suppose a boy is born a feeling type in an intellectually ambitious family. His surroundings will exert pressure upon him to become an intellectual, and his original predisposition as a feeling type will be thwarted or despised. Usually, in such a case, he is unable to become a thinking type: that would be one step too far. But he might well develop sensation or intuition, one of the auxiliary functions, so as to be relatively better adapted to his surroundings; his main function is simply 'out' in the milieu in which he grows up.[1]

Peter's horoscope (Chart 3) illustrates von Franz's ideas. His family led an upright existence according to Christian standards, held traditional thought patterns, and considered a social career an honorable pursuit. Peter, with his Aries Sun and Leo Ascendant both in fire, had trouble with this upbringing at an early age. He

---

[1]von Franz, M.-L. and J. Hillman, *Lectures on Jung's Typology*, Spring Verlag, Zürich, 1971, Part 1, p. 3.

had a strong need for inner freedom and self-expression, but because the Moon is located in earth (Taurus), he also had a strong need for security which is contrary to his fire Sun. In his case, the prominent earth-water houses clearly reflect his childhood environment, in which feeling, tradition, and security formed the pillars of the family. The circumstances that Peter grew up in meant he wasn't able to give full scope to his fire contents, although his parents were very cooperative in allowing him to develop himself.

At twelve years of age, he was introduced to the idea of missionary training; he let himself be talked into it and went to a seminary. He missed his home (Moon in Taurus) but enjoyed the possibilities and perspectives this training offered (fire signs). Within that environment, he gained prestige and belonged to the grown-up men. Yet, it didn't turn out to be what he was actually seeking; and, after a number of years, he terminated this study to begin a university education. To the great sorrow of his parents, he said farewell to the church.

During those study years, he indulged his potentially strong fire traits: the Sun doesn't allow itself to be repressed, especially when other contents, for instance the Leo Ascendant, are located in the same element. Yet the emphasis on the Sun gradually diminished and the water element became more prominent, which can be seen in a need to express himself artistically. Earth began to play a stronger role as well, although with difficulty, since it is an inferior element. His largely unconscious need for security will play an increasingly greater role in his life (strong earth houses). Indeed, we may say that upbringing and childhood environment are still working unconsciously, but if the fire houses had been stronger, the effect of childhood years may have been quite different. At birth, there was a predisposition for these experiences and for the tendencies of further development. The large role played by earth element in his psyche is strengthened by the fixed cross, which constantly brings the inferior earth element to the surface.

In the preceding chapter, we pointed out the strong possibility of making a changeover in this horoscope. In fact, a change already took place in youth, namely from traditional Christian to noncon-formist and non-churchgoer. This meant breaking away from the parental environment. Nevertheless, the battle between fire and earth will always remain important for him. This can mean that another period may occur in which earth becomes more important than fire, probably bridged by the water element. This changeover doesn't have to be lasting; rather, we can see him balancing on the razor's edge trying to keep his balancing through a strong auxiliary function—the element of water.

Von Franz has the following to say about the disadvantages of the distorted type:

> ...from the very beginning they cannot develop their main disposition; they therefore remain a bit below the mark they would have reached had they developed in the one-sided way. On the other hand they have been forced ahead of time into doing something which in the second half of life they would have had to do anyway...[2]

The intense confrontation with the inferior function, which forms the crisis around ages forty-two to forty-five, will mean that Peter will be going through something that he has known for a long time. All his life he has been wrestling with this duality, which is at the same time the source of his creativity. At that time, he may again make a temporary changeover, but in all probability his difficulties will not increase.

The fire element will continue to play a role in his new direction in life—music—a career which came after his university studies. He will probably continue to search for new possibilities and ways of expression within his existing framework. The storminess will gradually disappear and make room for more earth and (primarily) water contents to express. Peter is one example that shows how important the Sun is in element division. To the degree that the element division becomes more imbalanced, the Sun will more often be decisive, whether or not it forms any aspects or whether they are easy or difficult according to traditional astrological standards.

3. CONSCIOUSNESS AND THE MOON

By using the concept *consciousness* as defined in Chapter 1, we can better understand that the astrological content of the Moon, so

---

[2]*Ibid.*, p. 4.

closely interwoven with the unconscious, can also play an important role for consciousness. The Moon is a very personal content; it represents unconscious learned behavior, part of our past and our youth, and above all indicates the way we behave in order to feel comfortable or the attitude in which we feel best. Most astrologers agree that this attitude is of an unconscious origin. When these contents are brought to the attention of the ego through the function of consciousness, then the ego can have a much better image of its own psyche than when the contents of the Moon remain hidden, provided the ego accepts these contents as from itself. Someone, for instance, having a strong Gemini emphasis is very much involved in surroundings. This person wants to participate in everything, experience everything, and know and talk about it. In short, excitement and liveliness appeal a great deal. If someone had Moon in Pisces, unconscious enjoyment by withdrawing into peace and quiet to catch one's breath, not actively participating for a while, no matter how much a desire to participate is also part of the character, would be a part of the personality. This inner duality can be experienced as troublesome for the individual may try to identify with one of the two sides. However, this always leads to increased tension, since both contents are present and both pull on the psyche to be recognized. If the individual doesn't allow personal seclusion now and then, the ego fails to appreciate the contents of the Pisces Moon. The result is that the individual is less conscious than if a willing comprehension of both sides of character were recognized. The realization of the Moon can increase awareness and make a more balanced self-image. It may sound paradoxical that unconscious contents can also contribute to the broadening of our field of consciousness. It will be self-evident, however, that in order to broaden, expand, and deepen consciousness, certain components are necessary that we weren't conscious of before. We are hereby thinking of an expansion of consciousness in regard to components the ego can easily identify with or wishes to enrich itself with, as well as a deepening of consciousness in regard to components the ego could not or did not want to accept or comprehend before.

Perhaps we may restate the way the elements work on the whole psyche: consciousness passes information onto the ego, which filters it, *i.e.* assimilates, forgets, or represses the information. The *way* consciousness passes on information is indicated by the elements, while the crosses indicate the way assimilation or repression takes place afterwards. The role of the Sun, emphasized in the preceding section, can be clarified within the theory of consciousness: the Sun represents the ego or the self in the horoscope.

4. MERCURY AND CONSCIOUSNESS

Mercury is the planet that connects everything—facts, information, people, and things from the outer world, as well as contents from the inner world. Mercury is also considered one of the personal planets. It has a specific meaning in the relationship between consciousness and the unconscious since it maintains the interaction of contents and information from both. It can connect the Sun and Moon, and at the same time bring the Sun and Moon into contact with the outside world. In this way, the element in which Mercury is located plays a subtle role in the organization of consciousness. Strikingly, where there is a great conflict between the Sun and Moon, if the Sun is active in the superior and the Moon in the inferior element, Mercury's element will become prominent. In Peter's horoscope, (see Chart 3 on page 42), this is the case. The Sun in Aries and Moon in Taurus produces a fire-earth duality. Through Mercury's location in Pisces, water comes into prominence, to a much greater degree than Venus (also personal) does in the air element.

It is extremely difficult to give exact rules that would apply to each horoscope. Each horoscope has its own unique combination which demands that it be examined with all its own nuances. Nevertheless, the Sun, Moon, Mercury, and Ascendant deserve special attention in the element and cross divisions, as illustrated by the above remarks.

CHAPTER FIVE

SAMPLE HOROSCOPES

1. BACKGROUND

For the last several chapters we have been discussing how the planets and houses affect the personality in relation to the elements and crosses within the horoscope. For the sake of taking this discussion further, we will now examine three different horoscopes to see how the energy manifests.

People who are born at the same time and in the same place are called astro-twins in astrology. This happens only when two people are born at the same hour and at the same longitude and latitude. When this occurs, the lives of the two people will be strikingly similar. A similar circumstance can also occur when more than one person is born at the same Greenwich Time. In other words, although the location of the birth is different, the Greenwich Time used to calculate the planetary positions is the same. And to take this idea a step further, there are relationships and differences between people who are born at the same Greenwich Time, but in a different location. When such circumstances arise, a person will share Greenwich Time with another person, but the houses will be very different because the people involved were born in different places on the earth.

The individual with the same planetary positions, but with a different set of houses—meaning that the Ascendant and Midheaven would be different—create an interesting experiment for us to interpret, for we can see how the element and cross divisions would

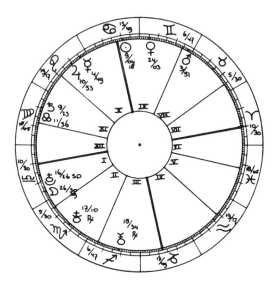

Chart 5. An imaginary chart created for Amsterdam.

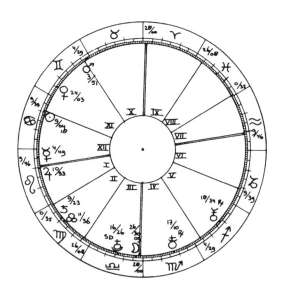

Chart 6. The same data as used in Chart 5, with the houses calculated for New York City as the birthplace.

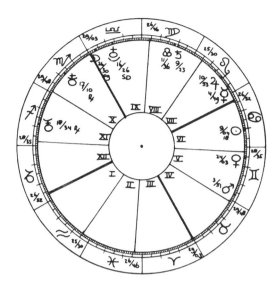

Chart 7. The same planets in Chart 5 and 6, but with the houses calculated as if Djaharta, Java was the birthplace.

affect such personalities. For the sake of a learning experience, I have provided totally imaginary horoscopes (Charts 5, 6, and 7). These three horoscopes have the same planets, but have been calculated for different cities. The change in birth location shows us three different people, who will express their natal energy through very different element and cross divisions as we shall see.

If all three people should become interested in astrology, they would read exactly the same interpretations in reference books: the Sun in Cancer indicates this, the Moon in Libra indicates that, and so on. The aspects between the planets will also be identical. However, the aspects to the Ascendant and Midheaven, as well as the house positions of the planets, indicating areas of experience, will differ. Because of this, they will become very different people, even though they share many characteristics. Their areas of experience will differ, and, therefore, their possible development and difficulties. On the basis of these differences, certain planets will appear more clearly in one horoscope than in another, as will be seen when we analyze the division of the elements and crosses. Try to answer some questions in regard to these horoscopes:

1. What does the division of the crosses and elements for each of the three horoscopes look like?
2. Are there notable differences between the horoscopes?
3. Briefly, how would we interpret the division in Chart 5?
4. What can be said about Chart 6?
5. What about Chart 7?

2. Notable Differences Between the Charts

In comparing the element division in Charts 5, 6, and 7 (see fig. 5.1), there are distinct differences that can be pointed out. Naturally, a number of points will be identical: the planets are located in the same signs in all three charts and therefore they will be the same in potential for the element divisions. The Ascendant and the Midheaven, however, are not alike. In Chart 6, the fire element receives enormous emphasis because the Midheaven and Ascendant are located in that element potential. This is not the case in Charts 5 and 7. In potential, therefore, Chart 6 deviates sharply from the other two.

A comparison of the circumstances (planets in the houses) reveals some notable differences. Chart 5, for instance has few possibilities to manifest the water element (in which the Sun is located!) by house, although the strongly-developing fire element can be of help since it doesn't conflict with the water element. Like water, the air element, equally strong by sign, has little possibility to express itself in house position. The water-air duality plays a clear role by sign (even more so since both the Ascendant and Midheaven are concerned), but it disappears almost completely by house position (circumstances). It gives way to a total fire predominance in which Mercury in Leo (out of an earth house) causes a duality in circumstances.

In Chart 6, fire is strongly developed by sign (potential), having Mercury, the Leo Ascendant and Aries Midheaven as its personal contents. The air-water duality also plays a role, although less strongly than in Chart 5 where the Ascendant and Midheaven were contributing. In contrast to Chart 5, Chart 6 can express itself well in circumstances: water is strongly emphasized, fire and air somewhat less, while earth remains in the background. The

a) Chart 5

Elements	Signs	Houses	Total
FIRE	☿ ♃ ♅	☊ ☽ ♂ * ♀ ☉	8
EARTH	♄	♅ ☿ ♃	4
AIR	♂ ♀ Asc. ☊ ☽	♅ ♄	7
WATER	☉ Mc. ♇	—	3

b) Chart 6

Elements	Signs	Houses	Total
FIRE	☿ ♃ Asc. Mc. ♅	♃ ♅	7
EARTH	♄	♄	2
AIR	♂ ♀ ☊ ☽	☊ ♂ * ♀	7
WATER	☉ ♇	☽ * ♇ ☉ ☿	6

c) Chart 7

Elements	Signs	Houses	Total
FIRE	☿ ♃ ♅	♂ ♀ ☊	6
EARTH	♄ Asc.	☉ ☽ * ♇	5
AIR	♂ ♀ ☊ ☽ Mc.	☿ ♃ ♅	8
WATER	☉ ♇	♄	3

Figure 5.1. As you will notice, the element division for a, b and c differ a great deal. Even though these charts were all calculated for the same day, the difference in birthplace has changed the emphasis of the elements. (*Denotes cuspal planets. See page 16.)

character in Chart 6 will develop more and more along the lines of a purely feeling person (water), with fire as an auxiliary function.

Chart 7 differs completely from Charts 5 and 6. Since earth has a strong personal content by sign (potential) due to the Capricorn Ascendant, this element gains more importance than it did in either Chart 5 or 6, and the difference becomes even greater when we relate this to house distribution (circumstance). Although Chart 7 gets little chance of expressing its nature (symbolized by the Sun) by circumstance—only Saturn is located in a water house—earth continually becomes more important, and this is an element that gets along well with the Cancer sun sign. The original duality between water and air shifts in circumstances somewhat, due to fire-earth duality playing a greater role in the house placements. Earth is now actually the strongest (in contrast to Chart 5). Mercury plays a different role: it is located in a fire sign (potential) and expresses itself in an air house (circumstances), an easy combination for this planet. But the basis of the horoscope is the tension between air and water, in which earth can make itself useful as an auxiliary function, but also as a means of escape. With this in mind, Mercury, because of its position in an air house, shares in the primary tension of the horoscope.

As a whole, the charts appear in a different light when we relate them to the cross division. See figure 5.2. We have already seen some large differences in the element division; the cross division indicates how these different attitudes are assimilated inwardly. Charts 5 and 7 both have a strong cardinal cross—besides the Sun and Moon, the Ascendant and Midheaven are located in that cross. Consequently, both horoscopes indicate an assimilation process strongly directed toward adapting to outward norms and values. In both horoscopes, we again find the Sun in a mutable house (circumstances), although the mutable cross is more strongly emphasized in Chart 5 than in 7. The planets located in mutable signs (potential) are located in mutable houses (circumstances) in Chart 5, but all of them are in fixed houses in Chart 7. Taken as a whole, this means that Chart 7 will be more fixed by that cardinal cross than Chart 5, creating a somewhat easier transition and a more flexible formation.

Chart 6 shows a rather broad distribution of the planets within the crosses, and both the cardinal and fixed crosses are well occupied with personal contents. Since the Moon is also located in the

a) Chart 5

Crosses	Signs	Houses	Total
CARDINAL	☉ Mc. Asc. ♇ ☽	♇ ☽ ☿ ♃	9
FIXED	☿ ♃ ♅	♅ ♄	5
MUTABLE	♂ ♀ ♄ ♇	♇ ♂* ♀ ☉	8

b) Chart 6

Crosses	Signs	Houses	Total
CARDINAL	☉ ♇ ☽ Mc.	♃ ☽* ♅	7
FIXED	☿ ♃ Asc. ♅	♄ ♇ ♂ ♀	8
MUTABLE	♂ ♀ ♄ ♇	♇ ☉ ☿	7

c) Chart 7

Crosses	Signs	Houses	Total
CARDINAL	☉ ♇ ☽ Asc. Mc.	☿ ♃ ☽* ♅	9
FIXED	☿ ♃ ♅	♂ ♀ ♄ ♇	7
MUTABLE	♂ ♀ ♄ ♇	☉ ♇	6

Figure 5.2. The division of the crosses changes when we look at Charts 5, 6 and 7. (*Denotes cuspal planets. See page 16.)

---

cardinal cross by house position, this cross remains strong. The fixed cross also acquires Venus and Mars, yet these planets are somewhat less important than the Sun, Moon, Mercury, Ascendant, and Midheaven. The importance of this cross, through the position of the Sun and Mercury in mutable houses, will increase as this person becomes older, so attitude and behavior may show an increasing flexibility. On the other hand, the fixed Ascendant produces a great deal of resistance.

In summary: with regard to the crosses, the distribution is most even in Chart 6, allowing more sides of the personality to be developed. In a very subtle way, however, tension, can also arise. The strong cardinal cross is located diametrically opposite the fixed cross, so the developing mutable cross will need to invest a lot of energy to keep the cardinal and fixed cross in balance.

3. Brief Interpretation of Chart 5

In Chart 5, we can say in potential that this is a feeling person who has difficulty expressing feeling judgments and evaluations of situations because possibilities for expression are lacking in the houses. Moreover, the urge to experience things through feeling (Sun) is strongly influenced by impulses from the air element (Moon, Asc.), so that the balance is shaky. The feeling evaluation of situations continually conflicts with the need to arrange everything mentally and to reflect upon events and situations. The contradiction between the Sun and the Moon unites itself by location in the fire houses with the result that this element probably will play an important role for consciousness at an early age. The shaky sign balance (potential) would cause the influence of the houses to be felt at an early age. Both the need to experience life in a feeling way and the need for logical reasoning can be satisfied by the fire houses. The search for possibilities, the chasing after future dreams, the fiery longings to experience everything, the desire to understand things is expressed through fire. Through this, the intuitive side can develop. Generally, the water element is known for its ability to sense and feel *through* certain situations or events. Fire's support in this horoscope makes possible further development and creates a growing understanding of why things happen. The practical side plays a subordinate role in this, because earth is hardly developed, even though thinking (Mercury) must develop in a concrete house. This Mercury in combination with a strong cardinal cross, can give a certain purposefulness to consciousness, whereby the mutable cross provides the necessary flexibility whenever desired.

Being in a fixed sign, Mercury has a difficult time in this horoscope, since it is connected with unconscious contents that can harass consciousness through the regressive movement of the fixed cross. Thus Mercury has a need for depth, both in thinking and in contacts, but because of its location in a cardinal house, this doesn't always work out. Even though its position in a fire sign is very promising, it must express itself in an earth house. This means the following is taking place in Chart 5:

a) a duality in potential between water and air, which leads to a shaky balance;

b) the fire element provides a good bridge and will continually become more important;

c) the strong cardinal cross energy causes the combination of elements to show an outward directedness: adaptation to the demands of the surroundings;

d) the mutable cross, which becomes stronger with age, makes this adaptation easy and creates smooth transition situations;

e) however, there are two difficult points:

• the element of water, so important for the Cancerian nature, has no possibility of expression, and this can give a gnawing feeling of not being understood, which, by the way, may stimulate this person to express via the fire outlets.

• Mercury is the central point of various conflicting tendencies: it shifts from fixed to cardinal and from fire to earth. Within this structure both the fixed cross need of depth and the fire element need of a variety of possibilities and grand future dreams cannot be secured without an arduous struggle.

4. BRIEF INTERPRETATION OF CHART 6

In Chart 6 (as in Chart 5), you see the duality between air and water. Here, however, the contradiction is not resolved by a strong fire element by house as it was in Chart 5, since it is clear that water houses are predominant here. Fire, it is true, is strongly represented by sign, with Mercury, Ascendant and Midheaven in fire, but it has difficulty realizing its potential by house position (cirumstances). Therefore, the search for possibilities and the reality behind appearances is not as much a means to bridge the duality here as we saw in Chart 5. In this horoscope, fire is much more an essential component of the psyche.

The circumstances this person will experience in a lifetime are those of water, in complete agreement with the Cancer Sun. The Moon, located in an air sign, will have to express itself in a water house as well, like Mercury, which originates in fire. Everything in this horoscope indicates that water, although having a shaky balance with air by sign, will rapidly crystallize into the superior function. Automatically, therefore, air becomes inferior and the occupation of the fire signs in potential makes one suppose that fire will crystallize rather easily into a first auxiliary function.

Because of the equal and balanced distribution of the planets in the crosses, the assimilation process will take place rather smoothly. The person will know how to withdraw in time and when to go ahead, as the moment may require. The cardinal cross has a slight upper hand, so that we may say this is a feeling person needing impulses from the surroundings and adapting accordingly. The goal is the outer world and by means of this the individual can give form to the self.

Through the combination of the strongest element—water— and the slightly predominant cardinal cross, we automatically arrive at the sign of Cancer, the water sign of the cardinal cross. This results in our having to interpret the entire horoscope in the direction of Cancer, despite the fact that only the Sun is found in this sign and even though it is hidden away in the twelfth house.

Of the three, Chart 6 has the basis most fitting with its Sun sign. This has a great advantage for the emotional life which therefore will experience less uncertainty and show fewer ripples on the surface of the water. The planets lying hidden under the surface in the element air, such as Venus and Mars, can call forth strong reactions from the unconscious. The relative harmony predominating in consciousness, therefore, doesn't necessarily apply to the whole psyche. One advantage is a balance in consciousness, but there is also a greater chance that attitudes become rigid, causing the unconscious to become more active and to undertake more counteractions. In this horoscope, we can deduce the direction of this action from the planets located in the air signs.

5. BRIEF INTERPRETATION OF CHART 7

There is an element duality between water and air, and to a small degree between fire (Mercury) and earth (Ascendant). Therefore, a double polarity exists in potential, whereby it is very difficult to determine which element will have the upper hand in Chart 7. There is little doubt about this in circumstances: the earth houses contain the Sun and Moon, thereby receiving the greatest emphasis. Still, Saturn and the Ascendant in earth signs are not sufficient to make this element superior. Through the house emphasis (circumstances), however, earth would eventually become superior in the course of life. By house the water element has difficulty coming into its own; air gets along somewhat better. This results in a continuation of the tension between the very important Sun and the air houses, so that earth can soon develop into an element of escape. In other words, out of a feeling/thinking duality there is a tendency to develop sensation as the main function, with feeling and thinking as auxiliary functions, the way of least resistance in this division. Just as in Chart 5, the essential nature—water—is not quite fulfilled, which can give rise to undirected feelings, such as not being understood. These feelings aren't necessarily expressed verbally; they may float through this person's experience like a haze, influencing behavior and thinking. Through the element of air, thinking will certainly show compulsive traits and can appear in uncontrolled spells; the earth element can be a hindrance in this, at least in an inhibiting way.

If Saturn played an insignificant role in Chart 6, here it becomes very important due to the earth emphasis and its possible development into the superior element. By far, Saturn can express itself best in this horoscope, especially since it doesn't form part of the unconscious as in Charts 5 and 6. Therefore, Chart 7 is much more directed towards the concrete, material, and practical, with an even greater purposefulness than the other two. However, this is partly due to the lack of the intuitive faculty that characterizes Chart 5, for instance.

The crosses show us that assimilation primarily takes place when progressive and mutable energy is addressed by the individual. Only when we view the totality does the fixed cross play a role later on. Strongly geared to the outer world, the cardinal cross has an easier time, since the Sun expresses itself in a mutable house. This doesn't alter the fact that this horoscope shows less flexibility than Chart 6. The mutable cross mainly serves progressive energy, but the fixed cross will continue to make itself felt in a subtle way in that planets in mutable signs must express themselves in fixed houses.

This gives a certain stability but also less flexibility than in the other two. There is already less flexibility on account of the element division, and the stability of earth causes a greater firmness in this case.

6. CONCLUDING REMARKS

From the preceding analysis, it may be seen that even though three people are born on the same day with exactly the same Greenwich Time and therefore exactly the same planet positions, their characters nevertheless will differ essentially because of the differing basis formed by the elements and the crosses. Chart 5 will welcome all possibilities in life as an escape from an inner duality. Chart 6, on the other hand, may spend quite a long time in a world of feelings and dreams created through its strong water potential. Chart 7 will approach life in a practical and concrete manner based on feeling, though more directed than the other two.

Therefore, although these three different horoscopes have the same planets and aspects, when their basis is thoroughly analyzed, one can see that certain planetary aspects will show up more clearly in one than in another. For example, seen in the light of the elements and crosses, the sextile between the Sun and Saturn should be considered more important in Chart 7 than in Chart 5. Every individual is unique, and the division of the elements and crosses in a horoscope indicates the direction in which we must interpret the aspects and significance of the planetary positions we have dealt with in a general way, in order to reconcile their contents with the unique and pure individuality of each human being.

INDEX

The
Houses and
Personality
Development

Karen Hamaker-Zondag

*Translated from the Dutch
by Transcript, Ltd.*

SAMUEL WEISER, INC.

York Beach, Maine

For Wim

TABLE OF CONTENTS

PREFACE

Even though astrologers have never been able to come to any agreement on which house system is best, houses seem to provide information we really need for a basic insight into an individual's character. In my opinion, it might be advantageous to use several house systems side by side; but that problem is too thorny to tackle here. House indications can provide a wealth of information; so — avoiding controversy — we will concentrate on the theory of interpretation and its fundamental principles as illustrated by my own practical experience in this book.

How do we determine the meanings of the houses? Are they concerned solely with external circumstances? What is their psychological background? These are some of the questions we shall consider. Houses form a distinct part of astrological interpretation and should be approached thoughtfully. The house positions of planets are always an entirely different matter from their sign positions; a fact which still receives insufficient attention in the astrological community.

There is often great disparity between cases that might appear comparable at first sight. Thus Mercury in the third sign (Gemini) and the 8th house is an indication that the mental and communicative abilities (Mercury) will be expressed in a fluent and versatile way (Gemini) and will be exercised mainly in the discovery of whatever is hidden (8th house). But Mercury in the eighth sign (Scorpio) and the 3rd house has an altogether different effect: here the mental and communicative abilities (Mercury) have an intensely emotional tone (Scorpio) and are concentrated on brief contacts and exchanges of information (3rd house). In spite of the fact that the 3rd house is the counterpart of the third sign and the 8th house is the counterpart of the eighth sign, the interpretations are completely different! We must bear this sort of difference well in mind when studying the techniques of astrological interpretation; otherwise we shall misinterpret the chart.

My purpose in writing this book is as follows: on the one hand, I want to draw attention to the houses in a much broader perspective than usual in order to show that there are numerous relationships and factors of interpretation that are generally overlooked in books of stock astrological meanings. On the other hand, I want to offer a book of exercises for the student so he or she can grasp the theory of house meanings and use this knowledge of the planets to work out what they signify in the houses.

In the chapter on combinations I have endeavored to demonstrate how wary we must be about adopting ready-made house meanings. In this connection, mention must be made of the rulerhips of houses. These form a study on their own and really call for much fuller treatment than can be given in a single chapter. A separate book on the subject is in the course of preparation.

My husband, Hans, has read the manuscript and initiated discussion, offered suggestions, and helped me organize the material here. I am very grateful to him for his help.

Drs. Karen M. Hamaker-Zondag

Easter, 1981

CHAPTER ONE

THE HOUSES AND ANALYTICAL PSYCHOLOGY

1. INTRODUCTION

We are born on earth and, as earthly beings, are irrevocably subject to all the laws that govern life. Astrological house division, too, relates to earth. Hence it comes as no surprise that the houses have always been associated with concrete events occurring in our lives. Sometimes these are events in which we play our part but are not able to change the outcome. We find ourselves in a world in which we have a role of sorts, yet sense that we have little say in what happens to us. This concept of fate may be very disagreeable for some of us.

"Why has this happened to me?" is a common response to bad news; yet the progressed horoscope would generally show that something was amiss. What, then, is the mechanism? The victim appears to do nothing, at least not consciously so, and yet what takes place demonstrably coincides with trends in a progressed chart. Events seem to be indissolubly linked with ourselves, but in a manner which is hard to determine. "Character is fate" is a popular saying in astrological circles; implying that everything that happens to us is determined by our own dispositions and that our dispositions (or characters) are represented (or symbolized) by the planets in the signs, the planets in the houses, the planetary aspects, and by a number of other factors. The houses form part of our character and so help to shape our destiny. Somewhere there is a connection between the course of life and the sort of person we are; and when we say "person" we mean the total individual with all his or her conscious and unconscious drives and motivations.

Since the houses have a decisive influence on our characters, they must also possess distinct psychological meanings. And so it is not enough simply to state that the 4th house relates to our domestic circumstances and the 11th house to our friendships. There must be some further reason why we furnish our homes in the way we do, and why we take to some people but not to others. The answer lies in our character type, and the obviousness of this conclusion suggests that we would do best to regard the houses as mirrors of ourselves. The external world and our environment mirror what is going on inside us, which means we can also view ourselves in them. Our choice of friends is a hard fact, an observable fact, and by taking a close look at our friends, we can learn a great deal about our personal attitudes to friends and to friendships in general. Each item in our surroundings can be treated as a looking-glass, and if we analyze our reactions and try to trace the reason for the kind of emotions it evokes, we shall discover that we need to delve deep into ourselves. Thus the houses provide an insight into the depths of the soul and, though ostensibly informing us about external matters, they mirror the inner life and character that we may not be totally conscious of. To consider the houses simply as your environment or sphere of life would be superficial; it would make the chart a static entity. And if houses are only indicative of a sphere of life, they would not show us how to learn to handle events, and we would have no influence on what happens to us. This would mean we were only the playthings of destiny.

Once we are able to comprehend the houses in a deeper perspective, that is to say, as revealers of internal or psychological processes, we shall suddenly get a grip on things. We cannot take our lives completely into our own hands for the psyche is too complicated for that. There are many factors liable to be overlooked or of which we are scarcely aware. What should happen, however, is a change in our attitude. When people realize that they are not just a part of the environment, but that the environment is also a part of them, then they see life in a new and dynamic dimension. We can make opportunities; we can make a mark on the world, rather than remaining a helpless pawn of fate.

How does this relationship between the psyche and the physical world work? Psychology will help us here. The psychic mechanism of projection may be the very bridge between the inner and outer for which we are looking. Let's therefore consider this idea briefly before beginning an examination of the houses themselves.

2. THE PROJECTION MECHANISM

Projection may be defined as an embodiment of subjective activity on some object (i.e., on some person, thing, or event outside oneself). It does not in the least matter if the activity has no true relevance to the object onto which it is projected. We see something in someone, we feel or experience something, and react to it in a certain way (not necessarily emotional). What we think we "see" may not be there in fact; however, it is there as far as we are concerned, it is *our* reality, a subjective reality which is *our* projection.

The projection mechanism enters into every circumstance of our lives from beginning to end. It is not possible to switch it on or off at will: it is part of our psychic functioning as long as we live. When we are in love, we project all our amorous and idealistic feelings on the object of our affections. What an apt saying it is that "love is blind": we project on the other person only what is desirable, good and ideal, and the power of the projection is such that we fail to notice many of their possibly unpleasant characteristics. The latter obtrude themselves later, when the intensity of the projection has waned. Then we complain that our loved one has altered, whereas the change is in ourselves. The mechanism is hard for us to comprehend because it eludes the conscious mind. It can withdraw us from reality, but compensates by presenting us with the hidden elements in ourselves (which we invariably see projected on external persons or things). Our reaction to these persons or things can give us considerable insight into the good and evil sides of our nature and our unconscious activities.

The projection mechanism plays a very significant part in our relationship with the outside world; so let us take a closer look at it. To illustrate this concept, think of a slide projector, a symbol that has become a favorite in analytical psychology because it is so obvious. The projector illuminates a white screen with colored pictures. All the screen does is reflect the light, and yet, as long as the transparency is being projected, the screen *is* the picture so to speak. Of course, we know that another slide will soon follow and the screen is no more than a device for making the contents of the transparencies visible: without the transparencies the screen remains blank, having nothing to display. Projected images can evoke emotions of all kinds. If what is being projected from some slide is very distasteful to us, we are hardly going to rush up to the screen and rip it to pieces; we simply move on to the next slide.

Life is remarkably like a slide show. We are continually projecting images from our unconscious self, and these images — composed of colors and patterns originating in the unconscious — may have nothing to do with the person and thing on which they are projected. However, there is a significant difference between a slide projector and the psyche: when transparencies are being projected we can know in advance, by inspection, what pictures are going to be shown. With the psyche this is not possible. We know neither the image nor its (emotional) coloration. Therefore problems sometimes arise.[1]

We can project our unconscious activities onto anything: onto individuals, things, or abstract ideas. What is important to observe is that we can be certain that we are making a projection whenever we experience an emotional reaction. To be sure, we react as if the object were eliciting our response, even though we ourselves are eliciting it in our unconscious. How often we misjudge and blame others on what we feel are perfectly adequate grounds when, in reality, they are not at fault or only marginally so. But we seldom suspect that we are tilting at windmills. On the contrary, we seem to assume that if we can remove the "screen" we shall thereby remove the source of the image. Alas, this assumption is wrong. As soon as a fresh opportunity for a projection arises (and we find ourselves a new screen) the whole process starts all over again and the "slide" is seen to be still in position.

So projections are hard to deal with, but they are also instructive. A strong emotional reaction is a sure sign that we need to think about the personified contents of our own unconscious. By reviewing all our reactions to the external world, we can get a good idea of what is going on within us beyond the reach of the conscious mind. Unconscious activities find in the projection mechanism their grand means of making themselves felt. This applies to everything we no longer want to know about ourselves — what we have suppressed or forgotten. These things are still lodged inside us, in spite of anything we can do,

---

[1]Compare with Fitzgerald's *Omar Khayyam* (1st edition) Quatrain XLVI:

For in and out, above, about, below,
'Tis nothing but a Magic Shadow-show,
    Play'd in a Box whose Candle is the Sun,
Round which we Phantom Figures come and go.

Here the analogy is being used to suggest that we ourselves are projections.
Tr.

and through projection they make themselves visible to us through our environment.

In this light, we can say that the more we isolate ourselves in order to play an empty role, the harder we make it for ourselves. At times, often without being aware of it, we all play at hide-and-seek with ourselves. The reactions of others to us and our reactions to them have much to tell us about the hidden side of ourselves with its problems and, yes, its gifts.

But there is something else we should know about the projection mechanism. Certain traits in the person on whom a projection is made may well correspond to what is being projected. The projection mechanism, however, exaggerates these traits. And this causes trouble: for when an individual is not aware that a projection is being made on him (or her), or if he has no adequate defense against the intensity of that projection, he is liable (consciously or unconsciously) to be taken over by it. The process is often more insidious than we think. In fact, a situation may develop in which the person making the projection encourages in the other individual (and unbeknown to the latter) the sort of behavior he would rather have discouraged. Also, a hero-worshipping type of projection can occur, in which the other individual is placed on a pedestal, and this too is detrimental. The unconscious is a part of character, and did not the ancients say that "character is fate"?

Esther Harding tells of a lady who, in a state of desperation, consulted a psychologist. This lady explained that her husband was a slave to drink and that his condition was deteriorating. She had been married before, but had divorced her previous husband because of his hard drinking. Yet neither of her spouses had shown any sign of alcoholism before she married them. She projected negative factors from her past on both husbands, and did so with such energy that the projection produced the very result of which she was so afraid: they became drunkards like her father. She had reacted to each husband — not as he really was when she first met him — but with the full force of her own projections, which were the consequences of her own repressed memories (she wanted to forget her father and her past, and this had not been wholly assimilated). She projected the unassimilated material onto her husbands and became very dominating towards them (so as to control any drinking problems that might arise!). The men had little choice: either they could try to stand up to her by having constant rows or else they could drown their sorrows in drink. Both opted to do the latter. Everybody thought the woman was the ill-used party, but she brought her troubles on herself by her own character. If we look around us we shall see that some people appear to suffer from repeated strokes of the same ill-fortune. In fact they are dogged by their own projections. Only when we reach a certain level of awareness can the vicious circle of events be broken . . .

Let's go back to astrology and look in particular at the houses. The houses traditionally symbolize our circumstances. The projection mechanism turns our environment into a key which can unlock the deepest recesses of our being. Therefore the houses have an inner side which should not be neglected. When we study the houses in depth, you'll see the similarity of their structure to that of the psyche in analytical psychology. It is the houses, then, which can give us, often better than we think, a working insight into unconscious attitudes, unconscious patterns of expectation or desire, and what we unconsciously attract to ourselves from the outside world.

CHAPTER TWO

THE SYMBOLISM OF THE HOUSES

1. THE DERIVATION OF THE MEANINGS

It is important to understand that the houses are related to signs. The 1st house corresponds to the first sign (Aries), the 2nd house to the second sign (Taurus), the 3rd house to the third sign (Gemini), and so forth. Each of the signs symbolizes a given area of life. For example, Cancer (the fourth sign) is often considered domestic, and the 4th house represents that area of life where domesticity comes to the fore, i.e., our home life. Of course this is not the whole story, but the principle is always the same — houses represent given areas of life bearing some analogy to the signs.

In this manner we can derive a whole host of meanings for the houses, but that is not enough when we want to use the houses to understand ourselves from a psychological point. We might be over-inclined to see the signs as merely internal, and the houses as merely external or material. Indeed, over the centuries, the material definition of house meanings seems to have predominated. This is very understandable. Only in our own century, with the advent and development of depth psychology, have we learned to regard ourselves from other points of view, to discover more within ourselves, with the result that we can now extract more sophisticated information from the chart. Studies of the projection mechanism discussed in the previous chapter, and the concept of synchronicity, have provided new insights into the relationship between inner and outer and between spirit and matter. Although the houses indicate external circumstances as the signs indicate internal attitudes, we should no longer think of the houses in terms of external circumstances alone.

A wide range of psychic processes precedes any manifestation, in whatever area of life the manifestation may occur because conscious and unconscious motives are interwoven. The manifestation actually results from an interplay between all the inner processes plus the environmental factor. For example, if someone had a broken leg which kept him housebound for some months, it is by no means unusual to hear him say, "Looking back on it, I know I lost much of the will to persevere. I was having to sit about, so keeping to any plan of action didn't seem particularly necessary. I was real glad to be off work, although I didn't like the way it had happened. But I have thought about it since then and now I see things quite differently. I can enjoy working again." Someone once told me, "I wish I had fallen off a ladder years ago. Then at least I could have started painting earlier and would have found myself much sooner than I did." A great change came over this particular man during the time he spent confined to his bed.

Was his fall due to bad luck? No, definitely not. Analytical psychology would regard it as a consequence. Unconsciously, my friend had been dissatisfied (as he later admitted), and the unconscious constellation arranged something in the outside world to force him to leave his job. His conscious mind would not let him see — or did not want to admit — that something had always been missing from his life, therefore his unconscious took a hand. If a normally careful person does not look where he is going, and steps under a car or falls from a ladder and breaks his leg, might there not be a hidden reason? The man in our example had to stay in bed for weeks, and this gave him the leisure to review his situation. The quietness and time spent on his own allowed more things to surface in his mind than could have surfaced in the hurry of his everyday life.

Some people might simply say that they were the victim of their own stupidity (by not paying attention), or of an error of judgment, or might lay the blame on the person who knocked them down; whereas, in reality, there was something inside that provided the opportunity for the accident, something in the unconscious . . . It is all there in the chart.

Another example illustrates a need for change provided by the unconscious. A perfectly healthy and cheerful man, who had never been ill in more than thirty years, gradually lost interest in the work he had always enjoyed. But being conscientious he kept going. Internally he was experiencing a marked change: he changed his vision of life and became interested in all kinds of human patterns of behavior. Then he fell sick and everyone thought he just had a cold. A pain developed in his back, hips and legs and this pain got worse. His doctor suspected a slipped disc but finally diagnosed sciatica. The man could no longer work and lay in bed a great deal. In his heart of hearts he was very glad to stop working, even though he was not quite so thrilled about the reason. Eventually he began to recover, though not completely; his improvement was extremely slow in spite of the fact that he faithfully followed the doctor's advice on diet and so forth. Consciously, he was doing his best to get well, but his unconscious mind was interfering with his external circumstances because his employment had completely lost its appeal.

Just as he was ready to return to work, he felt discomfort in his groin. The doctor diagnosed an inguinal hernia, and again the man was found to be unfit for work. An operation, followed by a period of convalescence, left him once more able to resume his employment. He faced the prospect bravely but with aversion. And, strange to say, he was rapidly gripped by a new disease and so was unable to start. Those who knew him were full of pity, and commiserated with him. "What a run of bad luck," they said, "and you so keen on your job!" But the man himself finally got the message, and commented, "It was as if I were being deliberately prevented from ever returning to work. So I have given up on it, though I shall have to find some means of earning a living." And so he soldiered on, still ailing, yet inwardly in search of fresh possibilities which had covertly been announcing themselves from the first.

If we wish to know what is liable to happen to us in the world outside, it is necessary to dip deep inside to see what is happening there. We shall learn that the unconscious, in a way that is sometimes very painful to the conscious mind, acts as a corrective and helps us to progress in life. The responsibility is ours to learn to read and acknowledge its coded messages.

It is gratifying to see that modern books listing house meanings are asking students to pay more attention to the inner, psychological aspect. Often we find a house described as "our attitude to . . ." followed by a list of the things belonging to that house. Well, it is true that the houses reflect our attitudes; but how often is an attitude really conscious? Sometimes we think we are espousing a certain cause, when deep down, our sympathies lie elsewhere, and perhaps are the direct opposite of what we think they ought to be. This concept was illustrated by our previous example of the woman with her two drunken husbands: ostensibly, she was hoping to settle down with a teetotaller, but the unconscious expectations arising from her fears and projections were such that she actually drove two successive spouses to drink.

Wherever, in what follows, the reader encounters the words "our attitude to . . . (something or other)," don't assume that the attitude in question is conscious, nor must you assume that we cannot relinquish or change it except in response to some explicit feeling. The word "attitude" covers both conscious aspirations and unconscious projections. Both aspects of the psyche help to shape attitudes, and the part played by the unconscious must not be underestimated.

2. The Houses

Let us now take a look at the individual houses. First we shall discuss traditional meanings in relationship to the analogy between houses and signs. Then we shall suggest the psychological counterpart of each house; for that will give us a synthesis of our internal and external worlds, two quantities which are not to be thought of as independent, static portions of reality, but as perpetually interacting.

THE 1st HOUSE

The traditional meaning of the 1st house is analogous to the sign Aries, a sign which makes itself clearly felt in the outside world. The cusp of the 1st house is called the Ascendant (sometimes the entire 1st house is known as the Ascendant), and the sign that happens to be on the cusp of the 1st house in a chart is termed the rising sign. The 1st house governs the way in which you approach and respond to the external world. Your behavior and attitudes are, so to speak, brought into line with, and channeled through, the characteristics of the rising sign.

Just as Aries reacts spontaneously to all kinds of stimuli from the environment, so the 1st house indicates your immediate response to the environment, and that in the widest possible sense. For not only do your reactions to stimuli from other people fall within the scope of the 1st house; so do your reactions to climate, the state of the weather, medicine or whatever.

Aries likes to plunge into anything new, and can exhibit unbridled energy. Similarly, the Ascendant shows *how* you utilize your energy. It naturally follows that the 1st house is an indicator of your vitality, power of resistance and love of life. Aries is self-assertive — sometimes unconsciously so out of pure enthusiasm—and we may infer that the 1st house has to do with your need to manifest and assert yourself. How you manifest yourself in the outside world is physically as well as psychologically determined; that is why the 1st house also has to do with your external appearance, behavior and physical characteristics.

*　　*　　*　　*　　*

The psychological meaning of the 1st house indicates primarily your ego-involvement in life. Much as Aries does, it represents the degree to which, and the manner in which, you give expression to this ego-involvement and present yourself to the world. Your mode of reaction to external stimuli, whether the latter be physical or psychic, is directly influenced by this ego-involvement. But we must avoid jumping to conclusions and branding ego-involvement as egotism—something essentially different. Rather it is an attitude of wanting to show what you ARE, of daring to stand up for yourself and going out to meet life.

If there is an attitude toward a still undifferentiated external world or toward still undifferentiated impulses emanating from the external world, there must be some underlying blueprint. The attitude and the mode of reaction as indicated by the 1st house are obviously not determined by the external world or by the nature of the impulses. You start with an initially unconscious and abstract psychic attitude toward yourself, the sort of person you are, the way you express yourself, and the way in which, or degree to which, you can hold your own (simply as individuals).

There are other horoscope factors which inform us about the degree of your ego-involvement. But, as the bridge to the external world, the Ascendant or 1st house is most directly concerned with how the ego expresses itself in the world. For instance, a strongly "I"-oriented Ascendant can occur in an otherwise "you"-oriented chart. In such a case, you would strike those who meet you for the first time as being rather wrapped up in yourself. When others know you better, and your altruistic characteristics have had a chance to show themselves, others will see how your ego-involvement (Ascendant) is placed completely at the disposal of others (rest of the chart). Although the 1st house is an essential part of everyone's character, the first impression conveyed by this starting point of the chart (and point of entry into the personality) need not tally with the remainder of the horoscope.

Because the 1st house has so much to do with the external world, planets in this house are very noticeable; they can project their energy straight outward. These planets can also stamp themselves strongly on the attitude and behavior of the person in question, and can alter the significance of the Ascendant according to their nature.

The 1st house indicates the extent to which we can hold our own psychologically. However, it also indicates how psychic conditions are reflected in material and concrete circumstances. The 1st house makes its mark on the body, and will often give a good idea of your physical condition and appearance. Planets in the 1st influence the body too. For example, when we read in some astrological treatise that Mars in the 1st makes one prone to injuries, you may ask why. Mars, the symbol of action and energy, can so accentuate the self-emphasizing of the 1st house (especially when the signs in the background favor the planet) that you may run into trouble because you are overly impulsive, extra daring or too quick to react.

Mars is also the planet that represents your self-assertiveness and need to prove yourself. It colors the way you present yourself, also your response to external stimuli. Responses may sometimes be too hasty, fierce or ill-mannered, with all the consequences of this.

But there is another factor to consider. Under the influence of the 1st house, you possess a certain abstract notion of how you encounter the world; which means that you have an at least partially unconscious pattern of expectation which you see reflected in the external world by the projection mechanism. It is as if what is outside reacts on us in the same manner as we do on it, because that is what we are expecting it to do. Therefore, people with Mars in the 1st house seem to have "a nose for trouble," although other horoscope factors would have to be present for the risk to become serious. Obviously, Mars in the 1st has its good side too: in this position it tends to increase energy and we can achieve a great deal. Any of the planets in the 1st house would affect vital energy in one way or another; Mars has just been used as an example.

House 1 indicates initial impulse and reaction to the external world, and therefore says something about the degree to which you hold your own, assert yourself or make a first impression on others. By studying it, one may easily deduce the bearing and style of your dress, which are merely the material expressions of what is internally important to you. Hence, subject to the modifying influence of the rest of the horoscope, the 1st house particularly represents the impression you want to make on the outside world. It represents your general attitude toward, and degree of adaptation to, your environment, as well as those unconscious expectations which, by their very existence, attract certain things into your life.

THE 2nd HOUSE

The traditional meaning of the 2nd house is analogous to the sign Taurus. Just as Taurus lays emphasis on material security, so the 2nd house is concerned with personal possessions, including money, valuables, securities and so on. The 2nd house indicates the way we look after these assets and the extent to which we are free to enjoy material things.

The 2nd house shows how self-supporting we are, our capacity for making money and how well we manage our financial resources. Consequently, it also reveals if we are liable to run into debt through mismanagement, all according to additional information shown in the natal chart.

*   *   *   *   *

From a psychological point of view, the 2nd house also deals with possessions, but from a different point. Whatever our conscious or unconscious attitude to material possessions, we realize that a regular process has gone into the formation of this attitude. Even when we unthinkingly or unconsciously react to anything, our reaction is based on some concept or value judgment. The structure of our value judgments determines our notions of the nature of things and what we can do about them. Each of us carries inside us a unique imagery that determines how we see our basic need for security. The need for material security leads us to associate values with everything that surrounds us.

It is these personal values — our own value pattern — grafted on the need for a firm base, which we find in the 2nd house. In this house we can also find the entire process for the formation of these values insofar as they affect us personally. Social values lie elsewhere in the chart.

This house is therefore the house of our personal wishes respecting material possessions and of our attitude toward them. But specific processes invariably occur inside the psyche before we adopt a stance on such things. Feelings of satisfaction and dissatisfaction arise, as they can do with regard to any of the areas of life represented by any of the houses. As soon as we become aware of our feelings of satisfaction or dissatisfaction, these feelings begin to affect our state of well-being and, with that, our means of subsistence. We can ascribe to the 2nd house a signalling function that is concerned with self-preservation in a material sense.

In the process of the formation and resolution of our feelings of satisfaction and dissatisfaction, a specific attitude develops which gives us our personal pattern of values. (This pattern is concerned mainly with practical and material affairs—in contrast to our 4th house concern with emotional matters. However, both 2nd and 4th houses may be regarded as pillars of an individual's sense of security). These values are very personal because they result from the picture we have of how we should maintain ourselves. Obviously, this picture will be modified by the rest of the horoscope.

Our feelings of satisfaction and dissatisfaction prompt us to take certain steps. The acquisition of knowledge and skill is one of the measures we can adopt. What we learn is often used as a source of income, and this introduces the financial aspect of the 2nd house. We must nevertheless bear in mind that the house really signifies our feelings of satisfaction and dissatisfaction in the external world, and that it is not a foregone conclusion that a strong 2nd house will signify riches or the possession of great knowledge and skill. The primary need for feeling secure prompts us to concentrate first and foremost on banishing whatever is dissatisfactory externally, and on gaining a comfortable personal identity which will lay a solid foundation on which we can build.

The motivation for what we attempt can be traced to feelings of satisfaction and dissatisfaction which incite us to action (behaving with restraint being a form of action too!), and these feelings determine our attitude toward everything that can give security and certainty. That is why the 2nd house relates to our sense of freedom to a certain extent. Erich Carl Kühr said that the 2nd house is a measure of the personal freedom found in possessions, whether material, intellectual or spiritual. More abstractly, we can say that when we deal with the sources of our dissatisfaction, we can enable ourselves to derive more satisfaction from our lives, and therefore feel more free.

Planets in the 2nd house tell us something about those processes which arise from the need for security; they tell us about the way in which we express this need, and about our personal values. Secondarily, planets in the 2nd house show how we handle finances, take care of property and — according to the nature of the planets — how much we are able to earn. Planets in the 2nd house can be just as decisive for occupation as planets in the house of work and working conditions (the 6th) or planets in the house of social position (the 10th). Finally, the manipulation of material things can be creative and artistic as well as financial.

THE 3rd HOUSE

The traditional meaning of the 3rd house is analogous to the sign Gemini. This house displays characteristics of that sign and signifies our possibilities for making contacts, gathering information, classifying facts, observing and combining. The 3rd house indicates communication, and provides our ability for making all forms of communication. It also indicates our means of communication, such as letters, telephone, books, and even how we deal with transportation. Brief contacts with the immediate environment (and brief encounters are typical of Gemini) come under this house, and so by implication our neighbors and our home environment are 3rd house concerns.

The comings and goings of Gemini have their counterparts in the various relationships signified by the 3rd house: in trade and transport, in social intercourse, by direct contact and by word of mouth. Languages and teaching are 3rd house matters. Just as Gemini likes to talk as much as possible and to tell the latest news, so the 3rd house symbolizes the exchange of information in any form. It provides an indication of our learning power, logical skills, mental activity and educational standard. Journalism is another feature of this house.

The need for contact is fundamental to human life, and contact leads to an exchange of ideas. The 3rd house reveals the extent to which we express our need for contacts; emotional involvement, however, belongs to the next house, the 4th.

The 3rd house has to do with the manner in which we approach and reconnoitre objective reality. Not only contacts with people fall within the scope of this house, but contacts with *all* perceptible reality. Objective reality signifies very little until we have made it our own. We are obliged to analyze and classify this reality in order to apprehend it, and the manner in which we do so is the manner in which we approach facts in general. So at the basis of the 3rd house is an individual or subjective picture of the way in which we try to classify and arrange objective reality; initially, that picture is more or less unconscious. Our partly conscious, partly unconscious pattern of expectation is reflected in the way in which we get in touch with others; including the manner of each contact, its subject, and its progress.

As an air house, the 3rd naturally emphasizes an interest in the ideas of others, and this makes for short, informative or fact-finding contacts without obligations. When the contacts are prolonged, as they are in the 7th or 11th house, other factors such as personal involvement, shared interests and the like come into play—factors which are absent from the 3rd house. The same considerations apply to short journeys, which relate to this house. Perhaps we can define short journeys as trips in which impressions are gained but not the sort of knowledge that we integrate into ourselves (9th house), so we don't gain a lot of experience or become too involved. The 3rd house also indicates basic education; that is to say, a learning process with the emphasis on spontaneous knowledge or on knowledge that we may not integrate into our philosophy of life.

Because this house shows our need for contacts and what we may expect from them, it also says something about the means we use for making them: about the way we write or communicate in general, about any love of language, about our mode of thought. Anxieties and frustrations, talents and opportunities, are to be found in the 3rd house.

The result of our thinking is largely determined by the 3rd house. This must not be confused with what the planet Mercury (mundane ruler of this house) does. Aided by the projection mechanism, we marshall external facts in a certain way as revealed by our 3rd house, and planets in that house influence action according to their natures. As far as Mercury relates to the 3rd house, consider someone whose Mercury, owing to its sign and placement, expresses itself in a very rationalistic fashion. If you add Neptune to the 3rd house, it is easy to see that the normally rational Mercury will not be comfortable with the non-rational information colored by Neptune that clouds the very issue of rational communication.

Thus the 3rd house tells us how you make sense of things, connect things or make contacts. When these activities are projected into concrete reality they are experienced as agreeable or disagreeable liaisons with others, as the consequences of your orientation to the world. Because it is a cadent house, the 3rd also expresses your ability to make use of its contents whenever and wherever there are connections to be made: in the compiling and classifying of facts, in the exchange of goods, or the striking of bargains between buyer and seller, etc.

Traditionally, the 3rd house indicates your natural relationships with brothers, sisters and neighbors. If it is true (as we shall see) that the 12th house represents the child's experience of the world via its unconscious link with its parents, especially the mother, we can regard brothers and sisters (if any) as the first new manifestations that enter our early lives. Since neighborliness and social intercourse in the home environment still exist in plenty, neighbors will belong to the 3rd house. Perhaps, at this point, it will not come amiss if we mention the significant role played by brothers and sisters in forming our attitude to the outside world, also the importance of a good neighbor for helping a child to begin to explore the world from the backyard.

In concluding this section, let's consider someone with Saturn in this house. Traditionally, it would be said that you are rather retiring and may prefer not to become too involved with others, or that you have no brothers or sisters or you have little contact with them. But what is responsible for this? Saturn emphasizes a particular response to life; therefore the native's expectations with regard to it are pitched rather high, and the fear of failure in the area is correspondingly great. You may be haunted by uncertainty, and if you do venture into new contacts you may prepare the step so carefully that your manner is far too constrained, and makes other people think you are cold or distant. Through projected uncertainty, anxiety or defensiveness, or through overcompensation, you may seem overpowering and will see this fact reflected in the attitude of the outside world. If you can manage to get in touch with people without forcing yourself on them, you will discover you can make solid and permanent contacts.

Behind our apparently unchangeable external circumstances there always lies a world of dynamic psychic processes. Difficult planetary positions need not prove as troublesome as is sometimes thought. What matters is the unconscious abstract pattern of expectation which we consciously perceive after it has been projected on our surroundings. In the case of the air houses, our surroundings act as a fairly clear mirror of what is actually going on inside us.

THE 4th HOUSE

The traditional meaning of the 4th house is analogous to the sign Cancer, a domestic and maternal sign. And so our early home life is represented by the 4th house, and it in turn also indicates our adult need to care and be cared for, our feeling for family, tradition, genealogy and the past. Then again, we find our old age and its circumstances symbolized by the 4th house—when our professional life loses its importance and we retire into the more circumscribed domestic sphere and experience the end of life.

The sign Cancer lives in emotional contact with its environment; similarly, the 4th house shows how we evaluate anything emotionally. Since Cancer creates attachment to origins, it is hardly surprising that the 4th house should be associated with the origin of things. Beginning and end lie in the 4th; it is our base of physical and mental operations. Land and houses (real estate), mines and liquids (petroleum!) all relate to this house in a mundane interpretation of the chart.

People with a strong Cancerian influence are so involved in the emotional situation of their environment that they often mask their own feelings when these are not in tune with it. They always rely on maintaining emotional links with their surroundings. This masking function is also found in the 4th house (reciprocally with the 10th house, as we shall see); where we find not only personal masks but stage masks, i.e., the theater.

More importantly, from a psychological point, here is the area where we experience the results of the unconscious inner processes of the 8th and 12th houses. To the conscious mind these results are irrational; nonetheless, they emerge from an inner world of subjective reality which needs to be explored as thoroughly as the objective world of the 3rd house. It may be assumed, therefore, that the 4th house indicates the way in which we face our subjectivity, that is to say, how we face the mainly emotional reality lying within us. And our approach is governed by a pre-existing frame of reference which determines how we view this subjective reality.

The 4th house indicates our sense of well-being, but the conscious mind will not always feel at ease when the subconscious mind's emotional contents proceed to make themselves known; especially as the latter are so unpredictable (e.g., when they take the form of changing moods). Whereas the 2nd house has to do with certainty, with having a *stable* existence, the 4th has to do with security, with having a *safe* existence, and this need involves us in the search for a solid emotional basis.

This house concerns our attitude to the world. As soon as consciousness begins to develop and the sense of safety derived from the unconscious link with the mother fades a little, the need for security (which is still there) makes us cling to our parents (not simply to the mother). That is why the security provided by the parents is traditionally assigned to the 4th house, for it represents not merely the security parents offer us, but also the security we seek from them — and the measure in which we obtain it. Thus the extent to which we experience the parental home as a place of safety when we are young is indicated here, and so is our later (conditioned) attitude towards domesticity.

We can tell a great deal about the occupant of a dwelling from its style of decoration. In fact, we can watch the decoration change as the occupant changes. Someone who has become very gloomy may choose to paint a room black or dark purple. It would be a mistake to say he was depressed by the color. No, the deathly color is actually a reflection of his inner frame of mind, and is just a single aspect of the expression of inner processes, in this instance a material expression of them.

Another mistake we could make would be to say that someone with Uranus in the 4th dislikes his family. Uranus in the 4th is more likely to indicate an insecure emotional base, which means that feeling "at home" is developed with difficulty. It is hard for this reason to look at his own home as a safe haven. Nevertheless, if he succeeds in establishing his individuality, then it is certainly possible for him to settle down, and to express what he has been trying to realize.

The unconscious, of which the 4th house is the tip (and the part we actually experience), contains not only personal factors but also factors that have been handed down from generation to generation. In addition to informing us of conditions in the parental home, the 4th house tells us about our sense of kinship, our links with the past, with tradition, and with our native land, all of which show how well we are rooted in our own family.

Now, on the one hand, our need for a firm emotional base leads us to adopt a certain attitude in the outside world and, on the other hand, it may make us feel vulnerable. This house reveals both the need for security and the ability to provide it; it indicates how we cherish and care for others, how we enter into their feelings — to "get inside them" — without losing ourselves in them. The ability to "get inside" someone else (acting is always associated with this house) also performs a social function. And yet, the feeling of vulnerability so characteristic of this house makes it difficult to commit ourselves emotionally.

In the interests of self-protection, we adopt a rôle, we create an image for ourselves, we wear a mask. Some such protective device is essential to help us adapt without trauma to the external and the internal worlds. But there is a danger that, like a performer, we shall be trapped in the part we are playing so that it takes us over. Originally so reassuring, the mask stifles us on the inside and provokes unwanted conflicts on the outside. This mask and the 10th house one that we wear to impress society are known as the Persona.[2]

Finally, the 4th house points to how we shall spend our old age. We are back at home base, we have lived life and are often dependent on the care of others, while our reduced participation in the community and a more philosophical outlook gradually deprive mask-wearing of its sense. Of course, the experience we have gained in the course of life will have its effect, but it is our own attitude toward life that will make of it either a tragedy or a comedy.

----

[2] A light-hearted fantasy based on the change produced in a man who wears a mask is Max Beerbohm's *The Happy Hypocrite. Tr.*

THE 5th HOUSE

The fifth house is analogous to Leo, the fifth sign, and so refers to self-expression. Our hobbies, creativity, our need for sport and amusement are closely connected with the latter and are traditionally shown by the 5th house, which is known as the house of pleasure. In this house our self-expression can take any of many different forms. Hence this house indicates how and to what extent we indulge in self-expression and assert our individuality. It shows how much we study our own interests and go our own way. A liking or talent for management and leadership is shown by the 5th house. Leo claims exclusivity; the 5th house, too, reveals the degree to which we are able to make our mark.

Children, as a direct and concrete result of the creative urge, are symbolized astrologically in the 5th house. The 5th house is concerned with love affairs and adventures — and with their consequences. And it often shows how we get on with children in general and with our own children in particular.

Human beings naturally strive for self-realization. But if we want to be ourselves, we must at least have something with which to identify, a system of ideas in which we can find and recognize ourselves. In these ideas, as mentioned previously, there is an abstract guiding image. C.G. Jung defines the "I" or ego as a complex of ideas which is the mid-point of the field of consciousness of the person concerned, for it appears to possess a high degree of inner continuity and identity. The psychic energy of the "I" or ego as so defined is represented in the horoscope by the Sun. However, the 5th house is that area of life in which we state our identity and it shows how determined we are to be our own person.

Uninhibited self-expression finds a natural outlet in our way of enjoying ourselves: in our hobbies, sports, entertainments and recreations. A willingness to show what we are made of and confidence in the result of doing so are sometimes reflected in gambling and speculation, sometimes to the point of rashness.

Each house requires us to give shape to something, and using our creativity is a 5th house matter. Such creativity can be seen in all sorts of original work, on either the material or the intellectual plane, and this creative expression may be amateur (done for fun) or professional.

By extension, the creative becomes procreative. Children and the begetting of them belong to the 5th house. Although this house concerns children in general, it has mainly to do with our own children. Quite often, it is possible to see prominent traits in children clearly indicated in the charts of their parents and, in particular, the 5th houses of the latter reveal the child's most troublesome traits, traits to which the parents, often unconsciously, react very strongly.

The result of our urge for manifestation is reflected, via the projection mechanism, in our environment. Someone who has unusual opportunities for self-expression generally radiates a self-confidence that compels respect, and is in a position to play a central or leading role. Leadership, authority, and the exercise of will-power are all associated with 5th house self-confidence. But, more than this, the confidence needs to be reinforced, because self-expression usually meets with opposition somewhere along the line. Thus there is a craving for recognition, and a search for reassurance. The projection has a very immediate effect.

Since self-affirmation plays a very important role in affairs of the heart, love-making and love affairs also find a place in this house, even though they do not relate solely with self-affirmation. The fun side of love, seen in flirtation and erotic play, is a typical 5th house phenomenon. But the state of being in love as a projection-process of the animus/anima, and sexuality as the surrender of oneself to one's partner, do not belong to this house, but to the 8th.

If the 5th house is strong (for example if it has a number of planets posited in it), it will show how we behave when attempting to assert our authority; also how we may expect the world to respond. Here is a case in point: someone with a configuration indicating that he has trouble deciding his personal identity and suffers from anxiety over the centralization function (because, say, of a difficult placement of the Sun and a weak Ascendant) can really run into problems when the 5th house is heavily tenanted. He has a strong need for self-expression in order to reassure himself (5th house), but the rest of his character is not in keeping with that need. Nevertheless he will notice that time and again he lands himself in situations where he stands at the helm, plays a leading part, and makes his presence felt (the 5th house again). The need for self-expression is not to be denied; but, because the rest of his character does not help him to understand that he has this need, he may stare in amazement when his companions tell him that he is sometimes too insistent on having his own way, or that he tends to ride roughshod over them just because he has taken control. He will probably find this hard to believe, until he watches himself closely!

To sum up then, the 5th house, the planets in it, and the ruler of the 5th, show what need we have for emphasizing our own personality and, even more, our own individuality.

THE 6th HOUSE

The 6th house is analogous to the sign Virgo; which is why we associate our job or profession with this house, as well as working conditions, state of health, our attitude toward health, and service to others. Analytical ability and a sense of method can also be assessed from this Virgoan house. And out of a gift for analysis spring discernment and the critical faculty. Therefore the 6th house is one of specialization. It is the house of the skilled crafts-person who pays scrupulous attention to detail; but (if the planetary constellation so inclines) it can also indicate the person who is a slave to his or her work; it can be the house of the drudge.

Virgo, as the sign of service, signifies usefulness and practicality, seeing that its work, like that of the 6th house, is designed to meet practical and concrete ends. In the 6th we find the objectification of facts, again very much in keeping with objective Virgo.

The 6th house indicates sickness, health, how well we care for our bodies, and our interest in hygiene. By extension, it relates to treating the sick (as a doctor, nurse, naturopath, acupuncturist, hypnotist, etc.). What is more, the 6th house represents the food we eat to sustain the body, and hence it represents the digestive tract, assimilation, diets, dieticians, reactions to food, and to whatever supports the physical system.

In the house opposite the 6th, namely the 12th, we find our link with the collective unconscious. The collective unconscious holds the so-called archetypes, or primal patterns of human behavior. An archetype is, so to speak, the "idea" of a certain type of behavior before this manifests itself in the outside world. (Compare the idea of a crystal lattice, which has a latent existence before its corresponding form ever crystallizes out of a chemical solution).

Archetypes are universal to humanity; but although their original contents are always the same, they are protean in the forms they take. So it is the contents, not the forms, which are universal. The latter differ from community to community and from individual to individual. The objectified archetypes within a given culture, sub-culture, or society, are to be found in the 6th house, the house of the collective consciousness. These objectified forms of underlying archetypes give us, so to speak, a pattern of norms and values which is part of a certain culture — the culture to which we belong. The collective conscious was described by Jolande Jacobi as follows:

> By 'collective consciousness' we mean the aggregate of the traditions, conventions, customs, prejudices, rules, and norms of human collectivity which give the

consciousness of the group as a whole its direction, and by which the individuals of this group consciously but quite unreflectingly live. This concept coincides in part with the Freudian concept of the 'superego,' but differs from it in so far as for Jung it includes not only the 'introjected' dos and don'ts of the environment, operating from within the psyche, but also those which pour in uninterruptedly from outside to influence the individual in his commissions and omissions, his feeling and thinking.[3]

The collective conscious is something with which we do not normally identify as individuals. In fact, the existence of a collective conscious in our psyches indicates that, as individuals, we must keep within certain norms to be able to function within a settled order of society. From these norms and values, and from our manner of functioning, we have within us an abstract picture guiding our behavior — a picture that is presented by the 6th house.

In order to function within a settled society, we must be able to view ourselves in an "objective" light. Objectivity, a sense of proportion, and a capacity for engaging in and coping with self-criticism are all contained in the 6th house. Using these mechanisms, we can produce other, more self-orientated contents out of our psyche (based on the rest of the natal chart), in such a way as to function to the best of our ability within our social framework. The 6th house does not refer to particular standards and values; these differ in every nation, culture and era. It does, however, tell us how we shall function in our own milieu. Being a cadent house, everything it indicates can be put to use. Of course, falling in line (where possible) with prevailing standards involves the sacrifice of a little bit of individuality somewhere along the line.

---

[3]Jolande Jacobi, *The Psychology of C. G. Jung* (London: Routledge & Kegan Paul, 1942) pp. 29–30.

In Western society, our functioning within the social framework is assessed mainly by our performance of our daily work. The 6th house supplies information about our attitudes about work and working conditions. Differences between norms that we are expected to keep and our abstract picture of them (guiding our behavior from within) can lead to reprimands from employers and even dismissal when these differences are unacceptable to society. Positive differences, however, could mean a brilliant career, if the rest of the horoscope is in support. The 6th house reflects our personal status as a subordinate as well as our attitude about holding an inferior position, and also the way we regard our own subordinates and the demands we make of them.

In the 6th house we encounter some very disparate factors, all of which have one thing in common: the contribution of our ego toward making flexible functioning possible within the social setting in which we live. These factors can come either from outside or from inside. From outside come the problems of environment, such as confrontations at our place of work, the degree to which we can fit in, and how well we accept criticism. Sound judgment (also a 6th house attribute) is necessary in order to make a realistic appraisal of factors that affect us to avoid false reactions. Therefore we find our power of discrimination, our power to analyze, to criticize and so on, all represented by the 6th house.

But there are mechanisms that operate from within, too (introjection).[4] These can range from self-criticism to self-

---

[4]Introjection was a term first introduced by Avenarius, and later defined by Ferenczi as the opposite of projection; namely an indrawing of the object into the subjective sphere of interest, while projection is an expulsion of subjective contents into the object. According to Jungian psychology, introjection is a process of assimilation, while projection is a process of dissimilation. Introjection is an assimilation of object to subject; projection a dissimilation of object from subject through the expulsion of a subjective content into the object. See. C. G. Jung's *Dictionary of Analytical Psychology*, published by Ark Paperbacks, a division of Routlege & Kegan Paul, London, 1987. *Tr.*

analysis, but only to the extent that our capacity for criticism, self-criticism, analysis and reflection is reduced, is there an increased chance that unconscious mechanisms will come into play. Our body is a significant instrument in this, and we can become ill or exhausted when the conscious mind refuses to consider some change that is important to the total psyche as we discussed in our projection example in Chapter Two. The inner self "pulls us up short" in order that an adjustment can be made. Thus illness and health are 6th house matters. What is more, the objectivity that is characteristic of the 6th house enables us to take a dispassionate look at our body in both sickness and in health. "A sound mind in a sound body"[5] greatly contributes to flexible, though certainly not impersonal, functioning in the group to which we belong.

THE 7th HOUSE

Libra is the sign that is analogous to the 7th house. And so we find in the 7th house whatever relates to our cooperative links with partners and companions. Since Libra is the sign most directly concerned with the life-partner, it is natural to expect that the 7th house will provide information about the partner and about the course of married life or cohabitation.

However, we find not only the life-partner in the 7th house, but also professional colleagues and, indeed, anyone to whom we are closely tied by some contract or agreement. Public opponents and open enemies are also indicated by this house, as are quarrels, lawsuits, etc., that might arise on their account.

---

[5] *Mens sana in corpore sana.* Juvenal. *Tr.*

The 7th house, as the house of contacts, shows our attitude toward the general public (which, according to Kuhr, is our collective partner); also the reaction of the public to us. This house literally creates in us the need to express ourselves with others. Libra is an esthetic sign and so, by analogy, we find in the 7th house certain things which combine esthetic feelings and beauty with public contact of some kind — art exhibitions are a case in point, as is house decoration or diplomacy. A willingness to restore harmony, even if we have to reach some compromise to do so, is typical of the 7th house.

Marriage, living with someone, or forming a working partnership, are always preceded by a regular series of events. The decision-forming belongs to other parts of the horoscope, but the result lies in the 7th house. Counting round the chart from the Ascendant, this is the first house where we are confronted with the "other" as a separate individual different from ourselves. The house indicates the way in which we prepare ourselves for confrontations. This implies that internally we have an abstract picture of how another person will manifest as an individual, and that we base our attitude or approach to him or her on this picture. Our pattern of expectations is reflected via the projection mechanism in our partnership(s) and engagements; which the 7th house registers in terms of such external forms as marriage and other alliances.

Now it is probably more difficult with this house than with any other to determine the level on which it will operate. Therefore we must never say, without more ado, that Neptune in the 7th house signifies a partner who is an habitual drunkard. A spiritual link with the partner, with no hint of the toxic qualities of Neptune, is equally possible.

In the 7th house, we go to meet the other person fully aware of individual differences. Despite our differences, we seek ways of enjoying their company or of working with them. The need to do so inclines us to promote harmony and to make concessions, so that the confrontation can be as flexible as possible. Also this shaping of the social scene is apparent in efforts to beautify our surroundings and to make them more pleasant.

The search for a way in which two different individuals may associate presupposes some motive for cooperation. A commitment, any form of concerted action, partnership, or enmity, always implies a common interest. This is essential to the functioning of the house. A wide variety of interests can enter into marriage. Both partners are interested in staying together, probably they want to start a family, and so they have decided to wed.

The origin of the community of interests lies in other houses. When two people marry or live together, these other houses can be, among others, the 8th (sexual attraction) and the 5th (liking or approval). And yet these very houses — the 5th representing recognition and authority, and the 8th as the craving for power and a susceptibility to neurosis — can also sow the seeds of conflict and enmity. We have, as it were, concerted action in which frustrations occur as a result of over-positive projections by one party which are not accepted by the other, or as a result of the projection of purely negative expectations. There is openness and frankness in the 7th house whatever else we may say about it: we do *see* the other person; but we can not count on joint efforts, partnerships, and other alliances always being as harmonious as they should be.

If there are many planets in the 7th house, there is strong involvement with other individuals. For example, you may find it hard to make your own decisions and may leave a great deal to your partner. On the other hand, this may mean a certain degree of dominance in the sense that too much is expected of the partner; in which case, the so-called benefic planets can be just as pernicious as the malefics.

Jupiter in the 7th house ought, if the books of stock interpretations are to be believed, to signify an ideal marriage; yet it does not always do so. In itself, Jupiter in the 7th is continually looking for good in another person, and often finds it because the attitude is positive. Nevertheless, for all sorts of reasons, the expectations can be pitched so high that the partner is constantly kept on his or her toes, and this can lead to tension.

In general, planets in the 7th mainly tell us what we expect as our right, what our attitudes are like as far as partnerships are concerned, and the consequences of this attitude. The influences are subtle and do not lend themselves to making arbitrary decisions such as whether or not it would be advisable to marry. Fear about Saturn, Uranus, Neptune or Pluto being in the 7th is quite baseless; these planets are counterparts of certain patterns of expectation which we will endeavor to express in our own way (although this may easily bring some grief or disappointment).

Uranus in the 7th, for example, is merely an indication that you will not allow yourself to be suffocated by a relationship, but will continue to foster your own development. If you find someone who accepts this, Uranus need not mean divorce! But if we become apprehensive about relationship possibilities because of all kinds of negative statements, then our attitudes and fears may project a divorce because we do not believe it possible to have a good relationship, or we don't know how to seek a relationship that will be good for us.

THE 8th HOUSE

The 8th house is analogous to Scorpio. Therefore whatever is concealed, mysterious, occult, or sexual is placed out in this house. It is the house of death, destruction, doom, regeneration, conflict, and winning through. Everything that lies hidden within us comes within its scope; therefore the 8th house is often indicative of complexes and repressions.

The fighting spirit of the 8th sign is reflect in the inner strife and the power struggles of the 8th house. But the investigative side of Scorpio, its endless digging for facts while chewing the cud of experience, leads us to conjecture that this house will determine how far we are capable of penetrating to the core of things while searching the hidden side of our inner nature and of the outer world. In addition, the 8th house is traditionally the house of our partner's money, of society (taxation), the house of big financial institutions (banks and insurance companies), and also of legacies or money received following the death of another. It is the "we have" in contrast to the "I have" of the 2nd house.

The 8th house is commonly a difficult house to understand. We could call it simply the house of death, but that would not get us very far. Its significance is much more comprehensive than that. The 8th house (like all the water houses: 4, 8, 12) symbolizes the unconscious. It comprises what we term our personal unconscious: things we forget, things we have repressed because we no longer desire to know them, and also our hidden potentials and gifts. The 8th house is our underground cellar, haunted by scary beings that fill us with dread, but it is also where the treasure and inheritance of the past lies waiting for us until we pluck up the courage to go there and look for it.

All kinds of instinctive reactions are found in this house, and it lends itself very readily to projection. It is linked with all the other houses of the chart in one way or another. Repressed experiences in life are stored in the 8th house. The latter, in its turn, can become so overloaded with all our problems and repressions that it ceases to function properly. Actually, the life-urge is expressed by the entire horoscope, but as we continue to repress, more weight is tipped into the personal unconscious, and more psychic energy is absorbed in the task of keeping repressed items from re-entering consciousness; the result being that the amount of psychic energy available to the conscious mind is reduced.

And so the life-urge (and animal spirit) can be blocked and its expression can be impeded. Death, as the counterpart of life, can take a form here which literally or metaphorically annihilates life. Before that advanced state can happen, the process has to be way out of control. Generally we see repressed factors from the personal unconscious projected onto the environment, so that what we find in our fellow men and women is what is in ourselves. Our attitude to others, and the reactions we elicit from them, confront us with ourselves in such a way that the conditions are created for gradually recognizing and solving our problems.

Usually, however, this beneficial resolution does not occur until some crisis (mild or severe) takes place, at which point some piece of repressed personality is assimilated and new life is breathed into the personality as a whole. The process is by and large a painful one, because the projection of repressed contents of the psyche on others often places them in an excessively unfavorable light. The strength of a projected repression exaggerates fancied negativity to such an extent that all kinds of evil are attributed to these people who carry the projection, and the recognition that the evil is really in us and not in "them" is very hard to swallow. The unconscious inevitably projects itself on the environment and, in practice, is encountered in the Shadow (someone of our own sex regarded as a scapegoat), or in unbridled infatuation (with someone of the opposite sex).

The deeply buried unconscious pattern of expectation we have of the other side of ourselves is projected on the object of our affections. Without knowing it, we recognize and encounter in the other an unconscious fragment of ourselves, named by Carl Jung the Anima (for the man) and the Animus (for the woman).

But because of this projection onto another person we are able to wrestle with ourselves through that person and eventually gain an opportunity to descend little by little into the dark and forbidding cellar of the unconscious. The manner in which we project and what we project, on the one hand, and our complexes, neuroses, and hidden gifts and talents, on the other, are connected with one another. When the individual (often through some crisis as mentioned earlier) no longer needs to confine his or her energy to complexes and neuroses, he or she can employ it creatively in previously unimagined profundities, insights and achievements. The newly released energy can be used in all sorts of ways, including a sexual surrender to the partner, where the ego undergoes an intense experience completely different from that indicated by the 7th house.

In the 8th house we see a struggle between the love of life and the death wish. When these two are held in balance, we have an individual who has the courage to go his or her own way without looking for death either literally or figuratively. But if the two urges, which are indissolubly bound together in the interplay of life and death, are not held in balance, the consequences for the rest of the horoscope can be far-reaching even without the intervention of astrological aspects and such like. For instance, we see someone who hides from himself so much that he lives a superficial life with no depth and no background, concerned solely with keeping himself alive, although he may subtly undermine this attitude with his projections. Or we see someone who gradually paralyzes himself and his activities because his repressions absorb more and more energy. A crisis could produce a possible solution in both cases.

A longing for death, and a fear of death, do occasionally perform a motivating function, so we must not treat them as entirely objectionable. How often do we not hear of the person who needs to do something significant in life, something heroic either great or small, for the sake of knowing that he or she has done a deed by which the individuality can transcend time?

Ernest Becker calls the fear of death one of the most impelling forces behind human activities. It produces the need to be heroic; hence the old astrological dictum that someone with a strong 8th house likes to take risks and flirt with death, for by doing so he or she can achieve more by living life to the full than the person who is timid. Therefore, by promoting self-assertion and a love of action (symbolized by the heroic), the fear of death or a longing for death can enhance life rather than threaten it. The challenge to be death-defying is accepted by many people in dangerous professions. In typical 8th house style, they make a living out of their fascination with death. Love of life and flirting with death go hand in hand literally as well as metaphorically. And victory over symbolic death can release enormous creative energies. This can explain the creative power and creative urge of the 8th house.

Finally, the secrecy of the 8th house can involve dormant paranormal gifts, hidden psychological insights, mediumistic tendencies (in combination with the 12th house) and magic. All this can come to the surface as complexes are resolved. Because they delve into such matters, psychologists and psychiatrists are symbolized by the 8th house, along with wizards, occultists, parapsychologists and detectives, not to mention nuclear physicists — whose attempts to penetrate to the core of matter lead them into the borderland of the occult and the invisible.[6]

THE 9th HOUSE

The 9th house is analogous to Sagittarius, a sign characterized by wanderlust or a love of travel. Hence the 9th house has always been taken to indicate the part played by foreign lands in your life. Sagittarians are inquisitive and keen on self-improvement, so it is not surprising that a penchant for fitting facts into some greater whole, or a general aptitude for study, including higher education, are 9th house features. The propa-

---

[6]Indeed, the famous physicist and astronomer Sir Arthur Eddington freely admitted this when he said: "But it is reasonable to inquire whether in the mystical illusions of man there is not a reflection of an underlying reality. (*The Nature of the Physical World*, Cambridge University Press, 1928, p. 319).

gation of gathered knowledge and discovered truths is also symbolized by this house.

Pursuing the analogy with Sagittarius, we find in the 9th house our ideals, philosophical convictions, our sense of justice, metaphysical, or religious outlook, plus all kinds of deep speculation. Journeying and learning, experiencing the distant, the strange, and the new, and incorporating these concepts into our personal scheme of things are part and parcel of the area of life represented by the 9th house.

Travel and study must have incentives, of course, and the desire to undertake either comes not so much from sheer willpower and perseverance or from the wish to climb to the top of the social ladder, as from the 9th house need to continually expand our horizons. Entering a wider relationship presupposes a great deal of comprehensive knowledge, and therefore the idea of expansion and widening in all respects lies at the basis of the 9th house. Journeys to foreign lands can certainly be implied by the 9th house; foreign climes are always a literal expansion of our horizon. But it is by no means everyone with a strong 9th house who goes abroad. The 9th house also represents the need to expand inner horizons, and may well indicate such activities as study, university education, research into metaphysics, philosophy, and so on. Travel, deep thought and religious outlook, however unalike they may appear on the surface, are all aspects of an expansion of personal horizons—either physically, mentally, or spiritually. The 9th house is involved with becoming conscious, that is to say, with placing facts and phenomena in a larger setting and then synthesizing them. It contains the abstract picture (or partly conscious, partly unconscious pattern of expectation) that guides the way in which we carry out this synthesis after we have decided what information is meaningful, necessary and useful.

The results of our travels, studies, and our efforts to make sense of these lie in this house; however, since it is a cadent house, we feel a need to make our results serviceable to the outside world. But when communicating our findings to others, we have to be careful not to make a nuisance of ourselves by pressing our opinions too forcefully on others. Opinions are formed on the basis of what we have discovered or learned. The 9th house symbolizes how we will form these opinions, and also how good we are at sticking to them or propagating them. That is why making up your mind and, even more so, speaking it freely are naturally referred to this Sagittarian house.

The development and propagation of synthetic truths are found in numerous shapes and forms in everyday life, including the activities of those who proclaim their own particular verities with relentless fervor. For example: someone with Mars in the 9th may feel called (the remainder of the horoscope permitting) to express his views in an emphatic and fiery way. By nature, Mars allows very little room for others and, in the 9th, can indicate proselytizing zeal, though with the best intentions. If repulsed, the person is still combative enough to press the point a little harder. By fighting for what he believes in he can sometimes provoke strong resistance from those around him, and other people may even take steps to keep him quiet. The world reacts not to the message but to the style in which it is presented.

We can expect the 9th house to supply us with information concerning our need for expanding our mental, physical and spiritual horizon, the way in which we shall do it, and the kind of reaction we can expect from our fellow men and women.

THE 10th HOUSE

The 10th house is analogous to Capricorn, and therefore supplies us with information about career, social position, and what we actually do for a living (although the latter also depends on other houses such as the 6th and 12th). Our reputation, the esteem in which we are held, and the recognition accorded us for our services are all indicated by this house;

which shows the extent to which we are our own boss and how we react to those in authority, also how much authority we ourselves possess. The 10th house indicates the impression we make on others and so can give us some idea of the mask we wear for the benefit of those with whom we come in contact, and whether this mask has the set expression of stiff cardboard or the easy mobility of supple rubber.

This house symbolizes our need for support, reassurance, and indicates what we expect by way of tangible results in the concrete "real" world. Therefore it has a lot to do with public life, and with entering society — in contrast to stepping out on an individual basis as in the 1st house, or venturing into the arms of a partner as in the 7th. We look to it for intimations of the opportunities we shall be given to rise in the social scale — which is as much as to say for intimations of how favorably the world will respond to the manner in which we present ourselves to it.

Like Capricorn, the 10th house is heavily self-involved: it emphasizes our personal position, but also our desire to know exactly where we stand, the limits of our authority, and the nature of our responsibilities. If the 10th house reveals how the outside world reacts to us, it must also reveal the reason for this: namely, how we present ourselves to the world. And if the 10th house is directly linked to our social status, we must have done something to earn our position. In short, we first have to work at our formal education and also at gaining the sort of self-knowledge that shows us our possibilities and limitations, and then we can begin to know the occupation for which we are really suited.

On the basis of this self-knowledge, we start to identify ourselves with certain things long before there is any talk of our participating in the social order. In other words, as consciousness unfolds, we form a certain picture of ourselves, and that picture is the basis of the 10th house. The 10th house shows the manner in which we see ourselves and the social position this leads us to accept (thus the sort of fight we are prepared to put up for the sake of our job or our place in society, the position of authority we can occupy, etc.). It indicates the picture we present to the outside world — like the flag flying from a castle keep when "the door is made fast and the bridge drawn up."

On first approaching our castle, the world is greeted by the flag and responds to that. The flag does not necessarily represent much that is inside the castle, nor do planets in the 10th house necessarily agree with the rest of the horoscope. The picture we paint of ourselves will usually more or less differ from our true image and, during the course of our lives, we shall no doubt keep touching it up as we see through our own disguise and come to know ourselves better.

The self-image leads us to play a specific role, and this role, or mask, is our Persona. Although we are usually well aware that we are wearing this mask, the Persona represents unconscious as well as conscious expectations. But expectations never remain the same: our attitude to the environment evokes reactions from the outside world, and these in turn help to change our self-image and decide our place in society.

From the point of view of the 10th house, an individual's self-image is the result of the interaction between self and the environment, especially in regard to social milieu. As Carl Jung said: "The Persona is a compromise between the individual and society over what happens to him." Hence it is a compromise between what society demands and the inner structural constitution of the individual.

A properly functioning Persona keeps in touch with three factors: the ego-ideal of the individual (house 10), society's notion of the ideal person (house 6), and the mental and physical disposition which governs the interaction between the ego's development potential and the social ideal (house 2). A harmonious relationship between these factors produces a harmonious relationship with the outside world. But if, for example, the individual concentrates on being the sort of man or woman admired by society, he or she runs the risk of becoming a "communal clone." If social norms are ignored, the Persona may become that of the individualist, the rebel, or the eccentric.

Thus, in the 10th house, the ego-image acts outward from within while itself being influenced by other factors from without. The Persona responds to our adaptation to the outside world and to society in general. Planets in the 10th supply us with this information. They show how flexibly we can adapt. Conflicts involving this house (and thus the MC) directly affect our role in the community, but tell us nothing about the good or bad sides of our character. Neither does the house give us any information about what conditions will be imposed by society; all it shows is the difficulty experienced in conforming to social standards and requirements in the face of circumstances.

The mask that forms over us in early youth originates in the parental home, which is why parental influence can be judged from the 10th house. The 4th/10th axis provides information about the two parents, but in practice it has been found very difficult to assign a given house to a given parent. This is logical enough since, during the most impressionable years the child sees its parents as a unit and only later differentiates between father and mother.[7]

Finally, the 10th house generally represents the remuneration and reward for our work within the framework of social codes and conventions (cf. Capricorn). But conventions are usually fixed and cut-and-dried, if not completely fossilized. Planets in the 10th house, therefore, often have something stiff and inflexible about the way they express themselves even

---

[7]The expansive tenth house is sometimes assigned to the father and the domestic fourth to the mother. But when the father is being physically and emotionally controlled by the mother, the roles can be reversed. The matter is by no means clear-cut. *Tr.*

when one of them is the Moon. Form and fixed outline take priority in the 10th house.

THE 11th HOUSE

The 11th house is analogous to Aquarius. Therefore we find social contacts and interactions in this house. It is the house of friends and friendships, of parties and partisans, of ideologies and ideologists, community work and democratization. It supplies information about the way in which, and the extent to which, the individual can form and keep friendships, can discuss ideas and opinions, or can work in a group of peers. It represents cooperation based on spiritual affinity and shows the degree of fitness for social life.

Thus the 11th house mainly shows how well we relate to others in personal contacts. (The 10th house shows a relationship with others arising out of the interaction of our self-image with social processes.) Also the 11th house can often say something about the type of friends we attract in consequence of our social position. Such friends can be foreigners as well as folk belonging to our own country because, like Aquarius, the 11th house tends to break through boundaries; in other words: in the 11th house all people are equal, and contacts are made on that basis.

To form friendships it is not enough to meet potential friends: certain expectations and a certain attitude are necessary. The significance of the 11th house can best be explained by comparing it with other houses. In the 7th we discussed association on the grounds of common interests and the sinking of individual differences. In the 11th house, however, these individual differences are the essential point of departure in a search for something that can be shared — something universally human.

The matter becomes even clearer if we contrast the 11th house with the 5th, the house of personal self-expression. The

11th house contains the self-expression of others, and measures our willingness to tolerate their self-expression as equally valid with our own (even when we have to adapt our behavior to suit them). And so, underlying all manifestations of the 11th house are abstract expectations which, in spite of individual differences, give a feeling of essential kinship, community spirit and solidarity.

Our behavior due to these conscious and unconscious expectations evokes reactions in the outside world, and so in the 11th house we also find our response to these impulses from those around us. To be more explicit, we find the measure of our ability to form and maintain friendships, also the type of friends we are likely to attract owing to our unconscious expectations, because this is always determined by the kind of self-expression we seek in others. A self-assured individual will attract friends who are completely different from those drawn to someone with a weak identity who is constantly looking for support from his or her circle of friends. The 11th house shows what our friends mean to us, and the wishes and longings we expect them to fulfill.

Aquarians display personal insecurity because — owing to their assumption that we are all fundamentally the same despite our individual differences — they are plagued by the idea that others possess the same rights as themselves. Added to their insecurity, they feel a need to discover in what this presumed equality or similarity really resides. In much the same way, the 11th house gives us a need to rid ourselves of personal insecurity by plunging into the community spirit. We turn for safety and support to people (not necessarily close friends) who meet our 11th house expectations and speak our language; in other words, we turn to those of a similar disposition who share our interests in clubs and associations (where the 5th house can be given full rein in a wider context). By discussing and doing things in company, we can adopt a certain identity as individuals within the greater whole. Hence our capacity to operate within a group, the degree and manner of our participation in social or fraternity activities, and the extent to which we share community ideals and aspirations, are all to be found in the 11th house.

This is a house where the limitations of the ego are transcended and we realize the extent to which others can play a part in our lives as real personalities.

Like the 10th house, which it follows, the 11th supplies information about our relationships with the outside world, but now on the basis of personality. These relationships can be many and varied: for example, the contact of the politician with his grass-root helpers, the rapport between the actor and his audience, and so on. The 11th house shows the type of contact and how well we succeed in making it.

Our circle of friends, the voters, the public, all perform a very special function: by their reactions they hold up a mirror for us to see our true image. Their reactions reveal a number of things of which we would otherwise remain unaware; which is why the (fixed!) 11th house plays a bigger part in our development than we generally suppose. It is no superficial communicative house, but a house that can confront us directly with ourselves and by so doing can set all sorts of things in motion in the rest of the horoscope.

THE 12th HOUSE

The 12th house is analogous to Pisces, and so is always regarded as hard to comprehend. In it we find our secret enemies, also prisons, hospitals and asylums, in short all kinds of institutions where our own individuality has no chance to express itself, and where collectivity, anonymity, and what is clandestine rule. It is a house which is not always well understood simply because it is allied to the hidden and occult.

It is the house of pain and limitations, the place of withdrawal from external life. In a positive sense, it is the house of self-sacrifice and community service — for instance, nursing the sick, or feeding and housing the destitute. Then again, it may reveal a desire to leave the world and enter a monastery. The 12th is the house of repentance, of the spiritual and the esoteric. Because contact with worldly things is renounced in this house, it is known as the house of the mystic and of the paranormal, and in particular of clairvoyance and other supernatural senses.

Because of its "fluid" nature, any planets posited in the 12th have few opportunities of making a clear impression on the world, and that is why this house is associated with grief and subversion. It can mean either the disintegration or the transcendence of personality; transcendence through following the spiritual, the mystical, the religious, or the occult path, and disintegration through poisoning, drug addiction, intoxication or lunacy.

In a world such as we know in the West, where great emphasis is laid on the value of the conscious mind, hard work, and worldly success, the 12th house poses quite a problem. Usually its role in our lives is not understood and therefore it is not given its true value astrologically. The 12th house represents a need for privacy and detachment, but certainly does not imply any desire to do away with oneself or to undermine one's life as an individual. Its operations are very versatile and full of meaning in themselves, although in certain cases, our consciousness can experience this as undermining.

The 12th house is a house of the collective unconscious, which is a psychological term for the deepest layer of the human psyche. In the collective unconscious lie the archetypes and as much of the deposit of human experience as can be brought to life. This archetypal unconscious is the womb from which the individual conscious is born; it is the breast at which the individual conscious is nourished. First and foremost, the 12th house shows our links with the collective unconscious. However, these links are very difficult for the conscious mind to visualize and can sometimes inspire fear; the conscious mind has a controlling function, but since it is only one part of the psyche, it has less control over our lives than it would like us to think. When it is opposed by the rectifying influence of the unconscious, the latter can certainly seem threatening and undermining. The psyche is always striving for balance, and an action which strikes the conscious mind as harmful may represent an improvement for the psyche as a whole.

Whereas repressions and complexes in the 8th house are personal, repressive factors in the 12th tend to be universal, and therefore have more trouble getting through to the conscious mind. However, the 12th house does manage to warn and advise us in dreams and premonitions. Through this house (and thus through the part of the psyche it represents), we make continual contact with what is beyond time and space, and simultaneously with everything and everybody. But, the unconscious being what it is, its instructions and warnings must reach us indirectly through pictures planted in the conscious.

The 12th house can confront us in a less pleasant manner too, by tempting us to fly from reality; one of its more sinister aspects is the present day escapism in our youth which leads them to experiment with drugs and drink, so that the formation (and bringing to maturity) of personal identity is undermined at an early stage.

The desire for "another world" is not something strange. Social pressures we are unable to influence individually give us the feeling of not functioning as we should. Furthermore, the need for a sense of unity with the whole human race (common to both the 12th house and Pisces) forces itself on our attention in proportion to the difficulty experienced in attaining it. For this reason, some people idealistically set out to right wrongs (through social work and the like) while others lose their self-control during periods of frustration and immerse themselves in various addictions. Addictions weaken the personality, yet their goal is reached even so: a feeling of unity unhampered by petty restrictions. But by taking this road, we fall into the hands of an invisible enemy more powerful than ourselves: the fluidity that seemed so innocent at the beginning sets to work insidiously and is virtually unstoppable. Secret enemies in the form both of other humans and of inimical factors inside ourselves are therefore to be found in the 12th house.

The idea of unity is very strong in this house. We meet it in various areas: unity within oneself produced by the harmonious association of conscious and unconscious, the unity of all humankind regardless of color, social class, or any other criterion, the unity between a man and a woman, the unity of the cosmos expressed by religion, metaphysics,[8] meditation and so on. Now, a belief in some underlying unity entails acceptance of the fact that we are not the be-all and end-all, but possess only a relative importance and, in certain respects, even no importance at all. Such a realization, as already pointed out, can be either constructive (when it leads to social work, relief work, meditation, the practice of yoga and the like), or destructive (when it drives a person to drink, drugs and other addictions). Whatever the case, the experience of unity reveals the relative nature of the consciousness experiencing it. The link with the collective unconscious is a link with what is universal, especially with what is universally human. At the same time, the 12th house shows what the individual expects of the universally human, however vague and hard to grasp this concept may be.

The link with the collective provided by this house plays, in a very concrete manner, a leading role in infancy and in the mythical phase of early childhood. From birth until the time

---

[8]We have to be careful here, because the term *metaphysics* means different things to different people. To the ancient Greeks, metaphysics was the study of "original causes" carried out by Aristotle in the sequel to his book on physics; this was purely philosophical speculation. Some modern teachers of the occult arts use the word in the sense of creative visualization, etc., with what justification it is difficult to say. In the present instance, it seems to mean any non-religious belief in a supernatural order of things. *Tr.*

when as a child we gradually experience ourselves as a separate unit within our environment, the unconscious has a decisive say. We make contact with our surroundings through the unconscious, especially through the unconscious mind of our mother. In the beginning we experience our entire environment, including our father, through her.

Planets in the 12th symbolize certain experiences of the first few years of life. But, since we were then so strongly bound up in the unconscious mind and emotional feelings of our mothers and of others around us, we shall find represented in the 12th house experiences which do not belong to us at all. Rather, they have to do with personal and mutual problems or difficulties our parents had around the time of our birth or in our earliest year(s), at a time a child has still no adequate assimilation mechanism and its personal unconscious (8th house) either has not yet been formed or else is in a very embryonic state. Many planets in the 12th house could represent childhood experiences that still bother us because we could not assimilate them early on. Usually they consist of tensions and difficulties in the parental home. Parents' problems easily leave their mark on children.

And so the 12th house informs us about how we reacted to our parents at an unconscious level when we were young. Youthful experiences reveal themselves in various ways. Generally speaking, we can say that planets in the 12th have to express themselves in a collective setting and that, as individuals, we find it very hard to recognize anything specifically personal to ourselves in them or to identify with them. The sheer elusiveness of planetary factors in this position, combined with the fact that they represent our earliest experiences, can lead to irrational fears and phobias; so that the child, and later the adult, can see phantoms where none exists, not knowing that the things which haunt them are coming from themselves. It is extremely probable that the development of a personal identity is hampered by such early experiences; which may, however, be brought to light under hypnosis.

Note that a whole process precedes any external manifestations. The 12th house also reveals something about factors we could not handle in our youth because we had no example to follow. For instance: with the Sun in the 12th, it often seems to happen that when the child was very young, the father was away a great deal, or was dead, or unable to give proper support to the family due to illness, alcoholism, etc.

Yet, in contacts with collective or universal humanity, the 12th house also has its good side. Hardships encountered in developing one's own personality create a need and often the capacity to empathize with others, and to remain open to covert influences in the environment. The early detection of hidden undercurrents which have not yet entered concrete reality can border on clairvoyance. Often there is a natural, though unconscious, decision to go with the stream which is one of the more positive and salutary results of the 12th house. The sensing of undercurrents can even loosen the individual's hold on contemporary life, so that he or she is ahead of time in the way he or she feels and acts, having tuned into some trend in the making which has not yet been perceived by society as a whole.

As we have said, however, planets in the 12th house usually have problems in manifesting in a definite form and can even prove downright difficult. Their mode of action is often very silent and indirect, which is why the 12th house has a somewhat exaggerated reputation for being sinister.

Another interesting feature of the 12th house is that it tells us what we are like when we are on our own; also what we keep to ourselves, what things offend us easily because we are hypersensitive to them, and what things we keep attracting from the outside world in order to confront ourselves with them.

Thus the 12th house is a gigantic reservoir of unconscious factors. As we learn to explore this little by little, we come to realize our own relativity and the fullness and depth of life itself. From this point of view, the 12th house is the womb of the horoscope. The ego feels constrained by it and spasmodically struggles to be free; in the end, however, it has to acquiesce in combined action — conscious with unconscious — so that total integration of the personality can be brought to birth . . .

CHAPTER THREE

HOUSE INTERRELATIONSHIPS

1. INTRODUCTION

We have seen that each house has its own symbolism and can be clearly distinguished from the other houses. Nevertheless, this does not mean that they have nothing to do with one another; they are in fact closely connected. The houses represent parts of our psyche that correspond to areas of life in the outside world. The psyche is not a rope of sand, nor are the houses. In studying them we quickly see that they possess a natural coherence, quite apart from the effects of aspects and other transient astrological relations.

Inter-house relationships occur in various ways, which we can subdivide as follows:

1. contiguity with the houses which precede and follow;

2. opposition along an axis;

3. analogy with the elements;

4. analogy with the crosses;

5. dispositorships;

6. derivative meanings (e.g., the 8th house can be seen in 2nd

house position to the 7th house, and therefore represents the financial means of the partner or companion, etc.).

The question of dispositorships and derivative meanings will be left for another book, since there is no space to do them justice in this one. The first four relationships are particularly important at this stage of interpretation, however, and so will be studied now in broad outline.

First of all, then, each house is connected with the one that precedes it because it is a reaction to the latter, and is connected with the following house because it prepares the way for it. Let us look at the astrological implications of this.

The 1st house is a reaction to the 12th. Whereas in the 12th house everything is impersonal and is reduced to its essence, in the 1st this essence is used as a starting point for discovering ourselves in the world. In the 1st house we are concerned simply and solely with manifesting ourselves. The 2nd house comes in as a reaction and to some extent as a continuation: without manifestation the 2nd house has nothing for which to provide security. Our 2nd house urge to provide security is a reaction to the lack of restraint exhibited by the 1st house, and makes possible the development of the 3rd: once we have established a fairly secure base, we can start making contact with the outside world. Our 3rd house contact in the world provides the opportunity for 4th house emotional reactions to what we find there. And thus we gradually become aware of our personal identity, as revealed in the 5th. The 6th house is a reaction to the 5th in the form of critical analysis of self and others. We experience our own relativity, and so are prepared for one-to-one relationships. Relationships with others are, of course, represented by the 7th house, which displays an openness that is a reaction to the reserved nature of the 6th.

The 7th house lays a foundation for the 8th because, although the outward aspects of association with the partner lie in the 7th, the inner assimilation and experiencing of that association are found in the 8th — the house in which we assess our worth and delve deep in order to understand ourselves, our partners and the meaning of life. Thus the 8th is not simply a continuation of the 7th, but a reaction to it: it is very private. The 8th prepares the way for the 9th, in which we bring into the open what we have found, make a synthesis of our knowledge and experience and endeavor to become more aware. However, we should not be able to do any of these things without our experiences in the 8th house. And, as our vision of life expands, larger groups of people become involved with us. Accordingly, in the 10th house we find structure, not only the structure of social units but the further moulding of awareness. Therefore, in the 10th we acquire a clearly circumscribed identity as opposed to the uninhibitedness of the 9th house. The 11th house, the house of friendship and group membership, reintroduces the need for relationships, this time based on recognition of the rights of others to an identity of their own which is often very different from ours. Being both a continuation of and a reaction to the 10th, it places much more emphasis on contacts. The 12th house resumes the theme of relationship and brings everything back to an impersonal core or essence. But contacts on a mental level are lacking here. In contrast to the 11th house, there is a very guarded emotional response, which is impersonally personal. And so the wheel turns full circle, with the 12th house preparing the way for the 1st house task of discovering the essential, unadorned self; a task the latter performs in an outward-looking and outgoing manner, in reaction to the reclusiveness of the 12th house.

It is clear then, that all the houses need one another either directly or indirectly and are, indeed, closely linked even without the benefit of astrological aspects. Chart reading is at times rendered rather difficult by this fact, since someone with a strong 8th house, for example, will not be influenced by planets in the 9th in the same way as someone with a weak 8th house. On occasion the difference is trifling, but it can also be quite marked. This is one reason why we should be wary of books offering cut-and-dried interpretations: these can never explain complex house interrelationships.

2. HOUSE POLARITIES

There are other connections involving the houses for houses in opposition influence one another, too. Like opposite signs, they share certain characteristics which they exhibit in contrasting ways. Their differences are not irreconcilable, however, since they supplement one another to form a fundamental duality.[9] Let us see how this all works out.

---

[9]The study of opposites intrigued the ancients and has occupied the minds of philosophers and logicians ever since. Aristotle, for example, writes in his *Organon*: "One thing then is said to be opposed to another in four ways, either as relative, or as contrary, or as privation and habit, or as affirmation and negation. Thus speaking summarily, each thing of this kind is opposed, relatively, as 'the double' to 'the half,' contrarily, as 'evil' to 'good,' privatively and habitually, as 'blindness' and 'sight,' affirmatively and negatively, as 'he sits,' 'he does not sit.' " (From Chapter 10, "The Categories," trans. O. F. Owen, Bohn's Classical Library, 1853). Now, for Aristotle, a thing could not be double and half, or evil and good, at one and the same time, nor could a person be simultaneously both blind and sighted, sitting and not sitting. In modern psychology, however, the conscious and the unconscious, thought opposites, can coexist. Leaving aside the Eastern doctrine of "I am That" (*So ham*), "the self and the other are One" or, in its extreme form, "the self and the other are None" (i.e., only pure being exists), it is easy to see that just as the world of unconscious is always there and the conscious emerges from it from time to time before sinking back into it again, so in the chain of humanity individual selves restore to the "other(s)" of a new generation the life passed on to them by the "other(s)" of an older generation. These two pairs of contrasts—the self and the other, and the conscious and the unconscious— are the root themes of the houses as explained by the author of the present book. As the reader will see from the following pages, the odd-numbered houses have to do with the "self" and the "other," while the even-numbered houses have to do with the conscious and the unconscious. *Tr.*

1st/7th AXIS

Our personal being versus the being of another. In the most obvious form of this contrast, the "other" is the partner, and the best course is to integrate one with another so that you can proceed as a unit. Planets in the 1st house will influence your behavior toward the partner. Not that such planets will have anything to do with what you expect of the other person or with how you respond to him or her; no, the matter is more subtle than that. These planets emphasize "you" and so modify the effect of planets in the 7th house. Conversely, planets in the 7th will affect the 1st: a cluster of planets in the 7th could center your interest on your partner, which would indirectly influence the way you present yourself to the outside world (a 1st house affair).

2nd/8th AXIS

Personal conscious versus personal unconscious. If there are many planets in the 2nd house, your need for material security is considerable, and you shall be motivated to obtain it; holding at bay anything that might seem to threaten it, in particular any repressed materials or any hidden talents that could disturb your motivation. Therefore a strong 2nd house can divert your attention from the 8th house and can produce an artificial sense of peace and safety. But, sooner or later, the 8th house will break through in certain experiences, and it will become possible to achieve true tranquility as the buried contents of the 8th house are integrated with the security provided by the 2nd. Of course, it is also possible to repress the contents of the 8th still further. On the other hand, planets in the 2nd house can make their presence felt even more strongly when the 8th is emphasized (e.g., when it has many planets posited in it). Given this advantage, the 8th house can make you discontented and insecure, and then factors (such as the Moon and the 2nd house) which have to do with security will become more prominent. Paradoxical as it might sound, a powerful 8th house can also lay emphasis on its opposite, the 2nd house.

3rd/9th AXIS

Being aware of others versus being aware of self. But also: the accumulation of information (3rd house) versus the arranging and synthesizing of information (9th house). If we become preoccupied with increasing self-awareness and widening horizons (9th house), the way in which we handle our brief contacts (3rd house) is bound to be affected. Irrespective of whether or not any planets are to be found in the 3rd house, we shall always be inclined to promote or try out our own personal vision at the first opportunity. But the 3rd house can be influenced in another way, too. The desire to expand one's horizons (9) frequently goes hand in hand with the desire for more knowledge in general (3), the 3rd house being activated by the 9th. Conversely, a strong 3rd house may mean that gaining experience, gathering facts, making contacts and holding conversations will take precedence over preparing a synthesis of what has been discovered; although it may also indicate that a synthesis will eventually be made. In this axis-working, opposite houses exert their influence turn and turn about. Planets in the 3rd can hinder planets in the 9th, but can also help them and *vice versa*. The psyche is always striving for balance.

4th/10th AXIS

The result and the expression of unconscious feelings versus the result and expression of conscious, identity-forming processes. With many planets in the 10th house, you may lay great stress on being open to opportunities, and on being a good allrounder (regardless of how far you manage to achieve these aims), and in doing so you may persistently ignore or neglect the 4th house (emotional processes, home life, and the experience of inner stability). In typical 10th house style, stability is sought in some social (or similar) position. The 4th house, however, can react by disturbing the mask function (4th and 10th together). You may lose enthusiasm or may feel defeated by your environment and the world, and the reactions of the world to this attitude may well throw you back on what you have been all along forgetting: your inner emotional basis. It would appear then that in its capacity as the resultant of unconscious processes in the 8th and 12th houses,[10] the 4th house can undermine the 10th, but can also support it and lay for it a solid foundation.

On the other hand, over-emphasis on the 4th house will lead to conflicts. Domesticity and security will be regarded as more important than social status, and because of the lack of a clear-cut attitude, the emotional activities of the 4th house may strike outsiders as rather chaotic and undisciplined. In this case, the mask function is mainly emotional, is ill-defined and gives an impression of emotional insecurity (of retiring into one's shell) or of play-acting (when one is over-excited). But, if the 10th house can introduce a little more structure, the 4th should develop properly. Conflicts between the 4th and the 10th can sometimes externalize themselves in a striving for social position at the same time as domestic harmony is being sought.

5th/11th AXIS

Your own self-expression versus the self-expression of others. The presence of many planets in the 6th house increases the need to live in accordance with your own insights and, in particular, to do what you think best as and when the fancy takes you. In this house you go your own road, and often try to

---

[10]See the author's earlier book, *Astro-Psychology*, Chapter 6, "The Structure of the Houses" (Wellingborough, England: The Aquarian Press, 1980).

arrange that matters will fall out as you desire. But the 11th house suffers accordingly, since that is the house in which your friendships can come into being with all their possibilities and problems. It indicates the extent to which you will allow folk to ripen in your friendship and what requirements you expect them to meet. A strong 5th house emphasizes *you*, and so deprives the 11th house of part of its development potential. Now, if you make too much of yourself, you shall soon see this reflected in the behavior of your friends: some will leave you and you may find yourself at loggerheads with the rest.

Anyway, the house of friends will soon show you your mistake. If you integrate the 11th house, the 5th will not be so prominent, and the improved state of balance will mean that although the 11th house sometimes inhibits the 5th, it also complements it. On the other hand, a heavily tenanted 11th house can for a long time distract you from yourself and even from your true will (the 5th house), with the result that you may go along with friends and groups more than is good for you. When the 5th house induces you to pay more attention to your own wishes, certain relationships may have to be sacrificed. But, if you dare to be yourself in a group or circle of friends, you shall eventually earn greater respect than if you are continually falling in with the plans of others.

6th/12th AXIS

The collective conscious versus the collective unconscious. This duality is not easy to interpret; especially as the 12th house seems never to come out into the open.

Many planets posited in the busy, menial and analytical 6th house can indicate that we are reliable work-horses; the danger being that, with the emphasis laid on work and service, we could lose all feeling for anything that transcends personality and for the unity that links us not only with the unconscious but also with what is universally human. A kind of fragmentation occurs in activities which, though useful in themselves, are not seen in a wider context. By unconscious opposition, the 6th house can then confront us (through illness say) with other values, but in that case the 12th house will already have had an undermining effect. However, if we manage to integrate that part of ourselves—our primary nature containing our past, present and future—the 6th house will be free to work and analyze in a much wider setting. On the other hand, a strong 12th house can divert us from reality, both in our social life and in our personal circumstances. It can prevent us from thinking and working in any practical way, so that the 6th house fails to show to advantage and, if the worst comes to the worst, we may end up being cared for in an institution. Yet a heavily tenanted 12th house can also, in an unconscious but clearly perceptible manner, cause us to treat personal reality as unimportant and to renounce our own interests for the sake of others, for an ideal or for some community goal. Depending on the rest of the chart, that goal will be sought along personal or along collective lines: along personal lines by sensing new trends for example and by helping to reshape social structures accordingly; along collective lines by retiring into obscurity, say, to assist development projects in third-world countries. In either case, what happens results from the effect of the 12th house on the 6th. As we have seen, either house can inhibit or stimulate the collective or individual activity of the other.

3. THE ANALOGY OF THE ELEMENTS

The following house relationships are based on the elements. Four elements are recognized in astrology: fire, earth, air and water, distributed among the signs and, in the same way, among fire, earth, air and water houses. Each house belonging to a given element has its own unique field of action, but interacts with the other houses of that element.

THE FIRE HOUSES

We find our own manifestation in the 1st house. It represents our individual physical appearance. But as long as it cannot express self-assurance, ego, and will, the 1st house has no form. If only for this reason, it reaches out to the 5th where the need to be oneself is expressed. House 9 enters in to evaluate how this is working out; it represents achievement of awareness in the widest sense, and tries to answer the questions, "Who am I? Where do I come from? Where am I going?" and "What is life all about?" The 9th influences both the 1st and 5th, our approach to the outside world as well as our feelings of personal worth, and these in turn influence the 9th.

THE EARTH HOUSES

Feelings of satisfaction and dissatisfaction, motivation, and the pattern of material values in which we find security, are found in the 2nd house. This pattern has a bearing on the way in which we see ourselves and on the social status we hope to achieve: both of which are expressed by the 10th house. However, motivation and our ego-image (2nd and 10th respectively) are influenced by confrontations with objective criteria and facts and with the work situation (6th house). But the 6th can achieve nothing without the motivation to work (2nd) and can engage in self-criticism only where there are clear-cut data to assimilate and judge (11th). Of course, when our ego-image changes so does our sense of security (2nd).

THE AIR HOUSES

When we learn to know others (3rd), this can lead to closer contacts from which friendship (11th) or partnership (7th) can arise. Contacts with others actually influence our thinking (3rd) which, in turn, can influence our behavior in contacts. Again, contact with our life-partner (7th) influences our treatment of our friends (11th) and also our thinking and our brief encounters (3rd), while friends in their turn can influence the 7th and the 3rd.

THE WATER HOUSES

These are the houses of our inner emotional basis, and emotional security (4th) is the resultant of psychic processes in the personal unconscious (8th) and the collective unconscious (12th). Soon after birth we are gathering experiences which belong to the 12th house right from the outset. Early in life we are still part of the collective psyche and participate unconsciously in the environment via our mothers. Positive and negative experiences are not assimilated by the ego at this time (since that is still unformed). Nevertheless, early childhood experiences can play a big role in later life as far as our sense of security is concerned (4th). In older children, personal problems can be repressed in the 8th, and so this house influences our sense of well-being as adults; disturbing factors here are easier to locate and understand than they are in the 12th. The 12th can act on the 8th: associations, premonitory dreams, hypnosis and the like offer the possibility of solving personal problems coming from the 8th. But it can equally incite us to fly from reality, so that we become ensnared by unreal and fallacious ideas when the connection between the 8th and the 12th is negative. However, the 4th, which experiences tensions as a reduced sense of safety, can always exercise an indirect influence. And when the 4th is strong and able to provide a firm emotional basis and a well-developed sense of security, it can also do much to solve problems: for the 4th affects the degree to which we are able to digest experiences from early and later life. When the 4th, 8th, and 12th houses are in a state of equilibrium, collective and personal factors can be used creatively and can enable us to face life with greater resilience.

4. THE ANALOGY OF THE CROSSES

It is rather more difficult to work out relationships in terms of the crosses. Houses (or signs for that matter) being arranged on the arms of a cross are either square or opposite one another, and are in a state of mutual tension. Let us not forget, however, that this tension can be very creative. In trying to understand the way in which the crosses work, we should refer back to what has already been said about house polarities, since the crosses are always a combination of two axes:

a) the cardinal houses (angles) lie along axes 1–7 and 4–10;

b) the fixed (succedent) houses lie along axes 2–8 and 5–11;

c) the mutable (cadent) houses lie along axes 3–9 and 6–12.

THE CARDINAL CROSS

In the cardinal cross, the dual action of our own being (1st) and the being of our partner (7th) influences our mask function and our emotional and social functioning (4th and 10th). But how we function, and the extent to which we feel emotionally secure, influence the way in which we present ourselves to the outside world (1st) and our reactions to our life-partner (7th).

THE FIXED CROSS

Our measure of success in solving life's problems (8th) determines the measure in which we can create security for ourselves and the degree of motivation we derive from our feelings of satisfaction and dissatisfaction (2nd). It has an effect on the extent to which we realize our individuality and affect others — especially friends, since these are close enough to us to notice our inner tensions (5th) and (11th). The ability to adjust to problems in a balanced way gives the self-assurance (5th), necessary for steady friendships. Good friends in turn can stimulate our self-assurance and can help us to experience concrete security (2nd) and to come to terms with life (8th). Once again, we are looking at a complex interplay in which one house is subtly activated by the others.

THE MUTABLE CROSS

Much that we read, write and think, and much of the information we gather, is fairly casual (3rd), but further reflection can stimulate us to synthesize visions of all kinds so we can widen our horizons (9th). However, unless we are critical and analytical (6th), there is a danger that this process will flounder in a morass of theorizing. The 12th house is also involved, because it links us with universal humanity (the collective unconscious). Problems in the deepest layers of our being can hinder us from making a critical assessment of ourselves or of the outside world (axis 12-6); but the 3rd and 9th houses act as correctives by supplying us with information about our problems (3rd), and by placing them in a meaningful setting (9th). Problems in judging some matter or in forming a reasoned opinion about it (9th) can be dealt with by analysis and critical investigation (6th), as we ask ourselves what went wrong and why. Transcending our problems in some way can lead to a unified experience unknown to the 9th house. The 12th house road to this unified experience can be found through meditation, yoga, prayer, service to humanity or self-sacrifice; there is no need to seek it through drugs and other abuses. The processes of experiencing and assessing (12-6) can stimulate the processes of thinking and synthesizing (3-9), and the latter in their turn can stimulate the former.

*   *   *   *   *

To sum up, the houses depend on one another in all sorts of ways, and those mentioned above are only a few of many; we have certainly not exhausted the possible combinations. For instance, the 5th and 10th houses are inconjunct by aspect and this indicates a fundamental tension between them. At times the tension can be quite marked and our ego image (10th) can then be completely different from what we express (5th) or what we really want to do (5th); our creativity and self-expression (5th) can lead us in a different direction from the one desired by the part of ourself that determines how we appear to the outside world (10th). And so it can happen that our mask (the 4–10 axis), with the 10th as its "mouthpiece," and our feeling of self-confidence (5th) will not necessarily coincide. What is more, the 10th also filters the data coming in from the outside world, so that certain things sometimes fail to register.

The 5th house is also inconjunct with the 12th; the relationship here being rather clearer. The group always seems to be in conflict with how we would like to express the self as an individual or, to put it another way, the 12th tends to undermine the 5th. Once again, two parts of the psyche are making themselves known in two discordant house meanings. Of course, the chart can have planets in both the 5th and the 12th, but what I want to point out is that these will influence one another indirectly through those houses even if none of them is in aspect.

Above all, we must not forget that the psyche is a unit made up of many components. These components are interconnected and must not be seen as independent: it would be an error to ignore this fact in interpretation. And what we have done with the 5th house and the inconjunct aspect can be done with every other house and aspect.

Astrology has to be learned a step at a time; which means that we have to study each house in turn. We shall eventually reach the stage where we can weave the various threads of a chart into a single tapestry to produce a picture of the individual that is much more than could be determined from its separate strands. Part of the weaving process is to reproduce the pattern of interlacing factors as they affect each house. Only then shall we be able to make a safe judgment.

Nevertheless, before we can see the composite whole, we need the basic knowledge of what each planet can mean in each house. This will form the subject of the next chapter.

CHAPTER FOUR

PLANETS
IN THE HOUSES

1. INTRODUCTION

It is impossible, in the following paragraphs, to set out all the likely effects of the planets in the houses. An entire shelf of volumes would be required to do them justice, since in every horoscope there are a tremendous amount of factors influencing the overall picture. However, a number of fundamental principles can be outlined. Each factor is governed by several basic rules covering one part of the interpretation. Obviously these rules can be refined still further but, in each case, they start from the same point. In discussing the planets in the houses, you'll find a brief characterization for each position and these characterizations will be illustrated by some possible consequences, but what I say must not be regarded as the last word! Later on you'll want to combine the meanings of planets in the houses with the meanings of their positions in the signs, while taking into consideration the planetary aspects with other planets in other houses and signs, these planets being rulers of yet other houses, and so on. But there is no cause to be daunted; everything will slot into place if you pursue your study one stage at a time.

When analyzing a planet in a house, it is important to bear in mind that a planet represents a certain type of psychic energy or reaction pattern which makes itself felt mainly in the area of life indicated by the house. Therefore the house never relies for its interpretation on the planet; on the contrary, it is the planet that relies for its interpretation on the house. Note therefore the following rule:

> The way in which a planet manifests is indicated by the *sign* in which it stands; the area of life in which its manifestation takes place is indicated by the *house* in which it stands.

However, the rule needs to be made a little more precise, because we are dealing with attitudes and patterns of expectation (conscious or otherwise) underlying the different houses, as you have already noted. The activity of the planets in the houses is colored by their placement in the signs, but the pattern of expectations and the way the planetary influences work out are both partly determined by the houses.

Thus Mercury in Gemini in the 8th house is totally different from Mercury in Scorpio in the 3rd house. It is the same planet, placed in signs and houses that are analogous (Gemini being analogous to the 3rd and Scorpio being analogous to 8th), but the individual's character and idiosyncrasies would be completely different in the two cases.

Mercury in Gemini suggests that you will be talkative, interested in gathering facts, and always on the look-out for something new. You will continually be contacting others to brief them on the things that occupy your mind. Now an 8th house Mercury focuses the center of attention on 8th house matters, which can be quite numerous. They include everything that is hidden, such as the subject-matter of psychology, parapsychology and the occult, also deep-sea diving, medicine, archeological digs, etc. With Mercury in Gemini the interests are multifarious and there is a chance that you will dabble in all these fields, but, because the 8th house (when emphasized) tends to make a person reserved, your inclination to communicate will be curbed somewhat and you will give the impression of quietly mulling over the facts in an effort to discover their whys and wherefores. The thought processes themselves play a more central role and are engaged in questions of life and death, profundity and secrecy, conflict and the core of things. Even though Mercury is in Gemini, there is a good chance that no one will really get to know you — you keep your mental preoccupations to yourself.

What now of Mercury in Scorpio in the 3rd house? Your first impulse might be to look for a similar effect, but you would be frustrated in the attempt. Someone with this placement is interested not in incessant fact-gathering but in experiencing the facts already found. With Mercury in Scorpio, he (or she) takes a long time chewing the cud of every fact he encounters, he feels and lives it, and is slow to express an opinion. Yet his assimilating, investigatory, experiencing and sensitive Mercury does express itself in brief contacts, in the urge to instruct, and in systematic data-sorting. And so the person with Mercury in Scorpio in the 3rd concentrates on information to which he feels able to relate and on whatever he can arrange and systematize. However, his interests need not lie in the fields of parapsychology or the occult but may involve computers or systems analysis. (Of course, someone with Mercury in Scorpio may have a taste for the esoteric, but this is not such a foregone conclusion as it is for someone with Mercury in the 8th house.)

On the face of it, the planetary placements we have just been discussing seem to have much in common, but their effects differ considerably. Mercury in Gemini in the 8th is open and versatile, and although it sometimes investigates the hidden and profounder side of life, it does so in a perfunctory way. Mercury in Scorpio in the 3rd, on the other hand, feels things intensely and works hard at assimilating and classifying its knowledge.

By this time, it will probably have occurred to you that a planet in a given sign might be more at home in some houses than in others. The point is one to which we shall be returning in the chapter on Combinations in Interpretation.

So what must we bear in mind when considering the planets in the houses? Briefly, the following:

1. The influence of a planet is felt in the area of life shown by the house where it is domiciled.

2. Since planets in houses become involved in specific attitudes and patterns of expectation, they can tell you how these affect the inner life and also how they affect your presentation of yourself to the outside world. (Note that the rulers of the houses are being left out of consideration for the time being; they will be fully discussed in a subsequent volume.)

3. Planets in a house indicate the type of psychic energy being used in it; that is to say, they indicate the kind of action taken or the attitude adopted in response to the circumstances represented by that house.

Armed with this knowledge, let us take a look at the placements of the planets in the houses not forgetting that ready-made interpretations are never completely satisfactory since, in a real chart, there are always plenty of other factors to complicate the issue. The outlines given below are merely guides to how meanings can be assigned to the planets in the houses; there has been no striving after completeness. The aim has been to avoid misleading catchwords and to show by example how interpretations are made.

2. PLANETS IN THE 1ST HOUSE

SUN IN THE 1st

The ego, the path leading to optimal development and the way in which you try to achieve self-realization, manifest here in the outer world and are necessarily bound up with your attitudes toward and behavior in your environment. A person with the Sun in the 1st has a presence that can be felt. Sun in the 1st expresses itself simply and naturally and you give the impression of possessing a strong personality and of being someone not to be trifled with. Also, given the great vitality implied by the placement, you can suddenly come to the front. You need recognition and respect in order to display all your solar characteristics. Ideally, you are warm, vital, brimming with self-confidence and will-power, in addition to showing loyalty and generosity. Quite often you endeavor to assume leadership. But, with a difficult placement, there can be parades of pomposity, tactlessness, egotism, ambition and tyranny.

MOON IN THE 1st

The need to express your feelings and emotional states as you react to the outside world and the need to forge a link with your environment are represented by the Moon in the 1st house. There is an immediacy about the way your unconscious emotional activities and your conscious and emotional responses impinge on the outside world from the 1st and color the way you appear to it. This Moon, as the need to protect and mother, and to engage in emotional exchange with the environment, will encourage you to adopt a maternal and caring attitude to those around; especially as the Moon represents the mechanism that comes into play as soon as you feel insecure. Sensitivity and emotionalism are clearly to the fore with this placement, which can either bestow warmth or indicate a craving for change and excitement. Since the Moon adapts well to most placements (with a few exceptions), it gives an accommodating and friendly approach in the 1st. Emotional undercurrents are quickly detected. What is more, the Moon here makes for good relationships with women, the public and your country, which explains why popularity is one of the things traditionally ascribed to it. When this placement is difficult, however, you may be exaggerative and moody, dependent on others, and over-sensitive; so that acceptance and popularity are sought at any price. You can then live on others.

MERCURY IN THE 1st

Stepping out into the world is governed mainly by a need to gather and assimilate information, to arrange and communicate facts, to make contacts, to analyze and systematize. Mercury itself is neutral, and you are just as likely to link two parties with one another as you are to associate either of them with yourself. Maintaining contacts and gathering information are important means of self-expression. Mobile Mercury in the 1st house makes you seem fickle and restless; it also makes you inquisitive and therefore rather knowledgeable quite early in life. But, unless Mercury is in a fixed sign, you may start projects without going on to finish them.

The Mercury-in-1 person eagerly takes up new projects, talks freely about everything and anything, usually has many acquaintances, and is good at dealing with unexpected contingencies. In the initial reaction to anything new, this person is often brisk and quick-thinking and soon marshalls the facts; perhaps for that reason he or she is disposed to "nerviness." When the placement is difficult, you may be superficial, garrulous, crafty or indiscreet.

VENUS IN THE 1st

This position indicates a tendency to give open expression to a need for secure relationships and for harmony and beauty in every situation; a need which strongly colors your behavior. You will endeavor to reconcile opposites and to strike the happy medium. Pleasant surroundings will be at a premium, and conflicts will be very distasteful — everything being done to create a genial and harmonious atmosphere. This longing for beauty and harmony reveals itself in a consistently amicable approach and in the obvious wish to make a good impression. Venus in the first is likely to indicate that you are friendly and amusing, cheerful and easy-going, but a difficult position may make you lazy, rude, vain or frivolous.

MARS IN THE 1st

Your assertive self-preservation instinct and executive ability are channelled directly into the outside world, where you hold your own by being rough-and-ready, vigorous and rather aggressive. Surplus energy may well spill over into impulsiveness. A person with Mars in the 1st is brisk, decisive, self-confident and sometimes so hot-headed that the world feels you are not in proper control of yourself. Martian fierceness can wreak considerable damage, if only verbally, for words can be biting, quick, inconsiderate and sometimes tactless. On the other hand, Mars in the 1st gives courage, daring, frankness, and fitness for the fray. You may find it easy to impose yourself on others and to take the initiative; in these respects, at least, you are a born leader. Quite possibly, you may prefer to live life with no strings attached; you may even be inclined to bid the world defiance or (on a less sophisticated level) may simply enjoy starting brawls. A difficult placement indicates bluntness of speech, recklessness, an explosive temper and violence. That people with Mars in the 1st are liable to get injured on this account is a truism of astrology.

JUPITER IN THE 1st

This placement indicates that entry into the outside world is influenced by a need to create space for yourself and to widen your horizons (literally and figuratively), so you are quick to arrive at a judgment, a view, a vision or a philosophy. Jupiter in the 1st often indicates someone who is positive and optimistic. When being expansive, you like to talk about your own insights, and prefer to rely on your own opinions. It is natural for you to strive for personal freedom.

In direct contacts with the world, you are ever ready to help by words of encouragement, instruction and so on. The danger is that, with Jupiter in this position, you will strike others as cocksure and a bit of a know-it-all. Expansiveness leads you to tackle big problems; but if the problems are too big, you may be arrogant, boastful and the like if the rest of the chart confirms this.

SATURN IN THE 1st

Here you would like to present yourself to the world as a perfect whole and want to be recognized as such, and this makes you vulnerable to some extent. You wish to appear serious, reliable, self-controlled, and persevering. When Saturn is in the 1st, the need to define who you are affects your behavior in the outside world. And so you are reserved, sober, composed and rather subdued or inhibited. You take grave note of the world — sometimes a little apprehensively — and expect the world to take you seriously in return.

Cheerfulness is not your strong point! A sense of responsibility underlies whatever you do or refrain from doing, and you want to perfect everything that you take in hand and, in general, you want to be well-organized. You have little spontaneity, but beneath your apparent composure you can be really churned up. Because you are afraid you will not be taken seriously, you like to stress how much depends on you. Worried that you may not make a good impression, you keep your own counsel until you are sure of your ground. Somewhat melancholy and pessimistic, often inflexible, you are also steady, patient, realistic and practical. Sometimes you are mistrustful and fear to show your real self to the world, and then you quickly put on a mask.

URANUS IN THE 1st

The desire to develop individuality as freely as possible has a big influence on the way in which you present yourself to the outside world. Great importance is attached to whatever is new, to whatever crosses existing boundaries (either literally or figuratively). Longing to make changes, clean breaks and break-throughs suggests that you will be original but erratic.

Your number one concern is to be yourself, and so you will tend to be unconventional, independent and pioneering; although this does not mean that your progress is always an improvement! You are likely to kick at old values in order to stress your own uniqueness. The flashing suddenness of this planet makes you lively, unpredictable at times, sometimes genial and sometimes crotchety, and those around you react accordingly. But, however you may react, with Uranus in the 1st you will cling to freedom of expression and will behave in keeping with your nature. "Liberty, Equality, Fraternity" are your watchwords, and you can be aroused by them to fiery acts of destruction and oppression. At best you will be very tolerant of the self-expression of others, at worst you may seek to subvert systems that lack your approval or may display anarchist or terrorist tendencies.

NEPTUNE IN THE 1st

Your entry into the outside world is very much colored by this softening, blurring and sometimes undermining, psychic factor. Your attitude, as modified by Neptune's diffusive, transcendent influence, is ill-defined but very emotional, and you pick up all sorts of subtle messages being silently broadcast by your surroundings. Neptune is impersonally emotional and so there is something mystical and collective in your approach, which (because Neptune is in the 1st house here) can be very personal nonetheless. This collective approach does not mean that you will see everything alike; you can project in many different ways.

Your attitude is friendly and receptive, and your "antennae" are up on all sides even if you are not fine-tuned to every station. But the nebulous influence of Neptune tends to veil the real person so that no one can properly get to know you. You can dream and fantasize your way through life (even drink through life in some instances) if the whole horoscope permits. On the other hand, the sensitivity of Neptune can produce artistry, musicality, spirituality and sometimes mediumistic gifts if the rest of the chart is in support. You can be full of self-denial, love and compassion, but also can drift along looking at the world through rose-colored glasses while amusing yourself with figments of your own imagination.

PLUTO IN THE 1st

A craving for power and recognition and the readiness to fight for a bigger share of whatever seems to be on offer strongly affect your approach to the outside world. Pluto bestows a certain tension, a certain vehemence, but also intense concentration and manipulatory skill. When in the 1st house, it displays to the outside world great force of character and self-assertiveness, and an enormous hunger for recognition, power and leadership. However, that leadership may very well be exercised behind the scenes: the Pluto in the 1st person can wear a bland smile to cover real intentions. Since it is so uncompromisingly placed in the 1st house, Pluto sets an examination, so to speak, for those with whom you come in personal contact: there are requirements others have to fulfill. You observe those around you, delve into their motives, and want to know what they have at stake. You have a good nose for following a scent and can use or misuse this faculty in a bid for power, for Pluto is the planet of the manipulator, and in the 1st house it has ample scope. You behave forcefully and self-assertively, and show that you are possessed of a very strong will when you want to get anything done.

But Pluto can also haul all kinds of hidden things to the surface, and the danger then is of sudden unbalanced or hysterical reactions and violent outbursts. People with Pluto in the 1st have something about them that attracts attention without their having to do anything. This placement often gives an all-or-nothing outlook.

3. PLANETS IN THE 2ND HOUSE

SUN IN THE 2nd

The Sun in the 2nd indicates a need to develop yourself by building up a secure existence and by creating a pattern of values on as broad a basis as possible, but with material wealth as the cornerstone. Personal priorities differ of course. For instance, there may be an urge to acquire large holdings, or to accumulate money or goods. Even family and friends can be regarded as property. But material things can play another role: instead of being a slave to matter, you can make matter serve you and can give it form; because artistry and an appreciation of beauty and of beautiful things are other significant results of having the Sun in the 2nd house.

The importance of developing a pattern of values that will give inner confidence and also outer security in the form of a steady income, a nest-egg and the like, is emphasized by the

Sun in the 2nd. With the Sun here you are often suited for 2nd house professions such as those of jeweller, broker, valuer, cashier, banker, etc.

MOON IN THE 2nd

In the 2nd house, emotional responses to the world and the need for an emotional stronghold (Moon) are bound up with the question of material security. Central to this are the development of a pattern of values and the laying of a firm and solid foundation. And because the need is an emotional one, you will be much inclined to surround yourself with things that provide a sense of safety. In fact, when you feel unsettled, you may even buy something (preferably fine or expensive) that will give a sense of security. The Moon, as might be expected from the regular waxing and waning of its light, can provide a fund of good things on one occasion and next to nothing on another; although, when in the 2nd, the Moon usually manages to find something in reserve.

The Moon is the great molder of forms and so, you may be artistic. But, as the Moon often represents the public or society, its placement in the 2nd may point to a desire to provide security for people; hence it causes no surprise when we meet government officials with the Moon in this position. The jobs and professions available are quite varied—among them those already mentioned under the Sun in the 2nd, although the positions held may be less important.

Feelings of satisfaction and dissatisfaction are intense when the Moon is in the 2nd house, and they beget a need to actualize; which is why the Moon here is a powerful driving force for getting things done.

MERCURY IN THE 2nd

Thinking, contacting, and the capacity to arrange, classify, analyze and combine are used primarily to build up a system of values, to create security and to develop proficiency. Mercury can even indicate the type of proficiency: journalistic, literary, mercantile, etc. The person with Mercury in the 2nd frequently has a good business sense or tries to earn a secure living by writing, analyzing, thinking, trading and so on. Although Mercury is a somewhat variable planet, and would therefore reflect fluctuating feelings of security and satisfaction, and financial ups and downs, any difficulties can be tackled with the business acumen of this selfsame Mercury.

With Mercury here, we tend to make financial capital out of our brain power and our way of contacting people: we seek to develop skills that could provide us with an income. Mercury here will often take special courses to help in business or professional career. However, the chief concern is to feel secure in whatever you are doing; you need to know you have a solid basis from which to operate.

VENUS IN THE 2nd

The need for harmony and beauty teams up here with the need for material security. Therefore, with this position of Venus, you are keen to learn skills that will provide security. In fact, the emphasis on security and on external form can become a main preoccupation. Venus in the 2nd is very liable to encourage a taste for luxury; it also bestows an appreciation of art and the ability to create works of art. You will feel at ease with everything to do with beautifying the external form and will enjoy learning how to ornament and embellish. Therefore we are likely to find that, with Venus in this position, folk will be earning their livings from art, fashion, cosmetics, luxury goods and so on.

The other side of Venus, the need for security within a relationship, is very physical in the 2nd house: your partner is an important possession from whom you expect to derive reassurance and comfort; which is why Venus in the 2nd is traditionally associated with sensuality.

Venus is an air planet, and is capable of making us waft along ignoring worrying problems. When the planet is in the 2nd house this can mean that outgoings are sometimes allowed to exceed income. Beautiful things are found very attractive, and the decorative instinct is strongly developed.

MARS IN THE 2nd

In the 2nd house, a sense of self-importance, executive ability, and a need to prove yourself are involved in the creation of security. With Mars in the 2nd, feelings of satisfaction and dissatisfaction are particularly powerful, and give rise to the desire to undertake and learn things that can provide a secure subsistence. Now Mars is naturally rather uncontrolled, so that its energies tend to be frittered away on too many interests; or else some newly won security is abandoned for the sake of pursuing other forms of safety.

These powerful feelings of satisfaction and dissatisfaction can also be responsible for sudden fits of rashness, and you can go through a great deal of money and so create problems. But since being short of money hurts your pride, you work hard to make good the deficiency. Even where finances are not directly implicated, Mars can often create problems in the material sphere, yet can also supply the energy required for solving them. Mars in this house may stir up the desire for money and possessions. But also, with Mars in the 2nd you may earn a living in martial or competitive careers such as the army or professional sport.

JUPITER IN THE 2nd

The need for expansion and improvement is deployed in the field of creating a secure living, of learning skills and of feelings of satisfaction and dissatisfaction. Jovian confidence can in itself give considerable security. By acquiring various proficiencies, you are often able to build up not only a solid system of values but also material security and, with Jupiter in the 2nd house, are likely to set about accumulating possessions. There is also a taste for luxury and a fondness for being surrounded by sumptuous and beautiful things. You tend to let others share in your expansive plans.

Jupiter in the 2nd points to an income from religious, intellectual, or similar horizon-widening activities, such as philosopher, lecturer, minister of religion, and the like. Yet the expansiveness of Jupiter here can also cause problems. If there is over-expansion (by gambling or speculation, say), much of what has been achieved can be lost. The rest of the horoscope should be examined to see whether this is likely or not. Generally speaking, Jupiter gives an inner assurance that all is well and, when it does, all usually *is* well.

SATURN IN THE 2nd

This demarcating and bounding psychic factor, which lets us know our limitations, gives form to the house relating to security and feelings of satisfaction and dissatisfaction. Saturn here reinforces any feelings of dissatisfaction and is a sort of sensitive spot which you actively endeavor to protect from potential injury; although ultra-anxiety sometimes attracts the very trouble you are trying to avoid. The placement is one that suggests you will have to work long and hard for a living and will not have money showered upon you. But this is also a placement typical of collectors, that is to say, of people who try to overcome apprehension concerning the future by collecting things they can touch and handle; preferably valuables to serve as something put by for a rainy day. With this position of Saturn some are said to be miserly, but are actually not given to a love of money as such — it is merely hoarded as an insurance against hard times. Possessions give material security and are treasured for this reason. As much cash is saved or invested as possible. In fact, with Saturn in the 2nd the provision of material security is the weak point in your character. Lack of means can throw you completely off balance. But Saturn here can represent other possibilities: either you toil away to make as big a pile of money as you can (to give security) or else you refuse to become a slave to uncertainty, part with all possessions and live as a recluse. In the latter case, you have not really overcome fear of material deprivation, but are simply running away from the unpleasant side of possessions — which is the constant risk of losing them when least expected. So we see the penniless hermit and the avid hoarder as extreme results of Saturn in the 2nd.

A steady income from Saturnian work is possible; for instance from work on the land and its produce (forestry, mining etc.) or from trading in real estate. An aptitude for structure and order combined with a great sense of responsibility can lead to a steady improvement in circumstances.

URANUS IN THE 2nd

You need to give to your search for security and skills a thoroughly original, independent shape, and in doing so can actually put security at risk. Strangely enough, however, there is a sort of security in the knowledge that the introduction of an element of risk gives needed tension. By unexpected actions or ideas, you can sometimes destroy in one fell swoop something you have carefully constructed, but you can also make a quantum jump of creativity. The capriciousness and unpredictability of Uranus produce sudden shifts in feelings of satisfaction or dissatisfaction and in basic concepts and values.

With Uranus in the 2nd, you may be inclined to earn a living in some unconventional manner. You can gain job-satisfaction by crossing frontiers either literally or figuratively. In a figurative sense, this frontier-crossing can range from aviation and electrical engineering to fortune-telling and astrology. The person with Uranus here often goes beyond the limits of his or her own certainty. You may play for high stakes and take enormous risks, and either ruin yourself or win a fortune.

NEPTUNE IN THE 2nd

The desire to refine and unravel, but also the tendency to see things hazily and to hallucinate, and the ability to empathize, appear here in the area of obtaining a secure subsistence and of feelings of satisfaction and dissatisfaction. The latter are quite important, but usually remain vague; the person being haunted by an inexpressible longing for "something" he (or she) cannot define. This can be a source of inspiration if he is an artist or a musician. However he has little understanding of material things, and does not know much about handling money. Neptune in the 2nd can sometimes indicate an intuitive appreciation of what is happening in certain situations, but it is hard to turn this to one's own advantage. With Neptune here, the attitude to material things, including personal expenditure, will be irresponsible or woolly-minded. One can lose money through sheer disorganization, and yet money can easily come pouring in again against all the odds. How this happens it is impossible to say. Sometimes you don't seem to know the difference between your own belongings and those of other people, and so fall under suspicion for dishonesty.

Neptune in the 2nd also indicates an idealistic attitude toward possessions, but you may find it hard to derive security from them. But the ability to shape matter in the realms of art and music may well be bestowed by the inherent sensitivity of Neptune.

PLUTO IN THE 2nd

The urge to achieve fluidity or transcendence by bringing to the surface things from our hidden depths expresses itself in the area of life concerned with achieving security and so can cause great insecurity. A craving for power, and the need to plumb one's own being come what may, can generate intense feelings of satisfaction and dissatisfaction in the 2nd house.

This placement indicates tremendous concentration on what you intrinsically want to possess. You are prepared to work hard for it, and have deeply ingrained convictions that wealth is power. Strong feelings of satisfaction and dissatisfaction stir various desires to learn or do things. With Pluto in the 2nd, you can display remarkable versatility if need be, in order to preserve holdings on the material plane. Thus you will expend a great deal of energy managing property and will keep a firm grip on all the things owned (including people), because you see them as forms of security. On the other hand, the person with Pluto in this house constantly discovers that material things fail to satisfy and will start looking for the values lying behind them. Eventually, you will encounter your own drives and feelings of satisfaction and dissatisfaction as they are brought to the surface by Plutonian activities.

Pluto in the 2nd is a placement that causes you to grope desperately for a secure handhold as you hang precariously over the abyss of your own passions; too often you may seek security in the crumbling material things close by instead of climbing on upward to transcend them.

4. PLANETS IN THE 3RD HOUSE

SUN IN THE 3rd

With the Sun here, you will seek to express yourself in the areas of communication, brief encounters, connections and information. You try to realize potential by keeping in touch with many friends and acquaintances, by exchanging news and satisfying immense curiosity about all sorts of subjects, by combining facts with facts (cogitating), by introducing facts to people (conveying knowledge), and by linking one person with another (making introductions). The processing of goods is a 3rd house matter too; so that merchandising, commercial travelling and the like all come under it.

That the Sun is here makes this house a very significant area in your life, and you will probably engage in one or more of the activities mentioned. The range of activities typical of the area is certainly wide, but superficiality is the danger. With the Sun in the 3rd you would like to be an authority on trade, communications, information and human contacts. If the aspects are good, there is a great thirst for knowledge, versatility, a talent for writing, mathematics, study, etc. However, where the placement is a difficult one, information gathered can also be used in gossip, or trickery. You will quickly adopt fresh interests, and are likely to be considered fickle.

MOON IN THE 3rd

The need to experience emotional security in communication, brief encounters, gathering and spreading information and making connections is indicated with the Moon in the 3rd, and you will probably use your formative and reproductive powers along these lines. You are likely to favor commerce and short journeys, and are good at conveying your meaning by talking and writing. The placement suggests versatility but a possible lack of depth.

At the same time, you can be plagued by uncertainty and will seek to restore emotional equilibrium by occupying yourself with various mental activities. Because the Moon is so changeable, facts are not always assimilated in a balanced way and, if the planet is afflicted, fantasy can play a big part in life.

The consequences can be restlessness, an inability to settle down, and rash undertakings and statements. On the other hand, the Moon in the 3rd indicates a talent for languages and teaching, giving you an instinctive knowledge of what people want to hear and helping clothe it in the right words. The thoughts expressed are rich in imagery, and so this is a good placement for authors and journalists.

MERCURY IN THE 3rd

Mercury, with its capacity for communicating, making contacts and collecting information, is on home ground in the 3rd house, and is in a good position to show all sides of its character, both its best (varied scientific research, clever journalism, linguistic skills, etc.) and its worst (slyness, rumor-mongering, etc.).

Obviously, Mercury in the 3rd has a lot in common with the Sun and Moon here, but differs from them in its approach. Self-expression (the Sun) plays no part here, nor does the uncertainty of the Moon; and, although Mercury can be very inconstant, it is remarkably neutral in this house. Mercury is not such a promoter of imagination and fantasy as the Moon, but deals more in understanding and logic, and that makes its placement here extremely good for scientific research: the studying, classifying and analyzing of a multiplicity of facts. Here too, we find a gift for languages, business acumen, and investigatory skill. You tend to be restless in mind and body, but are a fluent speaker (unless there are too many inhibiting aspects). You quickly catch on to the thoughts and ideas of others. However, with adverse aspects, reactions are sometimes too quick, too critical, too cool and too analytic, and either you silence the other person or give him or her no chance to get a word in edgeways.

VENUS IN THE 3rd

The need for harmony and beauty, and for emotional and physical security in relation to others, is expressed here in the area of contacts, communication, information and so on. You like to improve the external form of relationships and to keep the peace in a friendly and gentle manner, sometimes at the expense of talking problems through. Harmony in contacts is what Venus prefers to see or bring about. Therefore, the person with Venus in the 3rd gives the impression of being accessible and diplomatic without necessarily being deeply sincere. For deep sincerity other factors would have to be present in the chart. Since Venus, with her love of beauty, expresses herself here on the plane of (among other things) thinking and writing, this placement can give the desire to pen fine words, to construct well-balanced sentences, and to write and speak about beautiful things. In short a pleasing presentation is regarded as vital. Hypocrisy (making things out to be better than they are) can of course be present, but often there is a genuine ability to improve and embellish. The person with Venus in the 3rd enjoys having plenty of agreeable contacts, also more intimate tête-à-têtes, and is interested in improvements in our means of transport and communication.

MARS IN THE 3rd

Self-assertion, energy and executive ability find an outlet here in the field of communication, contacts, associations, thinking, information and so on. This means that you have great repartee, and considerable energy to invest in tracking down facts and connections, but can also be very sharp and fierce in debates or encounters. With Mars in the 3rd you seek to assert yourself by acquiring extensive knowledge of a host of different things in order to take people by surprise. You know something about everything but seldom delve deep. Without perhaps realizing it, you can cut the grass from under a person's feet by an impulsive, rather tactless way of speaking. Conversations usually end up as arguments.

With hard aspects, you may easily become offensive in speaking to and dealing with people — who may well be nasty back. What is more, you are liable to jump to the wrong conclusion and to put two and two together to make five: at the drop of a hat, you can dash off an angry or hurtful letter on some trifling theme. Because the 3rd house has to do with traffic, Mars in this position may indicate jaywalking and careless driving.

JUPITER IN THE 3rd

Jupiter in the 3rd house encourages you to express your capacity for expansion and self-improvement in the area of communication and brief encounters, of information and making connections. You can find these matters very absorbing, but there is a temptation to do too much. The planet's placement suggests many contacts, many-sided interests, and ready speech — sometimes too ready — so that a long-winded account takes the place of what could have been said in a few words. Yet listeners are slow to complain, because you have the knack of involving others in your plans for expansion. You like to help by teaching what you have discovered, and you learn a lot in the process.

Nevertheless, Jupiter is not at its best in this house. The planet induces you to synthesize things, whereas the 3rd house is involved in gathering isolated facts. Therefore you will run the risk either of being swamped by details or of overlooking them because they seem unimportant. Jupiter gives a desire to pass judgment on contacts or the ability to envisage how they should develop; therefore you are somewhat biased about them.

The influence of Jupiter will be beneficial, however, if you take care not to be too expansive. There is a danger you may boast and exaggerate, although you are usually prepared to give the statements and opinions of others a fair hearing. Other things being equal, success in 3rd house activities is quite likely.

SATURN IN THE 3rd

The need to search deep, to limit and demarcate, appears in the area of information, communication, brief encounters and thinking. This can lead to reticence, reserve and inertia, but also to level-headedness and growing insight in this area. You feel insecure and can exhibit this in a number of different ways, for instance by keeping your thoughts to yourself or by studying every question minutely before reaching a conclusion. From this point of view, the placement is a good one for a professional researcher (scientific or otherwise). Contacts are difficult, and so sometimes is learning. You might be so worried you aren't able to absorb everything you are learning, you may develop a mental block over it, or even suffer from some speech disorder.

The person with Saturn in the 3rd often has emotional inhibitions where others are concerned, and behavior may be cool and distant in consequence. You find it difficult to talk to people but, when you do, it is well-thought-out and sensible, if a little too cut-and-dried — because the thought processes run along fixed lines and are rather conventional. Saturn in the 3rd is not an easy position, but, if there are no further problems in the chart, it can indicate that you are well prepared, set to work carefully and responsibly, and prefer a solid enterprise to short-term success.

Usually as a result of overcompensation, Saturn indicates some disappointment in matters ruled by the house in which it is posited; here it is communication that is affected, often as a result of a defensive attitude.

Because of the cautious thinking typical of Saturn in the 3rd, you can express a well-considered opinion, but are liable to ponder too long for fear of missing some vital factor. If you write a book it is likely to be dry, or packed with so much information that the thread of the plot is lost. In the 3rd house, Saturn's need to dig deep and penetrate to the core of things tends to be frustrated by the countless facts and figures presented by the house, too many for all of them to be examined in depth.

URANUS IN THE 3rd

With Uranus in the 3rd house, you like to express your individuality, originality, unconventionality and reforming zeal in the area of communication and information. You think rapidly, are quick to make connections and ready to become involved in a variety of different things. But restless Uranus in this position can make you nervous and tense because thought processes are too highly charged. And yet the person with Uranus in the 3rd needs to be "wound up" and alert in order to be able to react swiftly and intuitively. We may expect a display of the most unusual and unconventional ideas and reactions. You solve problems on an *ad hoc* basis: a notion suddenly occurs and is quickly put into effect.

Contacts are lively — sometimes too lively — and the disruptive principle of Uranus also makes itself felt in the 3rd house by the severing of relationships and an impulsive rushing into new things: you are always on the hunt for something different.

With Uranus here, thinking follows unbeaten tracks and steps outside conventional boundaries; therefore this is a good position for reporters and communicators. Certainly, in this age of world-wide telecommunications, air travel, electronics and so on, there are plenty of practical opportunities to seize. At the same time, Uranian impulsiveness can lead to traffic and other accidents.

Since the thought processes are not tied to set patterns, Uranus in the 3rd is a placement that favors inventors. But it is also a placement that provokes you to act without proper restraint regarding contacts, or to flaunt individuality and originality in the neutral ground between one individual and another.

NEPTUNE IN THE 3rd

The urge to refine, disassociate, make formless, dissolve, or idealize works out rather elusively here in the area of communication, information, contacts and thinking. Such a placement can hardly be said to promote logic or clear argument. Fantasy, however, is well developed, and the mind can range idealistically in higher spheres, provided it does not content itself with building castles in the air, and there is a chance that emotional factors and religious or metaphysical insight can be given shape in the 3rd house.

Hidden matters, hardly susceptible of being run to earth by logical deduction, are ferreted out by Neptune in the 3rd. This position can bestow a rare gift of appraisal of irrational facts. For instance, a person with Neptune in the 3rd can usually distinguish between a genuine and fake clairvoyant, yet would find it very hard to give a good reason for the decision.

The thinking is fairly emotional, and sometimes verges on the vague and chaotic. If there are other difficult placements, there is a tendency to day-dream and to confuse dreams with facts. A positive form of expression, however, is writing about the rich world of reverie and fancy, for imaginative writing is distinctly aided by this position of Neptune.

PLUTO IN THE 3rd

The desire for power, the wish to get to the bottom of everything, and the longing for fluidity and transformation make a big impact on 3rd house contacts. You are alert and intense, and thoughts are uttered forcefully and with conviction; you do not relish having your opinions opposed. You search for the information you deem important and often amass so much material that others are completely bewildered by your data.

Even so, the person with Pluto in the 3rd is never satisfied, never relinquishes the feeling that there may be more to come, and can expend an enormous amount of energy looking for all possible connections and facts. Obviously, in the process, you will stumble on much that is concealed but, inevitably, will stumble on yourself. Pluto in the 3rd house is bound to confront yourself with yourself, because you rake up so much information and want to have such a grasp of affairs that you effectively isolate yourself from ordinary contacts. In spite of knowledge, you stand alone, and suffer for concentrating too much on facts and their communication. Yet, through this trauma, you can discover who you are, what you are doing, and a personal transformation process can be initiated.

Pluto in the 3rd is often the sign of a very persuasive and dedicated orator. It signifies big confrontations, but big possibilities for development, too.

5. PLANETS IN THE 4TH HOUSE

SUN IN THE 4th

The urge to be yourself and to realize your potential are expressed in the area of domesticity, security, caring, cherishing, and in the forming of an inner emotional basis as the pivot of the horoscope.

A warm domestic setting, a sort of shell you can creep into, a comfortable base, is very important for you to feel you can develop best in home surroundings. You try to create an inner dwelling, a fixed emotional center which forms a safe haven. Someone with the Sun in the 4th will frequently put down deep roots with friends, family and household arrangements, and also in personal emotions. Maintaining emotional contact with your own circle means a great deal, since this placement often denotes motherly or fatherly tendencies.

But the Sun in the 4th makes you rather uncommunicative. Your own being is expressed in emotional involvements, but these must not come under attack lest you feel like a displaced person. And so you often hesitate to reveal your true feelings however intense they may be. Thus reserve and role-playing are typical of this placement. The acting profession, in which performers hide their own identity by "getting inside a character's skin," is likely to prove appealing.

Among other things, the 4th house represents the result of unconscious assimilation in the 8th and 12th houses. This causes problems, as it has an emotionally unsettling effect and the individual is very sensitive to all sorts of inner (unconscious) processes both in her- or himself and others.

MOON IN THE 4th

A need for emotional security and a disposition to protect, cherish, adapt and respond emotionally, expresses itself in the area of domestic circumstances, the inner emotional basis, and the emotions. Hence this is a very sensitive placement. The 4th house offers the Moon the chance to develop all her characteristics to the full. But, because the Moon is here, you have great need of safety and certainty on the domestic front in order to feel comfortable and in order to function freely. Thus the Moon in the 4th, like the Sun here, is well suited to creating a comfortable home-life. The Moon needs to develop an emotional basis before doing anything else. The receptive and impressionable Moon has a particularly strong influence, sometimes causing you to be hypersensitive or even mediumistic.

The caring nature of the Moon makes you more hospitable, so you keep open house for anyone seeking refuge; which you do gladly because this placement imparts an emotional need to please people. Yet there is a qualification: the Moon is a changeable principle and introduces change, not only within you but in your domestic circumstances, too. In other words, the Moon in the 4th indicates that you are responsive to changes of atmosphere and attitude in surroundings. This also indicates alterations in your domestic circumstances, such as removals, structural alterations to the dwelling, etc.

MERCURY IN THE 4th

In the 4th house, the impulse to arrange, analyze, think about things, exchange information, make connections, and communicate operates mainly in the domestic sphere and is concerned with obtaining emotional security. That there is a need to cultivate most contacts within the charmed circle of the home makes Mercury quieter than usual. You do not hurry here, there and everywhere, but prefer to develop interests indoors. Quite often Mercury in the 4th likes to collect a fund of information at home, invites people in to chat and compare notes, or builds a small library at home.

Thoughts and conversation are chiefly taken up with domestic comfort and security, and are occupied with tradition, family and the past. However, if you take those interests a stage further, you may become a student of history, the world's cultural heritage and so on. This position gives a liking not only for historical records, but also for fairy tales, sagas and legends, and even a talent for writing such stories.

Since Mercury, as a quick-moving planet, embodies for us a spirit of restlessness, it is hardly surprising that it introduces a degree of restlessness into the home — an area where peace is so essential. The effect can be seen in frequent changes of residence and constant redecorating and refurnishing, or perhaps in lots of home activities, home study, etc. Consequently, you may be jumpy or tense, but an accentuated 4th house needs inward calm and a stable emotional base.

VENUS IN THE 4th

Here, where it is associated with an astrological house signifying safety and security, the Venusian desire for beauty, harmony and reliable relationships with others lends an interest in homemaking and in creating harmonious and friendly surroundings. The home will usually have an inviting air and, with its comfortable furnishings and fine ornaments, will make the impression of being a tastefully arranged whole.

Venus in the 4th also indicates a need to settle down happily with a warm-hearted and caring partner. Since this astrological house also relates to childhood, Venus here is very intent on enjoying a harmonious relationship with parents and is willing to make compromises in order to avoid any kind of rift. If they upset you, you will probably say nothing so as not to disturb your sense of security. Of course, this lack of frankness can eventually cause problems of its own.

If Venus is well aspected, you are usually amiable and unruffled. But if the aspects are hard, undue emphasis may be placed on domestic issues or on caring for loved ones, either overprotecting them or else withholding the very warmth you need to bestow.

MARS IN THE 4th

The wish for recognition, the desire to hold your own, to prove yourself or to display executive ability and energy are found here in a reserved, protective and emotional area of life. There are several ways in which this can work out: for example, your home may be turbulent or quarrelsome. Or you may have been bullied in the parental home. The individual with Mars in the 4th tends to concentrate energies on domestic matters: on do-it-yourself projects say, or on anything about the house that requires effort.

Another, very obvious, point is this: Mars, in keeping with its nature, will make you want to have your say in the home and to do your own thing without listening to advice. This can lead to strained relationships with one or both parents.

Provided the sign in which it is also posited is in agreement, Mars in the 4th is liable to make you flare up whenever there are emotional problems, but the rest of the horoscope must decide whether you give vent to outbursts in the form of direct aggression or rage, or whether you experience a hidden build-up of inner tensions which erode your sense of emotional security. Temperamental reactions are likely however, since Mars has difficulty remaining concealed in this house.

JUPITER IN THE 4th

Your urges to expand and widen your scope will benefit your emotional basis and domestic affairs. With this position of Jupiter you will try to improve home circumstances: also the inner emotional basis will be resilient, and you will probably be well able to cope with the ups and downs of life. We might say that this placement keeps you cheerful and confident — a state of mind that makes it easy for you to attract pleasant experiences. The ability to help, care for, and encourage others is well developed. In other words, you are able to share your own inner strength.

From a material point of view, a desire to spread yourself may lead to investments in houses and land but, in any case, your thinking will be expansive and harmonious.

If Jupiter's aspects are hard, you may lack moderation, especially where home and affections are concerned. You may overspend on decorations and ornaments for the home, or may talk so proudly about circumstances and antecedents that people refuse to take you seriously. Generally speaking, however, you find it easy to share warmth and jollity with others.

SATURN IN THE 4th

When Saturn is in the 4th, restriction and limitation play a large part both in household affairs and in the inner emotional basis. There is great need for a secure home-life where you can express feelings freely. But with Saturn there, in spite of this great need, you often seem unable to let people know what you feel. You can seem cold, aloof and forbidding, yet with a coldness really begging for warmth. It is as if, for fear of being emotionally hurt, you shut yourself up in your own little bastion from which you peer through a tiny spyhole. Emotional setbacks are hard to overcome, for emotions are invariably your weakest area, the area where you feel most insecure. Therefore you can suffer from a sense of loneliness, even in a big family.

Because you quietly keep your distance, and because you have difficulty in showing feelings, others find it hard to tell what you are thinking. Saturn here makes you earnest and completely unassuming. Often you may appeal to rules and social etiquette in order to justify a rather frosty manner.

When Saturn is in the 4th, you have a great sense of responsibility for everything that goes on in your home. You appreciate family life but, because you are so reserved, others are likely to be shy with you in turn and, although you are often greatly attached to your home, it may cause you problems there. Saturn's influence can take various forms. Plunging into a busy and demanding professional life in order to escape from emotional ties or staying indoors and never going out are extreme examples of this.

URANUS IN THE 4th

When your longing to be an original, independent person is active in the area of your emotional base and domestic circumstances, Uranus indicates that you will be so open to new ideas that you are ready to set aside any feelings for the old or traditional; at least, you may behave as if this were so. Uranus, with its scintillating and changeable influence, does not make for emotional stability. Sometimes you may be very responsive; at others cold and distant: you can run through the entire gamut of emotions. Because you enjoy variety you are not bent on building a cozy, conventional nest, and your domestic scene is liable to be greatly unsettled by tensions, frequent changes of address, or even by parental quarrels affecting you in your childhood.

Nevertheless, although this placement of Uranus does not augur well for the formation of a secure inner emotional basis, you need not be wild and unsettled. If you take the trouble to come to terms with traditional values, and if new ideas are enriching rather than startling, you will have few problems expressing individuality within the family circle, and may find it possible to develop inner peace. Then, even if you remain a wanderer, wherever you have the opportunity to be yourself you will feel at home.

NEPTUNE IN THE 4th

The desire to refine and to perfect, to disassociate and to blur, and the need to dream and idealize express themselves here in the emotional life and domestic circumstances. Neptune in this house can intensify emotional rapport with the environment to such a high degree that, without being told, you can feel and know what lies behind certain situations. The position is typical of clairvoyants and mediums.

The inner life is rich and comprehensive, but not easy to grasp. You may feel compelled to express it in one or another of the arts: in writing poems or tales of the supernatural, or in music-making or painting.

Domestic circumstances can be genteel — if a mite chaotic. The house may be so cluttered with knick-knacks that it is virtually impossible to lay hands on anything in a hurry. Possibly domestic life is bedevilled by a host of emotional problems or complex emotional relationships. Sometimes the situation in the home reaches the point where everything is vague and the problems are swept under the carpet: nothing is discussed any more. Or you might belong to a family with a skeleton or two in its cupboard. Even so, the person with this placement of Neptune can idealize either past events or the current domestic situation. In either case there is a danger that the emotional basis or domestic circumstances are not being seen in their true light.

However that may be, Neptune in the 4th certainly increases the range of sensitivity, so that the home is brought in contact with the unseen and the transcendent (with parapsychological studies and phenomena, say). This can be all very spiritual, but can also result in mayhem.

PLUTO IN THE 4th

The desire for power and the need to get right down to the bottom of things are expressed here on the plane of the emotions and of domestic circumstances. With Pluto in the 4th, the emotional life is intense, and you are subject to emotional confrontations that end up by being confrontations with yourself. Pluto creates an "all-or-nothing" attitude; so you need to feel things very deeply, and expect those with whom you are involved to react with a similar depth of feeling.

Pluto in the 4th delves into the emotions of others, studies the ways in which they reveal themselves, and at the same time demands constant attention. You can be very domineering in the home, and can play on and even manipulate the feelings of other members of the family, seeming to be impelled by a desire to see how far you can go. Pluto represents fluidity or transcendence and, with Pluto here you are so sensitive that the least thing can make a big impression on you.

Because of a stubborn streak in one or both parents, they are quite likely to spend considerable time on the quiet trying to get the better of one another. Pluto in this position always means a struggle; in the final analysis this is a struggle you will also have with yourself, a struggle you provoke in order to arrive at self-confrontation.

In the 4th house the struggle is emotional, and it eventually helps to uncover your inner roots. When this happens, you may realize that the struggle was with your feelings and inner problems.

And so, Pluto can signify transcendence in the sense of developing inner conscious self-control. You may feel invulnerable if not indestructible within your own inner emotional citadel. Yet there is a danger that you will then take such pride in having conquered yourself that you will involve yourself in a sort of collective power struggle, although generally things do not go as far as this. Since the person with Pluto in the 4th enjoys studying the personal emotions as well as those of other people, you can become a fine judge of human nature.

6. PLANETS IN THE 5TH HOUSE

SUN IN THE 5th

The Sun as the ego, the drive towards self-development, is well placed in the 5th house, seeing the latter has the same aims. In this house the Sun can express its nature freely. Sun in the 5th likes to play a leading role, likes to attract attention, to take the helm and stand at the center of affairs. You yield to nobody, and usually go your own way. When the Sun is in the 5th, will-power is strong and so are vital powers, since the hold on life is tight and the attitude towards life is positive.

Associated with the above characteristics is a love of pleasure and enjoyment; you seek adventures where you can throw off restraint and simply have fun. Creativity comes in here of course, and is seen in artistry, creative leadership, having children (the pleasure of procreation), and in the production of money by speculation, etc. Adventurousness, vivacity, and risk-taking are certainly part and parcel of the influence of the Sun in the 5th. However, it is not possible to forecast whether or not this influence will be beneficial unless the rest of the chart is taken into consideration.

The 5th house represents our attitude to children and our experiences with our own children. With the Sun here there will be an optimistic attitude and a naturally supportive form of parenthood, which can help children's development, even if in somewhat authoritarian style. In fact, the individual with the Sun in the 5th can get along with children splendidly.

MOON IN THE 5th

The Moon in the 5th house gives a need to express unconscious emotional reactions in the area that lays stress on self and self-expression, and you will tend to concentrate on what makes you feel safe and happy. Like the Sun in the 5th, the Moon here encourages leadership, will-power and so on; but more because you feel comfortable when you can display these qualities, and not so much because they are part and parcel of a clear-cut identity — as they are when the Sun is in the 5th. Since it represents a craving for position and recognition, the Moon will usually accentuate the characteristics of the 5th house, so this placement indicates something of a hedonist who enjoys love affairs and perhaps having plenty of children into the bargain.

This is a placement where you try to give shape to unconscious emotional behavior by showing off in sport, entertainment and the like. It is relatively easy to captivate an audience or the general public. Therefore you can be found engaged in activities where the emotions of the masses are swayed, for example as a film maker or screen star. In a humbler sphere, you may apply to run a nursery school or playground.

Opinions are often bluntly expressed, and this can make you seem fairly fierce. You are naturally quick and impulsive but, if the aspects are hard, you may be much too rash, or may be over-keen to hammer home personal views.

MERCURY IN THE 5th

Our urge to arrange and classify, to analyze and combine, to communicate, exchange and talk things over, finds an outlet here in the area of life that emphasizes self. So self-expression and developing a sense of authority become particularly important.

Likely activities have to do with literature, writing, language, communication and so on. The playful, neutral and fickle nature of Mercury produces versatility and a desire for change, which can be experienced in all sorts of adventures and sporting activities, also in a free-flowing style of leadership. You don't set much store by sitting at the head of the table, but do expect to be heard when it is a question of keeping deliberations and discussions on the right track, of keeping the wheels of commerce turning, etc.

Mental activity is a game and you express yourself by means of that type of game. Now because this is the placement of someone who is looking for opportunities for self-expression and for being his or her own boss, a child with Mercury in the 5th house may not be so quick to learn as we might hope. He (or she) does not lack learning ability, but mental activity is an expression of himself and, as soon as the attempt is made to harness the mental processes to rules, he rebels, because he prefers to make up his own. If lessons are fun, however, these children can progress marvelously as they try to compete with others.

VENUS IN THE 5th

The need for harmony, beauty, balance and secure relationships is expressed in the area of life where we attempt to assert and give shape to our own individualities. Venusian activities take the form of hobbies. You may have an artistic streak, but other horoscope factors must decide whether you will make anything of it, since Venus is not particularly enterprising or lively in herself. She can, in fact, incline us to sloth and luxury, or to the admiration of beauty.

Venus in the house of our leisure interests and creativity can indicate amorous tendencies leading to love affairs and a taste for pleasure and romance. Venus here also likes to surround itself with warmth, elegance and the good things in life. It may have little depth.

The placement can show a need to express oneself in activities connected with the provision of comfort, pleasure and joy. Therefore you may sometimes engage in charity work — the management of a charity shop, say.

MARS IN THE 5th

Aggressiveness, self-assertion, energy and executive power, or the need to prove oneself, are expressed here in a house that itself lays stress on individuality. The result is fierceness, vigor, perseverence, the desire to come out on top, and passion. The person with Mars in this position needs to let it be known who is boss. He or she has a strong love of life and great vitality, and may well show courage in the field of sport, and in other amusements. The evidence for this may be seen in a preference for games demanding strength and muscular control plus courage and the competitive spirit. The use of sheer physical force is a means of self-satisfaction and reassurance, but also of making sexual conquests and of obtaining other forms of gratification. Mars in the 5th can certainly help you to assert yourself sexually, but this is not its only form of expression.

When there is some problem to deal with, Mars as a self-reassuring factor makes you want to meet it head-on, to put the torch to the powder magazine if necessary and, with this placement, make no bones about it but takes the initiative and go straight to the point. You are energetic, rather bossy, and determined to let nothing get the better of you. Mars here is quite a good position for those who want to carve out a career, but we have to reckon with the fact that excessive energy can work against us.

JUPITER IN THE 5th

When our desire to expand, extend and improve is deployed in the area of self-expression, the result is a kind of natural leadership. In this position, Jupiter is truly jovial and full of self-confidence, and you tend to express accordingly. Hobbies, too, bear the impress of this planet, and there is a tendency to tackle everything in a big way, with plenty of enthusiasm. Sometimes full of bright ideas, creativity is strong, and artists with this placement are often prolific. This productivity may, of course, be more basic and may reveal itself in having a big family or in caring for other people's young children.

A planet such as Jupiter, representing the need for expansion and a continual hankering after more will, in the house of fun and pleasure, be likely to cause you to strive for satisfaction in everything: you may overindulge in luxury, sexual indulgences or fine food and drink, or gambling and speculation. In any case, you like to spread yourself.

Naturally, you chafe at restrictions; you like to live freely without too many complications. You want to cut a fine figure, to enjoy the good things of life and to share them with your friends.

SATURN IN THE 5th

The planet that induces us to demarcate and limit, and the house representing our need to express ourselves, are two factors difficult to reconcile. The powerful urge to express and let it be seen that we possess a well-rounded personality is hampered by a dread of drawing undue attention and by the feeling that we ought to curb desires. This 5th house can often be very ambiguous. On the one hand we hold ourselves in check and make sure (consciously or unconsciously) that we do not quite fulfill potential or enjoy ourselves too freely; on the other, we want to let the outside world know very clearly the powerful person we could be if we chose. And this uncertainty can make us fretful and insecure because we take the way in which we express ourselves seriously. The 5th house always reveals what we enjoy doing and, with Saturn placed within its borders, what we enjoy doing will be something serious, down-to-earth and conventional.

Even in the field of sports, games, and amusements, the behavior is dedicated and a little apprehensive. Either the individual will excel in these things or will avoid them and will withdraw into a shell. This placement is quite often associated with childhood problems; especially with a lack of understanding on the part of the parents. The child may not be appreciated or wanted by the father or mother. From the earliest years, a need for support and recognition has been unfulfilled, and this has become a sore spot. Therefore, the individual can sometimes appear to be hard, cold and egotistical, but this is nothing but a strangled cry for recognition and appreciation. He demands much of himself and others all because of his uncertainty and earnestness.

But, after the hard learning process represented by this placement, the individual is likely to develop into a solid, sober, well-rounded adult with an unimpeachable, serious, reliable and robust attitude toward life.

URANUS IN THE 5th

With Uranus in the 5th you need to display independence, individuality and originality in the area in which we take the initiative and try to structure our lives. You may appear ingenious and inventive, hobbies will be out of the ordinary, and you prefer to develop unimpeded by old-fashioned conventions. Uranus in the 5th has no scruples about going your own way without so much as a "by your leave." You have flair, and the courage to do original things, to break through existing borders and to introduce fresh ideas — some of which may be too Utopian. With Uranus in the 5th you may seek to express yourself in ways that are unusual, unfamiliar and eccentric, and, sometimes provocative. Hence, this position of Uranus may indicate that you go your own way in a conceited frame of mind, relying on intuition and on sudden brainwaves. You may enter the field of technology or electronics, or the occult (fortune-telling by cards, astrology, etc.). There may also be flashes of creativity; or fifth-house matters such as love-affairs, children and hobbies arrive on the scene very hurriedly.

Independent and unconventional tendencies can sometimes express in sexual perversions, or unusual sexual interests, but although Uranus can contribute to these trends, it does not confirm them unless there is evidence elsewhere in the chart. In any event, Uranus here may indicate an original view of love.

NEPTUNE IN THE 5th

When the need to dissociate, blur, refine, perfect and idealize but also to undermine things or to immerse in them are expressed in the 5th house, there is certainly a desire to give shape to your life, but it seems as if in one way or another this concept is difficult to visualize. Neptune here makes you very sensitive, and can also bestow great artistic talent. Where amusement or love is concerned, Neptune here is idealistic but also unrealistic. You may be too quick to put on rose-tinted glasses and become super-romantic, especially when affections are involved. Love affairs are not seen clearly enough and can end in disappointment and disillusion when Neptune is in the 5th. However, you do have a gift for creative self-expression. You delight in day-dreams, fantasies and the like, and need to realize at least some of yourself in your dreams. The rest of the chart must be studied to see how capable you are of making these dreams actual. Sometimes you do not even consider it necessary to realize them.

In some ways, Neptune here makes it hard to express in a solid way. It is not impossible to do so, but the process is difficult to handle, and you may have problems with experiencing yourself as a personality. Neptune in this house can refine the personality but can also make it more insecure.

PLUTO IN THE 5th

The need to win power and recognition and to bring the lowest layers of the inner man or woman to the surface and use them for self-expression in the 5th house imparts a strongly developed ego sense or, at least, your activities spring from a sense of personal identity. Pluto represents transcendence, fluidity, an all-or-nothing attitude, and that can mean a very concentrated and grimly determined approach to anything you want to accomplish. You like to take the reins in your own hands and keep them there.

Here is a powerful but not an easy-going way of giving form to oneself. Pluto in this house is liable to keep talking about a need for leadership, authority and so on. Even the mildest chart cannot disguise the power of Pluto here. You will make up your mind to live your own life and go your own way. Others may join you provided they do so on your terms.

You live life with passionate intensity. The love of life inherent in the 5th house is deeply felt and expresses itself forcefully in all 5th house activities: love-affairs, pleasure, sports, games, hobbies and self-assertion; and here, too, Pluto brings the most buried layers of the personality to the surface.

People with Pluto in the 5th do not play for the fun of it; they play to win. In point of fact they carry on a running battle with their own powers. They are continually finding out more about themselves and are seldom satisfied. Their feeling of self-importance is so great that in all the affairs of this house they want to do better than others. They go all out to excel and to become an undisputed authority in their chosen field. But this desire for success at all costs makes them so pent up inside that they become isolated. Pluto in the 5th can do just what it wants, but this is a volcano placement and needs to become conscious.

7. PLANETS IN THE 6TH HOUSE

SUN IN THE 6th

With the Sun in the 6th house, the ego, the symbol of the road to optimum development, occupies the house of self-analysis and self-criticism, of service, and of sickness and health. The Sun in the 6th indicates that you will try to shape your life by making yourself useful by helping others and, above all, by working.

We often meet people with the Sun in the 6th in one or other of the service industries, or as a social workers, physician or the like. For the Sun as an intrinsically free spirit, by no means points to subordinate work but often to self-employment, and the self-employed can benefit greatly from this position.

As the house of analysis and criticism, the 6th house makes you critical both of yourself and others; sometimes you are a perfectionist. Discrimination can be exercised in the areas of hygiene and diet, and you may read about these subjects to look after your health. But your nature can also reveal itself in a rather reserved and timid attitude.

The Sun in the 6th makes you sensitive to criticism from others and even in spite of yourself the ego responds to criticism in a very direct way. Physical reactions, too, are usually present when the Sun is here. Tensions and conflicts, internal and external, are reflected in the body. Disease can result as a form of adjustment. Many astrological texts tell us that the Sun in the 6th indicates a struggle with rather poor health. We accept this, with the added insight that it is due largely to the psychic warning mechanism just mentioned. The body is a gauge here for the state of the psyche. And that means that someone with the Sun in the 6th who goes his own way and develops according to his own nature will not, generally speaking, need to fear for his health, since he will not be living under stress.

MOON IN THE 6th

Our unconscious emotional behavior, our need for safety and the attitude we automatically adopt when we feel insecure encourage helpfulness and service to others when the 6th house is concerned. You feel safe and comfortable in regular employment. You like to make yourself useful and are easily satisfied with a subordinate position. But, because the Moon is so variable, feelings about your work and situation can alter too, and this can mean several changes of employment if there is nothing in the remainder of the chart to suggest otherwise. Your physical condition can also fluctuate. The Moon represents great sensitivity to "atmospheres," even though the reactions here are secondary ones. It is likely, therefore, that the state of health will vary with emotional ups and downs, and that you will be more susceptible to disease at some times than at others. Like the Sun, the Moon in the 6th can serve as a measure of your psychic well-being.

The instinct to care and cherish, also symbolized by the Moon, can find an outlet here in the fields of nursing, medicine and dietetics, and in those of animal husbandry, veterinary work and so on. With the Moon in the 6th however, you may be more likely to work as an assistant or employee than to be in charge of the enterprise.

Because the 6th is the house of self-criticism, self-analysis, order, usefulness and practical work, the Moon here will like everything well arranged and carried out according to schedule. You'll do everything in your power to ensure punctuality. And you exact the same high standards from yourself. You are very precise, painstaking and analytical and, in this respect, suitable for scientific or other detailed research; but you do need someone to spur you on.

MERCURY IN THE 6th

The dissecting, arranging, cataloging, and combining capacity represented by Mercury produces a very critical attitude when the planet is in the house that has to do with analysis. You have a keen mind and a gift for synthesis — no detail escapes your eagle eye. Mercury's reactions in this house are not quick but they are very precise. This rather inhibits the urge to communicate; but the gift for keeping people in touch with what is going on is still present to some extent, and you can exploit it by becoming a merchant or a shopkeeper.

As the possessor of an analytical planet in an analytical house, you can be a very logical and systematic thinker, especially along practical lines. Occupations centered on combining, analyzing, writing, and communicating (other than the communication of self) are very suitable with Mercury in the 6th house.

Sometimes you can be ultra-critical and too much of a perfectionist; this can prevent you from finishing what you start. You are always concentrating on details and losing sight of the whole: something which is potentially counterproductive. Nevertheless, you do feel impelled to become fully involved in everything that offers itself, especially when it has to do with work and service. You approach the question of sickness and health just as thoroughly. Because Mercury governs mobility and nervous energy, the nervous system is prone to disease. When you remain healthy, you may be nervy or tense due to your constant alertness, and this may need work.

VENUS IN THE 6th

The need for a secure partnership and the desire to experience harmony and beauty express themselves in the 6th house in a practical, matter-of-fact way. In this area of work and work environment Venus in the 6th likes to create a pleasant atmosphere and lays stress on the desirability of harmonious conditions.

Quite often, a love-affair with a colleague starts to blossom; but you may be wary where romance is concerned. Often you find it easier to bestow warmth than to respond to warmth from others; the sign in which Venus is posited will give more precise information on this point.

Venus in the 6th creates a liking for activities relating to harmony and beauty, luxury and fine things. The world of fashion may beckon, and so may the world of entertainment. You are interested in expressing only what is warm, attractive and pleasant at work, and hope to help others by doing so. There are all sorts of possibilities in this respect. However, Venus sometimes encourages idleness and sloth, so that the person with this placement is quite likely to work at a fairly slow rate. On the other hand, you may work neatly or settle in easily at your place of employment.

Self-criticism is not a strong point and, because you are often helpful and indulgent toward others, co-workers are reluctant to criticize, but may come round to doing so eventually.

Health is generally good, although over-indulgence in such things as sugar could impair it. The body seems to reflect the needs of Venus in a balanced way: a person with this placement does not easily fall ill and recovers quickly (provided, of course, there are no hard aspects to Venus).

MARS IN THE 6th

Our energy and executive ability, our feelings of self-importance, and need to set ourselves apart find an outlet here in the work situation. You are industrious and have a great zest for work, being quick, energetic, without being slapdash or undisciplined. But because Mars does represent feelings of self-importance and, in this position, can indicate possible resistance from colleagues, this is an especially good placement for those who enjoy a measure of independence in their work or have a clear-cut, individual task, separate from what co-workers are doing. For the person with Mars in the 6th will want to force the staff to work harder or will rap their knuckles over any inaccuracies.

Not infrequently, these people work too hard, although health can usually stand the strain. Of course, they may succumb to illness from time to time, but powers of recovery are good. In some instances, the placement may mean that they have a high-risk occupation and may suffer injuries — but this is not inevitable.

Disease, whether physical or mental in origin, is usually burnt up by a high fever of short duration. Illnesses are acute and go as quickly as they come (unless there are contrary indications elsewhere in the chart).

Mars is not a planet that encourages self-criticism. This individual prefers to throw himself into his work and into service for others. In fact he may exhibit a rather aggressive sort of helpfulness, and will meet with a few rebuffs before he realizes where he is going wrong and changes his tactics.[11]

JUPITER IN THE 6th

Generally speaking, the Jupitarian urge to expand, enlarge and improve brings a jovial, cheerful and enthusiastic attitude to the affairs of this house. But, under the influence of Jupiter, you "put two and two together," forming your own opinions, and prefer to go your own way. Since this is the house of service, your independent attitude can produce problems. Nevertheless, the person with Jupiter in the 6th will seldom laze about doing nothing; interest in work is too great for that. You do insist on one point, however: what you do must be meaningful. Only then can you get down to it properly — dull work will never satisfy.

Jupiter in the house of health and disease will generally bring good health and excellent powers of recovery. But overeating, indulging in candies, etc., can undermine the constitution and sow the seeds of serious illness. With this placement, we should not expect the body to function as an indicator of psychic well-being: it is usually fit enough to resist psychological stress. Therefore these people can keep active in a harsh environment. In fact, their ability to do so may make them slow to adjust, and they may cling to out-moded work-patterns. This ties in with Jupiter's disinterest in (self-)criticism

---

[11]Whether the native will change or not will probably depend on his or her degree of intelligence. Human beings have various faults and failings and for many of us the answer to the question, "Will they ever learn?" is, sadly, "No." *Tr.*

or fine analysis. Jupiter is the planet of broad vision and of synthesis and attaches scant value to minor details or to anything that looks like hair-splitting. What is more, the personal vision of life will clash with social norms and values on occasion. These individuals do not always take kindly to criticism. Possible opinionatedness and willfulness can get them into trouble in spite of essentially positive attitudes towards work.

SATURN IN THE 6th

The difficult processes of restraint and limitation are not particularly helpful in the house of health, disease, work, and working conditions. There is a chance that Saturn here will weaken the health and the powers of recovery, but above all is likely to produce limitations in employment.

Yet the influence does not always have to be so stark. Saturn, as our power to structure things, will introduce form and structure into this area of life too. We cannot expect quick work from people with Saturn in the 6th, but nor should we expect them to do anything by halves! Saturn in this position makes people serious, conscientious and thorough. This tallies with the fact that the 6th house is a sensitive area where Saturn is concerned, and can provide a basis for possible overcompensations.

Special care will be taken regarding work. Usually these people are much attracted by anything to do with the body and its functions, and with such associated matters as diet. But they do run the risk of looking at too many details. Once they lose sight of the broad outlines and of the relationships between the parts and the whole, of the difference between the goal and the means for achieving the goal, or of that between body and spirit, then they can fall ill in spite of precautions.

They display dogged determination, but will frequently get into awkward situations or will overload themselves with responsibilities — although it is also in the cards that they will face set-backs in finding work. That is to say they are so keyed-up over work that inner tensions are reflected in external circumstances. Until they learn to handle this weak point they may not experience good health or a secure job.

The thought-processes of people with Saturn in the 6th can be analytical, economical and practical. Their criticisms are often sound. Nevertheless, they have difficulty relating to the self, and self-criticism, or being the butt of someone else's criticism is very painful. Consequently, they will suffer a number of rebuffs before they can or will revise the self-image.

URANUS IN THE 6th

With Uranus here, you will give vent to originality, independence and individuality in the sphere of employment. Uranus puts you under a degree of internal strain, and makes you restless, active and changeable.

With Uranus in this house, difficulty is often experienced in sticking to work. You may be easily distracted by novelties, and being naturally inventive, would feel frustrated by a monotonous, undemanding job. Much better is varied, innovative work calling for resourcefulness and ingenuity. Since Uranus is associated with such things as electricity and technology, you may be attracted to work in related fields.

Incidentally, the placement is not ideal for underlings: you are too much of an individualist. In subordinate positions you are quite likely to ignore instructions and do things in your own way. If unable to inject some originality into what you do, you will find it hard to concentrate on either work or lessons.

Uranus indicates an unpredictable attitude to criticism and self-criticism. You can certainly be critical, if only by fits and starts. With Uranian intuition, you can sometimes see aspects that are useful for work; yet are not so good at planning. You may be quite prepared to listen to friendly advice, but it is unlikely to sink in very far.

In matters of health, this tendency to be "different from the rest" and to cross boundaries will be noticeable. The person with Uranus in the 6th house may sometimes suffer from a sudden physical reaction which is hard to diagnose and can recover just as suddenly. And because, like Mercury, Uranus rules the nerves, it can produce certain nervous conditions or unexpected motor disturbances — often coincidentally.

People with Uranus in the 6th are not more susceptible than normal to disease; they just fall ill without warning, usually because of restlessness and tension. What is more, they often respond well to alterative medicine. To the ordinary general practitioner they can pose something of a problem, due to their strong opinions and completely original approach to their own bodies.

NEPTUNE IN THE 6th

The dissociating, refining, blurring, idealizing, but also chaotic influence of this planet will operate in a rather strange way in the areas of work, working conditions, sickness and health. Your sensitivity, both physical and mental, is very great, which can prove useful in your occupation, since you go by feelings a great deal and have an instinct for knowing what to do — something that is particularly helpful in the service industries and in medical work. In certain cases, you may have "healing hands" or a magnetic touch. Sometimes, however, you can make yourself ill by your imagination, but can also cure yourself with autosuggestion. In addition, this is a stimulating position for the artistic professions. Neptune here is very unpredictable with regard to material concerns, but it can leave its mark on a whole host of things.

In the area of work there is a fair amount of idealism, and you tend to look through rose-colored glasses which make matters look better than they really are. You are easily swayed and may let yourself be hitched to some bogus ideal, or else exploit others. Any resulting disappointment can engender an escapist attitude, especially as the boundary between the real and the unreal is already rather indistinct.

The powers of discrimination and analysis are not well developed when Neptune is in the 6th, so there is no question of discerning self-criticism.

PLUTO IN THE 6th

Our power-drive, our need to get to the bottom of things and our wish to make things fluid and to transcend them, gives the Pluto in the 6th person intense energy and enormous perseverance in finishing whatever needs finishing. You always want to be just that little bit better; not much escapes you and you complete everything as well as possible. A sense of self-importance and craving for power involve you in ambitious schemes, which usually succeed in spite of the fact that they can arouse considerable opposition from colleagues. You can easily isolate yourself in this way; work is one place where self-confrontations will take place.

Pluto here is therefore not an easy placement as far as collaborating with others is concerned. You prefer to work alone and take work very seriously. The occupation frequently has to do with the delving quality of Pluto: research, psychology, occultism, etc.

Because you have a kind of all-or-nothing attitude regarding work, it is not inconceivable that several times during the career you will balance on the knife-edge of overwork, and your health may be undermined. The confrontations at work can also produce transcendent insights together with a wider view of how you fit in this area. Nevertheless, Pluto in the 6th always gives the feeling that there is more to discover, more to analyze.

Sometimes this placement bestows paranormal healing powers (which must, however, be confirmed by other horoscope factors) and a deep concern with health care.

Criticism, analysis and self-criticism will be accepted when you are in tune with your own insights. Sometimes, too, you will consider the results of your work or service more important than any criticism levelled at the (compulsive) way you tackle it. But when you see and accept that the criticism is fundamentally sound, you can deal with those things that gave rise to it.

8. PLANETS IN THE 7TH HOUSE

SUN IN THE 7th

The effect of the Sun, as the ego, in the house of the other person — especially the partner or some person with whom we closely collaborate — is twofold. On the one hand, we can achieve self-realization only when we have a deep understanding with someone — probably our spouse or cohabiter. On the other hand, the ego has such a powerful effect here that it stamps itself on the relationship. We want to express ourselves in the relationship and have things our own way in it. This ambiguity creates all kinds of problems, especially in regard to the areas where we are important and to where the territory of the other person begins.

Because people with the Sun in the 7th have this problem as an innate feature, they are able to understand a matter from various angles and like to look at everything from two opposite points of view. They can, indeed, work to create balance and harmony in the environment. Collaboration is possible only when they have a clear-cut terrain in which to prove their worth; not so much out of ambition, as out of the desire to develop and win recognition. If they have a cooperative circle in which they can be reasonably sure of themselves, then they will prove reliable.

Should there be many 7th house conflicts, the Sun can sometimes have an extreme effect, such as tyrannical behavior towards the marriage partner, or marriage to a partner who is domineering. The 7th house often supplies information about what we are seeking in a partner and about what may materialize from our search. With the Sun here, we seek someone on whom we can lean, someone with a strongly developed ego. That this requirement can conflict with our own ego-sense, which likewise takes shape in the 7th house, explains the need for (inner) balance given by this house placement.

THE MOON IN THE 7th

The Moon, as a representative of unconscious emotional behavior and as a symbol of the behavior we adopt whenever we feel insecure, gives in the sphere of partnership and collaboration an emotional need for another person, especially when we do not feel completely safe. In such cases the lunar behavior is always strongly emphasized.

With the Moon in the 7th, we look for someone who is caring and perhaps rather maternal, but also for someone with whom we can share our feelings and for whom we ourselves can care. We are always ready to find in our opposite number an outlet for our need to be caring and, in doing so, we can become very motherly.

The person with the Moon in the 7th needs confidentiality, intimacy and emotional warmth in all personal relationships, and also needs to share everything with the other individual. But this mutual sharing is governed by the emotions, so that the relationship can vary like the phases of the Moon. Other horoscope factors will have to point in the same direction but, in principle, the Moon in the 7th indicates emotional responses to the partner—sometimes violent, sometimes very loving.

The Moon also bestows the ability to adapt, and when in the 7th it points to quick and easy adaptability both in the partner and in others. When joining in with friends, at parties and entertainments, say, a person with this placement willingly accepts some task and appears to become thoroughly immersed in it; but often this is nothing more than a front, and here too the rest of the horoscope will inform us if an inner flexibility lies behind it.

MERCURY IN THE 7th

Our need to analyze, arrange, classify, communicate and combine is applied in the 7th house to the relationship with a partner, and shows what we expect from this relationship. Mercury, as the representative of the intellect and the reasoning powers, creates a desire for a partner with whom we can converse, someone who will discuss in a logical and matter-of-fact way any matters that may arise. We will probably try to get to know a prospective partner by talking about intellectual interests, instead of in the more romantic way. As a lively and stimulating factor, Mercury will encourage us to look for liveliness and stimulation in a partnership—if we can stay steady long enough to settle down!

People with Mercury in the 7th will examine a partner critically; sometimes too critically, so that there is a clash of attitudes and opinions. If there are conflicting aspects affecting the 7th house, then there is a chance that we have a fault-finding partner or are fault-finding ourselves. Sometimes such a placement indicates life-long discord with the partner. A young partner is probable; either younger in years or less mature in character.

With Mercury here, the intellectual, analytical and communicative faculties come to the fore in any relationship, and its presence in the house can reflect a fair degree of restlessness.

VENUS IN THE 7th

Venus, as the desire for beauty, harmony and balance, and for emotional and material security in relationships, operates in a harmonizing and diplomatically friendly way in the 7th house area of partnerships and collaboration. Venus expresses the need to help relationships to run as smoothly as possible, and to take care that the general atmosphere remains unruffled and that appearances are kept up. Therefore someone with Venus in the 7th is often more inclined to hush problems up than to discuss them publicly, because open discussion might reveal that things are more unstable than he or she would wish and, anyway, with the planet in this position being diplomatic is preferred to meeting difficulties head on.

Hence the person with Venus in this house could be well suited to all forms of collaboration and living together. The other side of the coin is that he or she will have small relish for solving life's inevitable problems. Consequently he or she places too much responsibility in the hands of the partner to save trouble and ends up always having to do what the partner wants and never getting permission to do what he or she wants.

Venus here tends to seek a friendly and tactful partner, someone who moves easily in society, and so Venus has traditionally been regarded as an excellent placement when in the 7th. But if the aspects are hard, the result can be laziness, love of ease, and superficiality both in the partner and in the person who has this Venus placement.

MARS IN THE 7th

Our self-assertiveness, executive ability and energy and the need to prove ourselves can, when thrust into the area of contracts and relationships, give rise to strife and conflicts, but also to activities in which we involve our opposite number. Traditionally this is regarded as a thorny position for Mars, because the planet introduces a brusqueness and pushiness which easily disturb the balance of the 7th house and may occasion differences of opinion, quarrels and fits of temper.

Mars in the 7th is really not such a suitable position for collaboration, because you will want to take the initiative and will sometimes do things without bothering to inform your partner. Nevertheless, in this house, Mars prompts you to look for a partner with martial qualities — for someone, in a word, who is aggressive and blunt, or simply active and enterprising, or anything between the two extremes.

Mars, as self-assertiveness, contributes nothing to a life of ease when it is in the house of partnership: as soon as you throw yourself heart and soul into a joint effort, into living together, you run the risk of asserting yourself so much that you leave the other person with little room to maneuver. If your partner, as is very likely, exhibits one or two strong Martian traits, some fairly vivid quarrels may result. But such tempests certainly need not end in divorce; they may merely clear the air, so that the relationship can be constantly renewed. Similar partners can grow very fond of one another, and the cherishing of a passionate affection for the partner is another quality of Mars in the 7th.

JUPITER IN THE 7th

The need for broadening, expansion and improvement, and also religious and spiritual needs, will express themselves in the 7th in some way that involves the partner. The attitude toward the partner will be jovial and optimistic, but expectations are high. The partner must have something to offer, either material or spiritual. In the 7th house, Jupiter's expansiveness seeks enrichment through or with the help of the partner; an enrichment that may be obtained in various ways.

You need a partner with whom you can philosophize and hold stimulating conversations; or a partner through whom you can gain access to higher levels of society (in the older

books this was interpreted as "marrying above one's station").
Sometimes, too, you may have several affairs at the same time
or in quick succession — but confirmation of this must come
from elsewhere in the chart.

With Jupiter in the 7th you can in general show to better
advantage through your partner, and thus function better, create a stronger financial base and so on. Jupiter does, in fact,
favor cooperation in marriage. On the other hand, if there are
conflicts in the horoscope, there may be a love of pleasure,
extravagance and the like, either at the partner's expense or on
the part of a spendthrift spouse.

SATURN IN THE 7th

The inclination to limit and define, to demarcate and shape,
will confront you with your personal weak point when it is
found in the house relating to partnerships. Cooperation and
partnership will be a difficult terrain because you are trying to
give shape to something that is your weak point, and this produces feelings of anxiety. Therefore, with Saturn in the 7th,
you often experience disappointments in love and partnership;
to some extent due to your own reserved and secretive behavior. This does not always mean that you marry late in life.
Marriage at a very early age, as an overcompensation, is sometimes found with this position of Saturn; as is marriage or
partnership with someone older or more mature.

Saturn in this house has its good side too, however. If you
can learn to be less apprehensive, then solidity, faithfulness,
durability and reliability can come to the fore. These qualities
will be sought in others, and you will display them toward your
partner. Lasting relationships are frequently found with Saturn
here but, to begin with, there will be one or two disappointments to get over.

Nevertheless, Saturn will always mean that some of the
form and structure that you give to yourself will be borrowed

from the partnership and thus will be determined or colored by the partner; in other words, you are inclined to choose someone of a Saturnian type or, anyway, someone who is melancholy, moody and so on. He or she can also be tyrannical and imperious and will keep you tied down as much as possible. But this extreme behavior will eventually produce a changed attitude toward the (inner) partner, which should eventually lead to an improvement in the structure of the partnership. Alternatively, you may find a partner who steers a steady course through life with a clear idea of what he or she wants, and expects you to play a supporting role. Therefore this placement need not be so dramatic as the older writers would have us believe.

URANUS IN THE 7th

The urge to develop as an individual, your craving for independence and originality and your wish for renewal do not seem very compatible with the qualities of the 7th house: living and sharing with a second person. Although Uranus indicates a desire for freedom and unconventionality, this need not stand in the way of a relationship. Any relationship is unlikely to be a conventional one, of course, but Uranus here is typical of a modern marriage to or cohabitation with someone who is friend and partner at one and the same time. The individual with Uranus in the 7th may well choose a rather unconventional, not to say provocative and eccentric partner.

The ideal of the person with Uranus in the 7th is for each partner to carry on with personal development and for each to retain a private area in life, while, at the same time, the two of them do much together. If this is not agreed, and your partner ties you down so that you no longer have any freedom of movement, you will not be able to develop and will probably display the explosive side of Uranus.

When Uranus is in the 7th, the partnership is seldom boring, since there is always something new happening. The placement can be very stimulating when freedom is enjoyed within certain limits. The partnership can then contribute a great deal to your development. You just have to remember that Uranus produces tensions every now and then: it is a factor that can make you easily irritated and full of nervous reaction, and can lead you to do things by sudden fits and starts.

NEPTUNE IN THE 7th

The propensity to disassociate, blur and make things fluid, but also to refine and improve form, operates here in the sphere of partnership and collaboration. Neptune in this position can mean that the partner is readily put on a pedestal and idealized, and that his or her real nature is not discovered until later. This is why Neptune in the 7th is considered a bad omen for marriage. Inevitably, the projection of the ideal and "heavenly" partner is doomed to disappointment as Neptune performs its typical undermining function.

Hence Neptune in this position acts like a pair of rose-colored glasses, though its effect need not always be baneful. The planet can also refine and improve and, when in the 7th, strives to produce the perfect marriage. If you search blindly, disappointment will be unavoidable but, if you keep in touch with reality, Neptune here can give a marriage that is not rooted in everyday values or material security, but in spiritual union, in which the almost telepathic link between the two partners goes beyond the exchange of concrete information.

The person with Neptune in the 7th is likely to look for a Neptunian partner. Their Neptunian quality can be intellectual (spiritual or metaphysical) but also difficult (bad habits, alcoholism, drug addiction, unfaithfulness), all according to other placements both in your chart and in that of the partner.

So Neptune here can serve notice of problems but, on the other hand, offers the possibility of a special union which may indeed be utterly romantic.

PLUTO IN THE 7th

Pluto, as a love of power and ability to resurrect suppressed and hidden factors, has a far-reaching effect on all connections, partnerships and working relationships with others. It is the planet that confronts us with ourselves and, with this placement, the confrontation happens in connection with our partner.

When Pluto is in the 7th, we are likely to choose a partner with definite Plutonian traits, with whom therefore we immediately come into a degree of conflict; or else we ourselves have these traits and want to impose our will on the other person and make them conform to our wishes. Generally, it is a question of six of one and half-a-dozen of the other where this kind of behavior is concerned. The relationship is very intense. We are very attracted by the other person and usually engage in an unconscious struggle with the partner to see who can gain the upper hand. At times a relationship of this sort throws up so much buried material from deep down in the psyche that it takes years to assimilate all the consequences. Our attitudes toward partners brings us face to face with the unconscious in all its facets.

If our tyrannical behavior becomes part of the power struggle between self and partner, open conflict is unavoidable as the partner strikes back. And then we are thrown entirely on our own resources. Pluto in the 7th will engender a tremendous inner revolution through experiences with partners or colleagues.

When the nature has matured through some such confrontation, Pluto here can forge an intense union in which deep but ripened emotional energy can work in a positive way. And, when older, former difficult experiences can give the ability to help others who are suffering from troubled relationships.

9. PLANETS IN THE 8TH HOUSE

SUN IN THE 8th

With the Sun in the 8th, the desire for self-realization and self-development seeks an outlet in the area of the hidden and the unconscious, of life and death, and of the core of things. The Sun in the 8th tends to shrink from observation but is nevertheless very active and inquisitive. You are not so much interested in externals, but want to know the essence of reality.

You keep ferreting about to get to the bottom of things, even if you are on the completely wrong track. And so you can sit brooding: all the more so as you do not usually commit yourself until you have carried thoughts far enough. Sometimes it is impossible to understand what is going on inside and you may even do a bit of play-acting to prevent others from doing so. Also you can seem rather cold and distant, but are in fact drawn with great emotional intensity to things.

You are likely to keep delving into what motivates yourself and other people. Thus the nature of the Sun here is to create an interest in psychology, psychiatry and the veiled world of parapsychology and the occult, etc. In a more material sense, this proclivity shows itself in professions such as archaeology, deep-sea diving, surgery and so on.

All this profound searching often confronts the person whose Sun is in the 8th with the transitoriness and finiteness of things, so that you become acutely aware of death in its various guises. This can turn you into a gloomy cynic but, at the same time, may incite you to defy death by doing some imperishable deed or by becoming someone famous.

The Sun in the 8th is compatible with a sense of self-importance, not because of social position but rather as an affirmation of the conquest of oneself. Probably you will seldom know contentment: there are always new challenges to face. You will sometimes have to struggle against inferiority feelings for which you try to overcompensate, but the creative urge and capacity for enquiry are great. You need to devote yourself to whatever is engaging your attention, to throw your very life into it so to speak.

MOON IN THE 8th

The emotional need for security will find little to console it in the 8th house of confrontation with hidden and repressed factors. This means that with the Moon here your search for security expresses in an area of life that can make you uneasy. Therefore you are subject to great restlessness, even though this will not be very apparent from the outside.

The Moon in the 8th also means a many-sided interest in everything to do with the hidden and the occult but in a more dependent way than when the Sun is there: the Sun in this house encourages research into occult phenomena, while the Moon encourages a wish to experience them, which points to mediumistic tendencies, etc.

If badly aspected in this house, the Moon as a sensitive and emotional factor can sometimes indicate uncontrollable passions and even hysteria. Yet these very intense feelings can make a powerful impression on the outside world and can manifest themselves as a great ability to express oneself—not so much verbally as in facial expression and gesture. Mimicry, imitation and also the femme fatale all come under the Moon in the 8th.

MERCURY IN THE 8th

Our need to research, analyze, combine and arrange facts will, with Mercury in the 8th, be directed toward everything that is concealed and repressed, and to the origin and core of things. Therefore, this is a fine placement for Mercury research in general. The planet, which makes us naturally inquisitive and thirsty for knowledge, will in this instance seek to bring everything to light. So the placement is favorable both for detective work and for biological or chemical research, for example, also for psychology and psychiatry.

Mercury in the 8th can be fascinated by everything lurking below the surface and can bestow great powers of concentration in one's search, as well as a firm sense of purpose. In the 8th, Mercury, so moveable and easily distracted when in other houses, is more determined, less communicative and more analytical, causing one to seek to understand and solve psychic and hidden problems. If there are hard aspects, this person could "drive himself mad" and become nervy and neurotic.

VENUS IN THE 8th

Our need for emotional and material security in relationships with others, and our need for beauty and harmony, will have an intense character in the 8th house. Venus will go to the extreme in a relationship in order to find out what the other person is made of. At one end of the scale, we may see a powerful sensuality and sexuality, at the other sensuous artistry. In particular, the emotional life is deep, and much is unconsciously demanded of the partner. We want to experience indissoluble unity with the partner. This can produce great warmth, but there is also a danger of jealousy and blind passion.

When the capacity for love seeks an outlet in the sphere of life and death, questions concerning the latter play a part in a relationship. This can reveal itself (though not invariably) in the belief in a karmic union, also in *crime passionel* or in suicide, following a stormy relationship or unrequited love. The intense, often sexual feelings of people with Venus in the 8th should not be underestimated. If we find it hard to realize ourselves, we may make every endeavor to repress everything in a Venusian manner by abandoning ourselves to pleasure, luxury and sloth.

MARS IN THE 8th

When aggressive self-preservation, executive ability and energy seek to realize themselves in the area of life and death, of what is suppressed, unconscious or hidden, one can display great passion when in love or when one wants to know, experience or attain something *per se*. Mars can cut like a knife through what lies concealed and must be brought to the surface; so this is a good position for surgeons and dentists, who are always physically engaged in work of this sort—and also for butchers.

In another respect, Mars in the 8th impels one to take risks and to discover the limits of one's courage. The urge to be active is considerable but, if there are hard aspects, this can result in uncontrolled activity, recklessness and sometimes in ruthlessness. The rash behavior can lead to accidents.

Like Venus in the 8th, Mars here can indicate great sensuality and sexuality. The creative urge given by the 8th house is expended chiefly in proving oneself, one's strengths, or abilities.

JUPITER IN THE 8th

Here spiritual and religious needs and a desire to expand seek realization in the area of life and death, and of the suppressed and hidden. Jupiter gives the need to view all problems from a psychological, parapsychological, and occult standpoint.

Hence this is a good placement for psychologists, and also for physicians who are able to effect cures based on insight into the mental causes of physical ailments.

Jupiter's expansiveness can enable you to take a broad view of your own problems and those of others. You like to look at each matter in as wide a context as possible in order to come to terms with it. By doing so, you can get things in perspective and can meet life with a smile. The planet in this position also indicates trust in another person's ability, and you have no problem relying on experts such as the physician or psychiatrist.

But Jupiter exaggerates and, by wanting to get too much out of life, you can magnify your own abilities until you lose all sense of proportion. Generally speaking, however, you face problems with confidence and do not mind sorting them out thoroughly — so you are not likely to be a candidate for neurosis. The main fault is a tendency to take things too easily. When this happens, Jupiter has a broadening and confidence-building effect but does not encourage the search for those true treasures which are deeply hidden and hard to obtain. And so you may see nothing of importance beyond material possessions.

SATURN IN THE 8th

When the drive to develop the ego, to carve out a clear identity, and to experience and accept one's limitations are expressed in the area of life and death and of those things that are hidden and repressed, the person concerned will feel his or her vulnerability very intensely. Saturn is a barrier that must overcome in order to live. The 8th house impels one to take risks in order to make headway, and that is something the conservative Saturnine nature can do only after a severe inner struggle. Saturn finds it hard to surrender either sexually or in life itself, and can therefore make a rather cold impression. Often one will seem somewhat hypochondriac and melancholy. The person with Saturn in the 8th often perambulates complexes and problems in front of him. Not that he dare not deal with them — when he starts to tackle them, he does so with great thoroughness — but that he experiences considerable difficulty in seeing what these problems really are. Deep-rooted anxiety over sharing feelings (sexual or otherwise) with anyone else will all too easily be projected on the other person, especially as he feels the need to overcompensate.

You are likely to have your share of confrontations and difficult experiences, sometimes in the form of hard knocks but sometimes in a more subtle form. He can even go so far, in overcompensation, as to travel the world in the guise of a hedonist or "Don Juan": on the outside enjoying himself but on the inside lonely, the overcompensating behavior being merely a mask.

With Saturn in the 8th you will feel vulnerable and insecure with regard to pleasure in life, the surrender of yourself to another, and the sharing of something with the community (whether this something is feelings or possessions). Defensive and overcompensating behavior in confrontations can simply drive you further into your own inner world, which you experience as so far away.

URANUS IN THE 8th

The urge to be independent and original and to break through forms and boundaries can, in the 8th house, indicate a need to make an original approach to hidden factors and to personal problems in particular. Uranus in the 8th is in a position to throw a surprising and unorthodox light on difficult, insoluble, strange, or hidden things; so that you frequently seem very intuitive and full of brainwaves. Therefore Uranus here is a good placement for creative research, for scientists and inventors, for psychologists and parapsychologists, for students of the arcane, astrologers, and card readers, etc. With the help of this house position, the background and essential details of people and situations can be fathomed and understood.

The suddenness of Uranus can produce sudden psychological insights, but also sudden collapses due to tensions. For, whenever there are tensions and problems, the individual with Uranus in the 8th will always be confronted with them unexpectedly however much he or she may wish to hide away from them. And repeated tensions can cause psychological conditions such as nervousness. The suddenness can also manifest itself in the form of accidents, explosions and the like, but this must be confirmed by other factors in the chart. Inner strain and intuitive Uranian clairvoyance are typical of Uranus in the 8th.

NEPTUNE IN THE 8th

The ability to disassociate, refine, idealize, and improve, but also to blur things, will make itself known in a rather elusive but inspiring manner in the area of life and death and of essentials. Neptune here can indicate an extremely wide-ranging but fairly impersonal emotional life, which may find an outlet in artistic and musical achievements both in the creative sense (composing, painting) and in interpretation (playing an instrument).

In this house, Neptune can penetrate to the deeper layers of the unconscious through dreams and daydreams, fantasy and association and, in doing so, may expose buried problems. However, the language spoken by Neptune is the language of imagery, which is not always easily understood by the conscious mind. This explains why Neptune in the 8th can also divert us from our problems and tempt us to slip away into an unreal world which may have close links with the occult. We can become involved in obscure sects, even though what we are trying to find is the mental and spiritual source of life. When several of the chart factors are in support, Neptune in the 8th can bestow clairvoyant talent and prophetic vision.

PLUTO IN THE 8th

Pluto as our love of power, our desire to transform things and to dredge up matters that lie hidden, can enjoy optimum development in the house that likewise has to do with the hidden and repressed and with metamorphosis. This placement also indicates someone who can go to extremes. With Pluto here, the 8th house becomes the area in which you confront yourself with yourself—which is no easy matter, for this house contains the things we all would rather not know about.

Pluto drags such things inexorably to the surface, and so can make you very insecure, although you will do your utmost to resist the feeling and will want to prove the opposite. Hence the person with Pluto in the 8th can appear to be very self-assured, sometimes "as hard as nails" and unyielding. You can stand on dignity or pull rank in order to hold your own. You are looking not so much for worldly power, as for power over yourself and your own life. Questions of life and death can occupy your mind a great deal.

The other side of Pluto in the 8th is your chance to discover your hidden gifts and talents, which always lie dormant in the personal unconscious. Pluto can help to bring tremendous concentration to bear on whatever interests and inspires you so you can penetrate below its surface. Therefore you have a tremendous capacity for research and investigative work, and can pursue your enquiries far into the unseen. Pluto can indicate paranormal faculties.

It is, however, a placement that gives little repose. There is a lot of commotion going on inside, and a restless search prompted by constantly recurring confrontations. From the latter can develop a deep knowledge of human nature but also overcompensating defensiveness, even to the point of ferocity, and a proneness to complain about everything without exception.

10. PLANETS IN THE 9TH HOUSE

SUN IN THE 9th

The ego, the urge to develop and to be yourself, operates here in the area of expansion and the need to widen horizons. This placement imprints the idea of travel very strongly on the character. This may mean real journeys but also travel in the mind in the form of study to expand the mental and spiritual horizons. Sun in the 9th is often a born student, and you can immerse yourself in thoughts about the meaning of life. The inner aspect in all this is what is chiefly important: the external aspects of study and travel are usually minor matters. You are endeavoring to synthesize knowledge: looking for the common thread that binds all things to one another underneath their differences and, by finding it, you hope to understand the why and wherefore of the entire cosmos. Therefore you are very open to fresh hopes and to fresh possibilities.

You will quite likely become increasingly tolerant as you grow older, having seen so many different things and having studied so many different opinions. You are also likely to have religious leanings (not ecclesiastical). However, if there are hard aspects to the Sun, you may tend to ride hobby-horses and to say what you think so dogmatically that you leave others with little room for maneuver. Tolerance is then no longer possible.

MOON IN THE 9th

When unconscious emotional behavior is concentrated on widening your horizons, you will be greatly attracted by the process of expansion, irrespective of whether this is physical (travel) or mental (reading and study). Also, the Moon, as the behavior we so readily adopt whenever we feel insecure, indicates a deep need for expansion, study, travel, philosophy and anything that leads to a better understanding of life, in order that we may have a synthetic experience of the meaning of things. The unconscious emotional attitude is future-orientated, since the Moon sees many possibilities ahead. But, owing to emotional coloration, these possibilities are approached too subjectively, and perhaps there are (rich) fantasies of the future.

The changeability of the Moon can make us rather more erratic than one who has the Sun here, but the Moon also desires to expand vision effectively, and if possible to develop, and so can have a great liking for travel to foreign countries.

The mobility of the Moon can, if you are prepared to study, give a ready capacity for assimilating information and will make you quick on the uptake, especially when emotions are stirred by what you are learning. But, as in many of its other placements, the Moon here often needs some external stimulus in order to develop the given area of life to the full.

MERCURY IN THE 9th

The ability to arrange and divide, to analyze and combine, to reflect and exchange, has plenty of scope in this house of synthesis, expansion and extension. The powers of association are well developed: you have a need to make as many connections between things as possible in order to widen mental horizons and to achieve the synthesis you desire. This can give rise to a love of travel and to a wish to go fact-gathering when on a trip (including the gathering of geological facts), also a love for making mental journeys.

You enjoy studying and reading serious books, and organize knowledge as objectively as possible. You try to rid yourself of subjectivity toward topics of study, since that would interfere with objectivity and might cause you to lose sight of it entirely. Nevertheless, if badly aspected, Mercury holds the danger that you will become absorbed in minor details or be too pedantic and opinionated.

The expansive 9th house can incline the Mercurial mind to impart its discoveries to others by tongue or pen; so this is a fine placement for writers on the subjects of education, religion, self-improvement, philosophy, pedagogy, etc. Mercury in the 9th may indicate a restless mind, always trying to identify relationships and, above all, always futuristic in its thinking.

VENUS IN THE 9th

The wish for emotional and material security, balance and harmony, beauty and warmth, gives in the 9th paramount need — even in a relationship — to spread oneself with ideas and theories about the meaning of life. Logic plays second fiddle here; since you are more interested in whether the ideas and theories have an air of harmony, and in whether any use can be made of them to reconcile apparently conflicting opinions by combining the latter in a more fundamental synthesis. Harmony is the criterion by which any such synthesis is judged.

Generally speaking, Venus in the 9th is tolerant of the opinions, notions and customs of others, provided everything remains friendly, comprehensible and harmonious. On its own, Venus is not a sign of persevering study, for it needs the support of other factors in the chart. Therefore, this individual is likely to prefer the more outgoing forms of expression such as travelling and hiking. You can satisfy a need for harmony by regularly changing circumstances; making daily life relative by placing it in a wider perspective.

MARS IN THE 9th

Mars as executive ability, energy, self-assertion, aggression, and the determination to hold one's own, gives in the area of expansion and of a philosophical approach to the meaning of life many possibilities for development. The individual with Mars in the 9th is an eager and energetic world-reformer who does not hide his light under a bushel. In the search for the connections between things and in his efforts to make a synthesis of them, he is frequently eager not only to learn but also to impart to others what he knows. The teaching aspect is liable to run into trouble, however, because there is a good measure of self-assertiveness in Mars and the sometimes rather emphatic proclamation of opinions that are not always to everyone's liking. He can react with some very quick repartee in debates and at times can be very pugnacious and sarcastic.

With Mars in this house, the need for space and freedom is very great. This can mean, literally, that you will emigrate to a foreign land to make good or, figuratively, that you will find scope for ideas in some philosophical field. Mars in the 9th can bring about great improvements, but you must take care that you do not spoil your chances by indulging in exaggeration or in undue self-promotion.

JUPITER IN THE 9th

Jupiter as our need for expansion and for intellectual and religious experiences can express itself particularly well when in its own house; the usual consequence being that one has a very good grasp of main outlines, backgrounds and relationships. This can make you very tolerant, so the placement is outstanding for anybody who is involved with the administration of justice or with religious, philosophical, metaphysical, or academic studies.

The need to place and experience everything, including yourself, in a greater and more comprehensive setting gives a love of travel and exploration and, by extension, an interest in widening the intellectual horizon by searching for a synthesis and for some truth you can call your own. Because Jupiter gladly shares knowledge with others, this is also an outstanding placement for educators.

However, if there are any aspects afflicting the 9th, Jupiter can overdo the expansive urge and can encourage conceit, swank, bragging and arrogance. You are then inclined to pass judgment too quickly or to be very intolerant of the opinions of others.

SATURN IN THE 9th

The urge to define our egos and to delimit and structure things will, in the 9th house, be particularly sensitive in regard to the widening of horizons both mental and physical. Therefore the person with Saturn here will be inclined to think hard about everything, to chew everything over, and to study it in detail before making a judgment. He has difficulty in recognizing broad outlines and connections, and this makes him cautious over forming and expressing a opinion.

Sometimes, because of inertia, he is loath to forsake established routines just to start a new way of doing things. It may prove impossible to wean him from his pet subject. He can cling convulsively to his opinions, and can turn himself into a narrow-minded champion of some dogma. Then he misses the deeper insight he is really seeking. Instead of broadening vision in true 9th house fashion, he becomes blinkered and fixes his gaze on a single point. Other opinions are seen in a bad light or, at the very least, are viewed with mistrust.

Saturn in the 9th is a good position, however, for assessing the value of all kinds of high-flown ideals, Utopian schemes and the like; since Saturn is interested in concrete results and will always induce one to aim for some useful and realistic goal which is likely to make sense in the long run. In this case, single-mindedness may even bear great fruit.

URANUS IN THE 9th

The urge to be original, to transcend boundaries and to bring about renewal generates, in the house of the expansion of mental and spiritual horizons, a large number of new, original and intuitive ideas. Therefore, Uranus in the 9th is a position encountered in inventors, creative thinkers, and in those who lead an unusual or inspired life. The placement is not a peaceful one, however.

Uranus is usually tense and electrically charged and, in this expansive house indicates intense and restless mental activity, or flashes of interest in new and future possibilities. That is to say, Uranus in the 9th is concerned with possibilities and with the future in general, not with specific aspects of these things. Hence one is very intuitive and may well see unusual connections and be remarkably quick on the uptake.

On the other hand, with hard aspects, this is a poor position for making careful judgments. Personal opinions are formed all of a sudden, generally without much weighing of the pros and cons, and this can sometimes give rise to quarrels or broken friendships.

Religion and metaphysics are studied or experienced in a fresh, unorthodox way, and one feels free to scout the rules of religious institutions in order to experience the universally human. Speculation along these lines is more attractive than are rules and dogmas for which the Uranus in the 9th person does not care.[12]

---

[12]He may also be ultra-orthodox and accuse the "orthodox" of his own day of having departed from the true, original faith. *Tr.*

NEPTUNE IN THE 9th

The urge to disassociate, to refine, to improve, but also to blur issues is, in the house of expanded horizons, scarcely concerned with real journeys (trips abroad, say), but the individual feels particularly drawn to all kinds of trends and ideas in the fields of religion and metaphysics. He or she has a feeling for, and experiences, a sort of "unity in diversity" in religious and other movements.

When Neptune is in this truth-seeking house, little is needed to make one an idealist, someone to whom reality seems more beautiful than it really is. These people are perfectly happy looking at ideals from a distance, but, when it comes to putting them into practice, resolve will need strengthening by other horoscope factors. This is why Neptune in the 9th is commonly said to signify impractical dreams.

Neptune here enjoys exploring the human world in general, and thus travels beyond his own small ego. He wants to study it, usually because of a need for unity or because of religious feelings. With hard aspects, there can be a touch of fanaticism and he runs the risk of drowning in his sense of oneness. That is a special danger in this house, because it has to do with our becoming conscious and with the expansion of consciousness. Chaotic and erroneous judgment-forming can be the result.

But if the aspects are easy, we usually see a subliminal appreciation of underlying connections, which serve as the starting point of a vision of life — though the latter may prove hard to express in concrete form.

PLUTO IN THE 9th

The will to power, the desire for transformation, or to bring the deepest-buried secrets to light, gives the person with Pluto in this house of the expansion of horizons a strong incentive to look a good deal further than the end of his nose, to engage in self-development, but also to meddle with a lot of things that are none of his business. With this placement, he can confront himself with himself by tensions resulting from a drive for power, for example, in the areas of propaganda or study.

He has many of the qualities needed to make a demagogue; since he can make his vision so convincing to others that they have difficulty in controverting it. Yet because he has such a burning desire to share with them his vision of life as it should be lived (or rather to force it on them!), he frequently turns against him the very people he would like to help. Hence Pluto in the 9th tends to create differences of opinion or confrontations where a philosophy of life is concerned.

But Pluto in the house of study also has another side, and indicates a compulsion to know how everything fits together and what the underlying thread is that runs through everything. You will therefore be exceptionally well suited to studies which combine depth with versatility. But the aspect of extension plays a part, too, in this house, so that Pluto likes to put knowledge to practical use. Advertising, psychology and politics are among the fields in which you can deploy insights, and satisfy the need for power or conviction or promotion.

11. PLANETS IN THE 10TH HOUSE

SUN IN THE 10th

When the urge to develop and to be yourself is found in the house of demarcation of self (and others), of social position and of rank and hierarchy, you shall need to form a clear-cut picture of yourself and consequently to take a recognizable and well-defined position in society. The Sun in the 10th is therefore an indication that you can rise in the world, because you need to develop in a position that holds status, honor or credit.

The 10th house is where you experience yourself as distinct from other people. The Sun in the 10th does not usually permit itself to take advice: you will decide things for yourself and will arrange life in accordance with your own interpretation of current standards and structures, your idea being to secure a position in which you can adopt a certain identity and can organize others. This aim often brings success in society, through a sort of natural ascendancy that is openly displayed, provided the rest of the horoscope is in accord.

The Sun in the 10th also points to a disciplined manner of working and to a striving for authority within a given field. Political and social ambitions frequently go hand in hand with this placement. In general, the Sun has a strong self-image which is projected to the outside world.

When the aspects are hard, we may anticipate ambitious striving for the above-mentioned goals, sometimes with domineering or arrogant behavior; or else, if, say, there are further identity problems in the horoscope, one has a consuming interest in the question of current status and of what is expected of him.

THE MOON IN THE 10th

When the Moon, symbolizing the need for emotional security, stands in the house of self-demarcation and social position, we will want to be able to rely on a safe social position in which we are accepted as a fully-fledged member of society. If we have a clearly recognized place in society, we shall feel comfortable; however, the Moon is a precarious factor and will not always impart stability to this house. Your ego-image, the pattern of expectations, and ideas associated with this, can alter periodically through contact with the world—especially with women (the Moon!). And so we see a person with the Moon here frequently changing job or profession before finding something for which he or she is really suited.

The Moon in the 10th can be a stimulating influence for the placement indicates a certain warmth and responsiveness towards the environment. However, with hard aspects, this positive behavior can be converted into emotional ups and downs, fickleness and indecision.

MERCURY IN THE 10th

When the need to analyze, arrange, think, exchange and communicate, expresses itself in the area of marking out the limits of our personal identity and of striving for social status, there is a likelihood that we shall search for many contacts, especially in the professional sphere. In general, these contacts will be brief and will have to do with intellectual topics. The person with Mercury in the 10th is keen to acquire all kinds of information and knowledge in the course of a career—also to acquire knowledge that has nothing to do with work at all.

Gaining and assimilating impressions is a way of giving form to yourself; which means you are often quick and adroit where work and position are concerned. Research and scientific work, also trade, transport, authorship, journalism and so on, are all possible occupations and, quite often we see someone with this position engaging in more than one occupation during the life, and sometimes one has several part-time jobs at the same time.

With hard aspects, given the restlessness of Mercury, we may expect this individual to be a jack-of-all-trades and master of none. Mercury in itself imparts little perseverance and he or she is easily distracted. Any number of projects can be started only to accomplish next to nothing—the rest of the horoscope will show how this will work.

VENUS IN THE 10th

With Venus in the 10th, the need for beauty and harmony, and for secure relationships, is directed into the area where we carve out an identity for ourselves and strive for social status. This status can be achieved in an easy and flexible manner by expressing and giving shape to Venusian factors such as artwork and other forms of beauty, to clothing and fashion, cosmetics, interior decoration etc. Through insistence on harmony and beauty, the person with Venus in the 10th often gives the impression of being balanced, friendly, and well adjusted; therefore Venus usually promotes the career. But with hard aspects, Venus can also make you lazy, uncaring, or indecisive as far as social position is concerned.

Generally speaking, however, Venus here radiates amity, and your self-image as a friendly person evokes friendly reactions from those around. You can also show to advantage in situations where harmony is essential or where mediation is required. Hence this is a good placement for a diplomat or a justice of the peace.

MARS IN THE 10th

When Mars is in the 10th, you need to deploy executive ability and forcefulness, self-assertion and ambition, in the field in which you demarcate your identity and strive for social position. This combination tends to indicate that you are combative, ready for battle, ambitious, and ready to invest a great deal of work into getting what you want. Mars is more goal orientated when in the 10th and, because its indefatigable energy, is much better disciplined than usual here, it can raise you to considerable heights in society. You must, however, be careful not to elbow too many people out of the way during the upward climb; also you need to make more of an effort to understand others, which is something you may easily fail to do since both Mars and the 10th house encourage a strong self-fixation.

Problems and obstacles are overcome by tackling them with terrific energy. Mars does not always set to work wisely but, if the other placements are good, any incidental damage is quickly repaired. Matters do not always turn out so well if aspects to the planet are hard. Then roughness, thoughtlessness, recklessness and opposition to others can create enemies, of whom you sometimes try to rid yourself by unscrupulous means.

Professions in which energy, activity, power of command, competitiveness and honor play a part will prove attractive to the individual with Mars in the 10th. Sport and the army are examples of these.

JUPITER IN THE 10th

Jupiter's need for expansion and improvement finds its outlet in the 10th, mainly in the acquisition of a social position that will offer you opportunities to show what you can do. The self-image is often of someone who is affable, optimistic and good-hearted. If there are one or two hard aspects, you may feel superior to those around you, and your somewhat inflated ego may make you patronizing or sometimes bombastic.

In many cases, however, Jupiter in the 10th obtains what you want because of a hopeful attitude and a feeling that, by and large, nothing can go wrong: success seems to drop into your lap in fact. Because things run fairly smoothly, there is a likelihood that you will think very highly of yourself, will have little humility, or will be elitist. Quite frequently, religious, metaphysical or ordinary humanitarian ideas enter into the formation of the social position, and so you could be a preacher, a teacher or an employer with a social conscience.

However, with hard aspects, this social conscience may be nothing but a hollow sham. But usually Jupiter here displays genuine friendliness and is joviality itself.

SATURN IN THE 10th

When the need to develop ego and the urge to demarcate and define yourself appear in the house that has a similar content, we may anticipate a powerful expression of Saturn. Saturn, a planet that usually causes problems, will to some extent be a weak spot. When it can develop well, both its structuring and form-giving qualities, and its restricting and restraining characteristics will come to the fore.

Because Saturn in the 10th has a reputation for making you work hard and long, final success should be assured. In this house, Saturn emphasizes the importance of a clear-cut identity so strongly that it often gives great ambition, the set goals being striven for with iron discipline and perseverance. With hard aspects, you may be unpleasantly grim and, if the goal is reached too quickly and at the expense of others, the result can be a fall.

In this house, Saturn gives a need for a personal identity: you want people to see that you amount to something, that you are a cut above the common herd. The formation of a separate identity is crucially important. It is a remarkable fact that children with Saturn here often have to do without the support and structure normally provided by one or both parents, and that they try to make up for this later in life. A position of honor means much more to them than respect alone: it is an affirmation of the self. A responsiveness to compliments is frequently met in this position of Saturn.

Once you find a form in which you can experience yourself as a complete individual, you can act quietly both on yourself and on the environment in a guiding and structuring way. Frequently, too, you bring about permanent improvements in your own circle (usually in the social or occupational spheres), especially with regard to structure, building up and methodics.

URANUS IN THE 10th

The urge to be original, renewing and barrier-breaking, to go beyond the bounds of current usage, can have a startling and sudden effect in the area in which we carve out a personal identity and acquire social status. Uranus is restless and changeable, but very inventive; therefore, with Uranus in this house, we can give shape to all kinds of new ideas and inspiration in our work and so keep things on the move. But there is seldom any clear-cut ego-image.

Uranus in the 10th gives the need to go through life without any hard and fast commitments, and to find work wherever there is an opportunity to use your ingenuity freely. Stagnation and idleness are pernicious to the person with this placement. New techniques and anything unusual and unconventional hold your interest. You like to see yourself as someone who has a renewing and pioneering function within the existing structures, and will act accordingly.

You can be an avowed revolutionary, but can also be one who works for change democratically in the fields of industry, teaching and so on. Or you can adopt some unusual profession such as that of a fortune-teller or astrologer.

With Uranus here, you have a need for change and renewal, also for what is unusual, and you set small store by the establishment. Owing to unconventional views and general interests, the person with Uranus in the 10th is in a position to take a fresh look at people and their motives, and could therefore be eminently suited to the world of advertising.

NEPTUNE IN THE 10th

In the 10th house, with its emphasis on structure, form, identity and social status, Neptune, as our urge to disassociate and refine, but also to make things fluid and to blur them, can find it hard to make its influence felt. Consequently, you have a struggle to understand yourself.

You may be very sensitive to atmospheres and to the influences around you. In an intuitive way, you penetrate to the core of things and get very clear feelings about other people; yet can find it hard to discover your own part in the world, your own identity. Hence the usual rigidity of the 10th house is weakened by Neptune, so you either adopt an altruistic and self-sacrificing stance in the outer world and fall in with the world's wishes and requirements, or else are led astray into a false idea of self and start inhabiting unreality (perhaps as a result of drink or drugs).

Provided the planet can make its presence felt, we often see with Neptune in the 10th that social and community affairs prosper marvelously, in spite of the occurrence of chaotic situations or of situations that turn out quite differently from what was planned. Neptune here can also bestow a measure of clairvoyance or some mediumistic ability, but this has to be confirmed by the rest of the horoscope.

PLUTO IN THE 10th

In the house of identity-formation and of the bid for social status, power-hungry and willful Pluto has great scope for development, and we may safely surmise that individuals with Pluto here will usually have considerable ambition and feelings of self-importance. These people want to be lord and master in their own territory and do not readily tolerate anyone sharing this authority. Since the planet makes them so thoroughgoing, they will literally do everything in their power to turn the spotlight on themselves and to put themselves in the right, and will do so in a very subtle, though convincing, way.

With hard aspects, the gloves will really be off, and they employ intrigues, gossip, scandal-mongering, etc., as instruments with which to eliminate a rival who stands in the way. These people have their own methods of keeping the reins but, in doing so, will provoke power struggles.

Pluto here gives great powers of concentration and perseverance in reaching goals, and much can be accomplished. The ability to fluidify and to transform can stand them in good stead when they wish to make important changes in community affairs or within the profession. However, they must take care not to be too doctrinaire and not to ram home opinions too forcibly; since this might raise up opposition that could even ruin the career—which is precisely what they do not wish to happen. But also, in this house, Pluto's forcefulness and all-or-nothing attitude will finally confront these people with themselves.

12. PLANETS IN THE 11TH HOUSE

SUN IN THE 11th

With the ego, the desire to develop and to be ourselves in the house of friends, associations and kindred spirits, we are in a position to participate as conscious individuals in contacts that go deeper than the superficial contacts encountered in the 3rd house.

The person with the Sun in the 11th likes sharing interests with others, prefers to work out ideas and opinions in groups, unions, or party conventions, and likes to make a mark on the activities of these groups. The Sun points to qualities of leadership and, when the placement is positive, there are many profitable contacts with like-minded people. Quite often one makes friends with people who are able to advance the career.

With the Sun here, you are able to form and maintain friendships, and this gives a great deal of self-confidence. If the position is strongly emphasized, you run the risk of making so much of yourself that your familiars will be hangers-on rather than genuine friends. But, generally, you attract those who are well matched and who are stimulating company. With this Sun position you will certainly expect no less!

You clearly recognize that others have their own individualities and their own special needs. Your attitude is a little ambivalent here, but if you are prepared to concede this to them, in spite of your sense of your own importance in social contacts, you will usually let others have their place.

With hard aspects, you will either impose yourself on others so determinedly that little is left of the democratic and humane side of the Sun, or you will, through shame and disgrace, learn wisdom in friendship and social ties.

THE MOON IN THE 11th

With the Moon symbolizing unconscious emotional behavior, the behavior you adopt whenever you feel insecure, sitting in the 11th house, you will be very fond of friendship. In order to be at ease, you need friends and acquaintances to whom you can speak on the same level, and with whom you can do everything. This placement does not have the depth given by the Sun in the 11th, since the Moon typifies changeability. Being easily upset, you are somewhat temperamental with your circle of friends. But once friends are made, you are usually much attached to them.

You can exercise your caring propensities on friends or, more widely, in community life, where helping and becoming involved with others hold a central position. If you enter politics, you are apt to stress those points that are most in keeping with this factor: child care, nursery schools, homes for the aged, maternity work, nursing or anything else represented by the Moon.

If there are hard aspects, you need to beware of gossip and mischievous chatter within your circle of friends. Either you yourself sin in this respect, or you become the target — quite often because of your rather capricious behavior toward those whose good will you need so much.

MERCURY IN THE 11th

The desire to analyze, arrange, classify and consider, and also to exchange findings, can, when expressed through the house of friends, hardly do anything else than promote friendships on the basis of similarity of thought and mental affinity. The mobility of Mercury may indicate a great deal of change in friendships, some of which are superficial.

You expect your friends and kindred spirits to be good talkers, and you yourself talk readily and volubly on many different subjects. You need friends who are mentally stimulating. But you may be too excitable, too capricious, and, sometimes, too interfering — Mercury loves to poke its nose in everywhere.

On the other hand, the mutability of Mercury can make you versatile, both in contacts and in activities on behalf of groups, clubs and so on. Also, judgment on matters unconnected with this house is basically sound because you know so many facts; you do not, so to speak, pluck an opinion out of thin air. Mercury in the 11th indicates many friends engaged in Mercurial activities, such as reporters, merchants, scientists and so on.

VENUS IN THE 11th

When in the house of friends and friendships, Venus, our need for secure and pleasant relationships, and for harmony and balance, tends to surround us with people with whom we have definite emotional links. We lay prime emphasis on harmony and peace in friendship, and are affable, accommodating and ready to compromise. Therefore we usually form agreeable and warm friendships. Yet even in the favorable atmosphere provided by these, the Venusian nature finds it hard to thrash out any problems that arise, since this would disturb the atmosphere too much. And so we are inclined to preserve the appearance of friendship even when brooding inwardly over something that must eventually lead to open conflict.

As already mentioned, Venus here certainly does need warm and friendly contacts, and will be accommodating in friendship without being so changeable as people with Moon or Mercury in the 11th. Individuals with this placement often meet with support and help when there are difficulties or when trying to start some new project.

With hard aspects, Venus can signify problems with friendships; for example, through friends who are nothing more than parasites, or because the native profits from or preys on friends.

MARS IN THE 11th

When the aggressive urge to look out for number one, the executive ability, the energy and need to establish self work out in the area of life where friendships and associations comes into play, there are likely to be clashes, so that personal relationships do not always last long. But when Mars shows its good side, you can be enthusiastic, warm, enterprising and energetic, and can do much for friendships. You can take a good deal of initiative in lodges, fraternities and associations, and may therefore have a very stimulating life. Through enthusiasm, you may gain considerable respect, and your occasional quick-tempered outbursts and expressions of irritation will be tolerated.

With Mars in the 11th, you are fond of engaging in group activities with friends, and look for companions who are lively and sporty (Mars characteristics). When the planet's positive qualities come to the fore, the sudden quarrels and differences of opinion will generally blow over quickly and be soon forgotten. With hard aspects, however, they can destroy the friend-ship.

This somewhat ambiguous placement can make you want to argue your own ideas and opinions and to initiate far-reaching discussions. You frequently see confrontations as a challenge, but this energy is often misunderstood by friends and acquaintances. Thus you can isolate yourself, or perhaps will become the headstrong leader of a small like-minded group.

JUPITER IN THE 11th

When the desire for expansion and extension is deployed in the area of friends, you can generally count on enjoying fine friendships which reflect your charming and tolerant attitude toward companions. Jupiter imparts a desire for friends with a similar outlook on life. But, in addition to wishing to share your views with friends, you expect a lot from them and are quite likely to cultivate people in the higher echelons of society who can help you ascend the social scale.

With hard aspects, your naturally forebearing and jovial attitude can quickly be replaced by fussiness and pomposity, egotism, or intolerance. You can regard yourself as one who knows it all, and affably invites the rest of the world to share your wisdom. Or you look for friends with a rich and extrava-gant life-style, a life-style that is really in conflict with the inner potential of synthesis-seeking Jupiter. Whatever the case may be, Jupiter in the 11th needs richness in contacts that can be intellectual or spiritual as well as material. Therefore you can form friendships of both kinds.

Your approach is welcoming and jolly and your pattern of expectation usually matches what you get. Occasionally you will be disappointed after pitching hopes too high, but you possess sufficient optimism to recover from any setback.

SATURN IN THE 11th

When the desire to limit and confine, to demarcate and give form and structure, makes itself felt in the house of friends, you will be rather reserved and secretive about friendships. You may be painfully self-conscious, or find it difficult to commit yourself to a group of any size.

Although you would like to enjoy membership in some larger whole, you often hold aloof and live as an individual. Not that you are without friends, far from it; you have only a few, it is true, but you are exceptionally faithful to them. You look for something *more* in a friendship. Others have to release feelings in you that go well below the surface; only then do you value them. Yet what they release makes you very nervous, and you do everything in your power to avoid showing feelings to others.

The person with Saturn in the 11th is tormented by the conflict between the fear of being, and the need to be, something in a greater unit; wondering whether he would be accepted as a member of as an individual. A rather defensive attitude can provoke similar reactions in those he meets, and this is why Saturn is traditionally said to produce difficulties in the circle of friends. The difficulties, such as they are, arise from one's guardedness.

Even if he brings himself to feel more relaxed in groups, clubs, or friendships, he will still be fairly unassuming and will seldom act in an exuberant manner. Usually there is something paternal in his outlook, and this is often reflected in the type of friends chosen, who tend to be people with whom he can converse seriously—sometimes older and more mature friends who face life with a sense of responsibility.

Saturn here occasionally behaves as the life and soul of the party, and can be completely sold on communal living, but this is only an overcompensation to cover a deep sense of loneliness — which will rise to the surface immediately his attention wanders and the control of his conscious mind is released.

Nevertheless, with good aspects, Saturn in the 11th will give lasting friendships and will also lend form and substance to group activities. With hard aspects, however, we see the loner or outsider, who never feels himself to be part of a group.

URANUS IN THE 11th

Independence, originality and individuality are expected of our friends, when Uranus is in the 11th house, and you need to express these personal characteristics in associations and friendships. This can mean many changes, usually sudden changes, in the circle of friends, and also points to unexpected new friendships.

You wish to share the unusual and the unconventional with others, with people prepared to be themselves — an effect that Uranus invariably has when in this position. Such things as rank and station do not impress you in the slightest. There is an air of idealism and fraternity about this placement, but the changeability of Uranus can spoil the game. That is to say, Uranus here can make you an unpredictable friend or associate, who is blunt and quick-tempered, not to say capricious. So that, with hard aspects, you may be disliked or even dreaded by those who know you.

Uranus in the 11th looks for free spirits who are idealistic and out of the ordinary. Hence you can boast of an unusually lively and stimulating circle of friends, who may however turn out to be fickle and unreliable if you are not careful. Occasionally, Uranus in this position indicates membership in a revolutionary group, but this needs confirmation by other factors in the chart.

NEPTUNE IN THE 11th

The ability to refine and improve, to disassociate and idealize, can promote warm and spiritual friendships in the 11th house, and friends for whom you are prepared to sacrifice everything.

Sometimes there may be telepathic links between friends. You expect a great deal from friendship, and hopes in this regard will not always materialize and you will suffer disappointment. Especially as the other side of Neptune is undermining and fluidizing. Therefore, with Neptune in the 11th, you need to be careful not to choose friends who are bad, not to expect too much of them, and to see to it that they do not exploit you. On the other hand, you yourself can be guilty of taking advantage of others if the rest of the chart points in this direction.

You look for a meaningful environment, and material things or status holds no attractions for you. What you value is the inner bond, the sense of community. This can be obtained by having close friends, but also by becoming involved in circles where addiction is rife. You may lose friends as a result of dishonesty, irregularity, drink or drugs, if the planet is afflicted by hard aspects.

Neptunian characteristics are also sought in friends — characteristics that can vary from criminality and addiction to artistry, musicalness and spirituality. You look for unusual depth in all companions and generally get what you want.

PLUTO IN THE 11th

The power-drive and compulsion to haul unconscious factors to the surface of the mind, give, in the house of friends, the chance of struggles, especially power struggles, but also of making friends who will exert a far-reaching and often transforming influence. The person with Pluto in the 11th house is certainly not looking for superficiality in others. Friends must pass muster and must be seen to be worthy of friendship. And although the "examination" of candidates in this regard is held unconsciously, it is very thorough.

Pluto in the 11th prefers a few deep friendships, preferably with those who are well matched, are not easily offended, and can give as good as they get. You live for confrontations; not that you derive any satisfaction from opposing others; no, not at all, you are simply trying to draw them out whether they wish it or not. You may even do this so subtly that the other is unaware of being manipulated.

But you are not satisfied with this: you still keep on looking further and further, and are in danger of finding things that do not exist. Therefore you can repel friends and isolate yourself. And, although you can easily live on your own, you do need friendship and community life in order to develop inwardly. You will undergo maximum inner change by confrontation, which is why you prefer friends who act just as drastically on you as you do on them.

You search into what is deep, dark, hidden and secret in your friends, and are not content with a superficial acquaintance. Thus you can make friends in the world of politics, occultism, psychology, parapsychology, and feel the need to probe deeper into a person than might appear at first glance. You will have to live with the fact that your intrigues and the use you make of your investigations will not make you universally loved and can also create powerful enemies.

13. PLANETS IN THE 12TH HOUSE

SUN IN THE 12th

It is not very easy for the Sun, as the representative of our urge to self-realization and self-development, to express itself in such a collectivist and impersonal area as the 12th house. The ego is then formed with difficulty. Very often this is the consequence of experiences lying in infancy and early youth, during which the father was unable to give a confirming and supporting example because he was away much of the time due to his occupation (e.g. as a sailor), to illness, or to other reasons, or because he was dead, and had little or nothing to do with the child's upbringing. The difficulty experienced in forming an identity can in later life produce anxieties and inhibitions, because you do not know how to conduct yourself.

On the other hand, it is entirely possible that you discover at an earlier age than usual how relative everything is (including your own ego), and become aware of yourself as part of a much greater whole. The Sun in the 12th is then in a position to build a deep inner life, in which the unity of all living things has a central place. From this experience of unity and from the need for this experience, you may be drawn to prayer, mysticism, meditation, yoga, or the like.

Relationships with everyday reality and society are loose. The Sun in the 12th inhabits a world of your own, perhaps a dream world or fantasy world in which you escape from reality. But it is equally possible that you will keep your feet firmly planted on the ground while sensing that there is something more to life, so that you like to peep behind the scenes so to speak and, from time to time, can become so engrossed in your own thoughts that you are oblivious to all around you.

Your need to be part of a greater and more inclusive life makes it possible to open up to others and to appreciate them. Therefore you can be eminently suitable for social work in an unobtrusive way. Because you find it hard to express your identity, you often do not know who you are, and so keep quiet about yourself and appear sly and underhanded, although the reputation is seldom deserved.

You may gain an important position and can do outstanding work in the background, but there is always something infantile about you, even something awkward or clumsy, since the practical side of life is not your strong point.

It goes without saying that not everyone with the Sun in the 12th ends up in a prison, cloister or asylum, as so many of the older astrological writers would have us believe. Such an outcome is possible only when the rest of the chart points in the same direction. But you may be moved by compassion to visit jails and other institutions where human beings are confined.

Nevertheless, you will always have an identity problem of some kind and, since this house is such a retiring one, you will not be easy to understand as an individual. Difficulties in contacts are highly likely—especially as you have an extremely hazy notion of the status of your solar ego, and can emphasize it so much that you sometimes appear egotistical.

MOON IN THE 12th

The Moon, as the symbol of the search for emotional security and comfort, looks for safety in the house of the collective, the impersonal, the secluded and the disassociated, as one might look for the bottom of a bottomless well, and this creates continual unease and insecurity. Often its presence in the 12th signifies that there was something amiss with your relationship with your mother. Either she was not there, or she was unwell or incapacitated, or else you remember her as an icy lady who succeeded in completely dominating you. Whatever the case may be, you are unable to imagine what it would be like to have a loving, caring mother, and suffer from attendant problems that can persist long after you have grown up. For example, you may shy away from any emotional relationship with women because you fail to understand them and see them as a threat. Also you may not want to have children. Everything to do with the manifestation of the Moon can generate a vague anxiety or bewilderment, even though this is such a sensitive placement for the planet. There is much greater turmoil taking place in people with the Moon in the 12th than they would ever dare to admit.

When you have the Moon in the 12th you are on your own, all feelings come to the surface, and the emotional life can be so far-ranging that there may be mediumship, clairvoyance, etc. But the surge of emotion can, with hard aspects, also lead to great sensitivity and self-pity. Because a planet in the 12th indicates the kind of things with which you are unconsciously occupied, the Moon here will make an emotional impact on those around you and will demand a great deal emotionally even when you hide your feelings.

Nevertheless, your feelings and capacity to immerse yourself give you an outstanding opportunity to do social work and service and, although you may sometimes seem rather shy, you can mean a lot to others. You sympathize with them over their problems, see through their disguises, and can understand them so well, that you can help them on their way. Often you penetrate to the core of your own emotional difficulties and to your deep need for cherishing by doing this for others; thus the Moon in the 12th may well solve the problems it creates.

MERCURY IN THE 12th

The need to analyze, arrange, classify, reason and exchange expresses itself with some difficulty in the 12th house, which unsettles everything and is the house of seclusion and of the collective and the impersonal. You are unlikely to be particularly communicative and, although you may fill your listeners' ears with a stream of small talk, you will confide your profoundest ideas only to someone with whom you have a firm emotional relationship. For the rest of humanity, your world of thought is a sealed book.

That you can develop best in solitude can be seen from the fact that you find it hard to concentrate when surrounded by other people or by hustle and bustle. You must have peace and quiet or the pleasure of listening to your favorite music, and then the words simply flow from your pen. For, just as you find it hard to express yourself in front of large groups of people, so you find it easy to put things down on paper. Thoughts can soar like no one else's and you are poetic and romantic. In the stillness, the nervous and tense planet Mercury comes to rest.

With Mercury in the 12th communication sometimes runs along other than verbal channels. For you, the emotional content of a conversation is just as important as the words themselves, and you can sometimes pinpoint unfailingly what is going on in the other person's mind. Thus you have a gift for relating to the unspoken needs of others — although even you do not always guess them: you must be able to talk with the people concerned and to sense the atmosphere surrounding them. Yet you will understand little of yourself and your world of thought, and this can work out in two ways: in feelings of inferiority in regard to mental and communicative ability yet, at the same time, in the wish to have a say in conversations along a certain line. Mercury demands to express itself, and you can be more Mercurial than you might consciously think possible.

VENUS IN THE 12th

The need for comfort and security within relationships, for warmth and beauty, balance and harmony, has a rather impersonal form of expression in the collective and reclusive 12th house. Venus in the 12th channels feelings of love more into life in general and less towards a special person, although frequently one person is elevated to a symbol of it and is so idolized that their real nature is veiled, so to speak, in a cloud of incense. Venus in the 12th also makes you very impressionable, and this can show itself in artistry and musicality among other things. But the sensitivity of Venus goes further. Like any of the other planets in the 12th, Venus can signify unconscious trends and emotions in the environment and, because of a desire for harmony, you are always prepared to help when required. You have a great leaning toward self-denial and self-sacrifice. People in need, regardless of race, country, political allegiance, etc. will be safe with Venus in the 12th.

Venus, so concerned with relationships, in the 12th will seek the universal beloved with whom to experience divine unity. You will not know that this is well-nigh impossible and will keep on looking for it. In older literature, this placement is said to be typical of clandestine love affairs, but this certainly need not always be true. Of course, it is possible that, while searching for the ideal state of bliss, you will become discontented with a perfectly good existing marriage. In that event, a secret affair (even if simply in the imagination) is quite on the cards; but so are other outlets in the form of music or art, if only as a passive enjoyment.

Sometimes you will find it hard to say in public how fond you are of somebody: you prefer to leave this for the intimate moments with your partner. And this makes it difficult for the world to gauge you.

MARS IN THE 12th

When the urge to prove yourself or to express your executive ability, energy and ambition is in the 12th house (the house that conceals everything from view), you will have difficulty in giving form and direction to it. Rather than stand up for yourself, you may creep away or withdraw into a shell, only to venture out again when the coast is clear.

Mars in the 12th certainly has feelings of importance but they are difficult for you (and others) to grasp. You prefer to work alone behind the scenes, where you can shift mountains of work. You can do much good in the field of service and as an auxiliary, also in the 12th house areas of metaphysics, occultism, psychology and religion, and can win a place in society by earning a living in these fields.

The Martian initiative, enthusiasm and pioneering spirit do not vanish when Mars is in the 12th; they merely retire from direct view. Inwardly, you are busy with a thousand-and-one things, full of new projects which usually have to do with 12th house matters, and are often occupied on the quiet. You are unlikely to sit still and do nothing, but break your silence only when certain of producing results; until then you are generally too unsure to face objections that might be hard to counter.

You are often troubled by the feeling that you are doing too little and cannot do more: the 12th house seems to swallow up your efforts like a bottomless pit and you do not know what to do about it. You are constantly trying to prove yourself in a rather indirect manner. You side-step confrontations but, by simply carrying on with what you are doing, you eventually reach the goal. Typical of Mars in the 12th, therefore, is the avoidance of conflicts and the attainment of ambitions by a circuitous route.

In addition, you could be capable of using means such as manipulation or sowing discord in order to gain your ends without confrontation, but this must be confirmed by the rest of the chart. The individual with Mars in the 12th is often very interested in the world around him and especially in the background to events, but mainly because he wants to understand himself. Mars promotes self-concern here just as much as it does in any of the other houses.

JUPITER IN THE 12th

The need for religious and mental values, the urge to expand, widen and increase often impart a feeling for social issues when expressed in the house of collectivity. In this house, the planet gives a sense of all-embracing life, together with a desire to improve things and to relieve social hardship. But you must take care that your kindness is not abused: you can sometimes overdo open-handedness, generosity and joviality.

Jupiter, the eternal seeker for the synthesis of things, can pursue its quest outstandingly in the 12th house, because the latter is concerned with the experience of unity; and sometimes there is further involvement in prayer, meditation, life in a religious order, mysticism, yoga, and similar activities. Psychology and dream-analysis are other terrains in which the person with Jupiter in the 12th can do well. The only danger is that you may be swallowed up by the rich inner world you experience and become impractical, or lose all interest in everyday concerns. A good solution is to work in some area you find inwardly exciting—some work of a 12th house type say, from social service to mysticism.

It is not easy to gain access to your deepest thoughts and feelings. Generally you let little of your inner life transpire, perhaps because unfortunate events in childhood have made you wary. You abide by your own sincere inner moral code, but may have been misunderstood by parents; they may even have made fun of your code, so you decided to keep it to yourself.

You want to deepen your life, often not externally, but intellectually and spiritually; yet, in the abyss of the 12th house, you are never satisfied that you have progressed far enough. This gives a sense of being lost and weak. You never manage to enter paradise and, as long as you remain outside, you do not let it appear that you know anything. Nevertheless, it is such a preoccupation that you may become self-absorbed and strike others as an impractical and idealistic dreamer. You never betray the secrets of your inner realm.

SATURN IN THE 12th

The urge to limit and demarcate things, especially your own ego, and to give it form and structure, is extremely hard in such a collective and impersonal area as the 12th house. There is no proper handhold there, and the formative powers of Saturn have no solid basis on which to work. Therefore you encounter many problems in the ego-forming process, and may wonder who you are and what you really want to do. Many times we find this placement in the horoscopes of people who have experienced little security or stability either during infancy or, possibly, in the years after.

Quite often, for some reason or other, the father played too insignificant a role to impart structure and a feeling of self-respect, or else he was too repressive. In this respect, the placement is rather similar to that of the Sun in the 12th, with this difference, however, that the Saturn person experienced something more traumatic and retains a very ambivalent attitude towards the father until late in life. Often you are left with a deep-rooted conflict or incomprehension; but equally often with some compulsive link. This results from the fact that the father is so successful in the community that you have a notion that you ought at least to achieve something similar, and wrestle early on (even in childhood) with inferiority feelings, or with feelings of guilt because you think you are incapable of doing so.

Whatever the actual cause, you frequently experience a sense of loneliness, disorganization and of not being understood, as well as the vague feelings of guilt already mentioned. In this condition, you will often find comfort in being associated with a matronly woman who is able to look after you and bring some order into life. On the other hand, you may meet a partner who is so dependent that you have to make strenuous efforts to cope with the situation, and this forces you to develop a more regular lifestyle, however painful the process may be.

Saturn in the 12th has difficulty in expressing emotions and prefers to do so in an impersonal manner along with the crowd. Yet you may want to mean something to your fellow men and women and are capable of giving them valuable help—but always in such a way as to disguise any personal feelings. You seldom betray the latter but, because you are so preoccupied with what is going on inside, you will sometimes strike others as serious.

All in all, Saturn in the 12th presents great possibilities for spiritual growth, even though this usually occurs through painful experiences. The individual with a well-aspected Saturn here can move mountains single-handedly by hard work and plenty of perseverance; although it will take time to reap the benefit of these efforts.

URANUS IN THE 12th

Even the gift to be original, independent and individual, and to break through limitations, does not easily take shape in the 12th house. It has no concrete handhold there and finds it difficult to manifest itself directly. Nevertheless, when you are with your intimates or on your own, Uranus in the 12th may suddenly be visited by inspiration; often as you are daydreaming, in the morning, say, just after rising, or while in the bath. The renewing and pioneering capabilities of Uranus should not be underestimated, even when the planet is in the 12th. Even there it exerts its influence suddenly and unpredictably.

You have a passion for immersing yourself in the irrational, or in subjects which are recondite and provide a deeper insight into people, life or into the unity of the cosmos. But Uranus in this sensitive house makes you very restless and, although you like to occupy your mind with subjects that transcend ordinary intellectual limits, you gain little peace or satisfaction from doing so. You are forever looking further afield, and this restlessness may even cause you to suffer from nervous ailments.

When Uranus is in the 12th, your character is almost a complete mystery to your parents; often you are quite different from the rest of the family and, sooner or later, will go your own way. With hard aspects, Uranus can have a compulsive need to be provocative and defiant, to which you give full rein as it is much stronger in you than in the average person. A growing feeling of unrest comes over you, though with what result it is hard to say. Essentially you have a pressing need to be yourself, but probably lack a good opportunity to satisfy this need or dare not do so immediately.

You participate unconsciously in the life of the greater Whole, and this is why you can get sudden hunches and insights into things, the existence of which you never suspected, insights bordering on the clairvoyant.

NEPTUNE IN THE 12th

The urge to disassociate and refine, to idealize and improve, but also to blur and fluidify, is at home in the 12th, in an area of life having characteristics that tally completely with those of Neptune. We may safely assume, therefore, that anyone with Neptune here will be very easily affected without understanding what makes this so. From an early age, you will be more sensitive than you show to the outside world; which is hard, since the planet concerned, Neptune, is difficult to know and identify.

With Neptune in the 12th subtle atmospheres are detected and there is a response to small changes, attitudes and feelings in others. However, it is a long time before you realize that some of your feelings and frames of mind come, not from yourself, but directly from those around you, with whom you are connected through the unconscious mind. You are *one* with these others, whether you like it or not. Hence Neptune here is a very sensitive placement to have, and its sensitivity is strongly present even in childhood.

The placement is that of the mystic and the yogi, although not invariably so. You are not exempt from life in the everyday world, where Neptune can bestow a pure artistic gift in a quiet way, an ear for music, and a love of life expressing itself in caring for every living thing that needs help — all this in a manner of which you have scarcely any awareness or comprehension.

The great sensitivity of Neptune in this position can give escapist tendencies, both in the form of fantasies and daydreams and in that of addictions; yet you will find that some of your fantasies turn out to be prophetic visions. If you care to develop this aspect, you can integrate metaphysics into your life and can gain a deep emotional understanding of existence in general, and of your own existence in particular. But the first task is to recognize and learn to cope with Neptune's vagueness, incomprehensibility and enormous sensitivity.

PLUTO IN THE 12th

The power complex and urge to uncover every hidden thing receive scant encouragement in the 12th house of the collective, the impersonal, the secluded and the disassociated. Whatever Pluto disinters tends to remain wrapped in a shroud. The planet certainly gives a strong need for power, but not for personal power. Pluto in the 12th causes you to sample life and you are not satisfied deep down until you can enjoy power over life. However, you have difficulty finding out what motivates you, and what you really want. You experience an enormous restlessness inside, a powerful urge to do something without knowing what it is. Thus you live on top of your own volcano.

We need not be surprised, then, that the person with Pluto in the 12th can have a great need to make his or her influence felt in the community, generally without knowing that this is so. Now and then, this placement is found in individuals who have a large following and are sometimes even idolized. This admiration has to do with something collective that they radiate or represent. The individuals, as individuals, need not be at all imposing or impressive and may even provoke opposition. Usually they are unable to exploit their influence or to manipulate the public. And neither do they comprehend their success, for they persist in entertaining the idea that they have got next to nowhere and have achieved far too little.

Pluto in the 12th has a problem in telling apart the feelings that well up inside him from the trends and feelings impinging on him from the outside world. Above all, he is very sensitive to clandestine power-struggles in the environment. Quite often there are deep-rooted, serious, and sometimes unspoken conflicts aroused by the birth of the child with Pluto here. The placement generally gives deplorably little security. In their different ways, none of the 12th house planets have much security, of course, but their significance for the personality can still be understood. Pluto, however, is already scarcely comprehensible to the conscious mind, and here there is a danger that it will cause an uncertainty deep-rooted enough to produce disorientation. But this will need confirmation by the rest of the horoscope.

The person with Pluto in the 12th can be tempted to get a grip on himself and on life through magic and occultism, and may seek to penetrate the laws of nature and the universe. From this can come unlimited insights promising great psychological growth, which usually will not occur until many inner problems have been overcome; one problem being a volcanic restlessness which is rather hard to describe. So Pluto here can indicate emotional inhibitions caused not so much by anxiety, as in the case of Saturn, as by the pressing need to hold himself in check. With Pluto here, there can be an obsession with sex accompanied by a problem in becoming completely sexually mature. However, the individual will without doubt radiate sexuality and those around will certainly respond to it.

What is more, as long as you have not mastered uncertainty, you will not only be troubled by a need for power to which you find it hard to give direct expression, but may also stoop to crooked dealings, manipulation and intrigue. Pluto avoids face-to-face confrontations and gains entry by the "side door." He is stronger than one might think, and has an incredible reserve of talents and abilities which he can put to wonderful use in the service of humanity — but only after clearing away the rubbish in himself.

Chapter Five

Interpreting Combinations

1. Combinations of Planets in Signs and Houses

The house positions of the planets do not provide us with an independent system of interpretation. It cannot be emphasized enough how everything in the chart hangs together. Therefore, when we have gained an impression of the potential effects of the planets in the houses, we must combine our results with other factors such as the planets in the signs, the elements and crosses, the polarities, etc. The special importance of the planets in the sign is that they always reveal the way in which a planetary factor will manifest itself. On combining this with the house placement, we identify the life-sphere in which this mode of manifestation of the given psychic factor will occur. This point has already been considered in Chapter Four. For example, there we saw the difference in background and effect between Mercury in Gemini in the 8th, and Mercury in Scorpio in the 3rd. In order to deal methodically with the problem we can set to work as follows.

First we examine the natural disposition and significance of the planet itself. Having made sure of this, we then take the sign in which the planet stands and relate the mode of expression of the sign to the nature of the planet. We have already gone into this in Volume 2 in this series, so there is no need to dwell on it here. Once we have combined the nature of the planet with its mode of expression as given by the sign, we can determine the trend as given by the house. Therefore, when we know the key-notes of the planets, signs and houses, we can work out the meanings and effects for ourselves without having to rely on any reference work. By way of example, let us look at the Sun in Aquarius in the 5th house.

A person with the Sun in Aquarius needs to express his ego and identity in an Aquarian way by conceding to others the same right to stress their individualities as he exercises to stress his; therefore his personality can be insecure. As an air sign he enjoys thinking about many things, and it is important for him to identify emotionally with the subjects of his thoughts. He likes to reflect on people's attitudes and reactions, and has a penchant for psychology, and an uncanny knack of knowing what is going on in others under the cloak of external behavior. He can chew the cud and brood over it for a long time (the fixed sign influence!). This, together with a natural communicativeness, is responsible for his love of freedom and belief in the equality of each individual. But he realizes only too well that we all have our human problems and shortcomings, and that simply calling people free and equal does not necessarily make them so. Fixed cross people care little for outward show when this does not serve some inner purpose. Hence the Aquarian can create the impression of being someone who subverts authority and social mores. This is both the result of the notion of the intrinsic equality of all men and women, and an expression of the struggle within himself, in which the authority of the conscious mind is continually challenged by indefinable emotional factors emanating from the unconscious.

Turning now to what is implied by the Sun in the 5th, we may be struck by the apparently contradictory nature of the placements. For what is going on when the Sun is in the 5th? In the 5th the Sun promotes full expression of the individuality:

the person lays great emphasis on himself and wants to take the lead, to be the kingpin and so on. But this is something with which the Aquarian Sun does not feel entirely comfortable. The Aquarian Sun is in accord with adventurousness and a love of life indicated by the 5th house, but is not so well suited to the power-loving and leadership side of the house. So what does he do? Does he decline to take the lead, or does he fail to behave like an Aquarian? Such questions are based on a mis-understanding. All too often, unfortunately, the mistake is made of thinking that conflicting factors cancel one another out and omitting them from the overall assessment of the chart. But this is an infraction of the rules of interpretation. Each psychic factor always seeks to express itself in its own fashion, because each factor is irreducible.

What is the actual effect, then, of the Sun in Aquarius in the 5th? For its own part, the Aquarian Sun encourages him to grant free scope to others, to let them seize their opportunities and to treat them as equals. However, he will not realize that at the same time he is hogging the limelight, is occupying the center of the stage and is either taking the initiative in some-thing (probably to do with reform) or, at the very least, has leadership pretensions.

It is remarkable how little he suspects what he is doing; invariably he completely identifies himself with his Aquarian Sun sign. When the truth is pointed out, he will look amazed, since this was never his intention. And yet he will persist in taking the initiative — even though he may have some qualms about it — and will head some movement, exercise a measure of authority and, whether it is his intention or no, end up sitting on governing bodies and committees. But all this is done in an Aquarian manner, so that he goes through the motions of being democratic even though he is acting in a very 5th house way.

As the above example illustrates, certain combinations of sign and house are not entirely easy to handle, and sometimes they are downright problematical — and this is before the aspects are taken into account! Also, it will be evident that a Leo Sun in the 5th, although seeking to develop in the self-same area of life, will have an effect that is quite different from that of an Aquarian Sun there. Therefore interpretations of the planets in the houses can never be the same for everyone: the background influence of the signs has to be considered before we can see the whole picture.

In the light of the foregoing, it is easier to understand what is meant by the older astrological texts when they inform us that a planet creates difficulties when it is "bad" by sign but "good" by house. Certainly there is no need to worry ourselves sick over a bad placement, for what is meant by its being bad? When, according to traditional astrology, a planet is in its detriment by sign, this means that the planet finds it hard to express its essential nature in that sign. An obvious candidate is our example of the Sun in Aquarius. The Sun is a psychic factor that indicates the self; it emphasizes the self. An Aquarian finds it impossible to concede this power to the Sun, since he sees all too well that others have their own egos and are also wishing to develop. Thus the Sun will not feel completely welcome in Aquarius. But this certainly does not mean that all Aquarians are bad by definition or that they function unsatisfactorily.

And so we have to treat sweeping assertions of this sort with great circumspection. As our short study has shown us, someone with the Sun in Aquarius in the 5th house is striving for a more forceful expression of the Sun than he can manage or even conceive. This can create problems, but not invariably so. And, anyway, several other factors in the horoscope have to point in the same direction. However, we can safely say that a Leo Sun feels marvelous when it is occupying the 5th house. But this is no guarantee that the owner of the chart will be equally happy. For instance, he can have such an overwhelming need to feel important that he can become frustrated if he is not the permanent center of attention, or if he is not cast in the starring role. That would be a situation with which the person with an Aquarian Sun in the 5th would find easier to cope with.

To sum up: all according to its nature, a planet in a given sign will find it easier to realize its potential in one house than in another; yet the planet does exercise some influence in the house in which it is posited regardless of whether or not the background is in harmony with it. Therefore, although a tense background can create problems, there are a number of situations in which the tension can offer the ideal solution for certain problems, so that it is not always desirable to have a planet in its own sign and house. Exaggeration of the planetary symbolism can then take place all too easily, with the individual becoming the author of his or her own troubles.

Hence it is best to refrain from value judgments such as, "This planet is well placed and that planet is badly placed," because the issues are much more complex in practice and much more finely balanced. It is far preferable to say, "The pattern of your psychic contents is so and so, and you operate with them in such and such areas." This is a professionally neutral statement and does not convey a sense of fate or doom.

2. SPECIFIC INTERPRETATION DUALITIES

As we have seen in the above example, certain factors can have conflicting sign and house positions. A quite lively conflict occurs when different elements are involved, so the following placements are liable to bring problems which are different in kind from the opposition problem in the foregoing example:

a) planets in fire signs in earth houses, and the reverse;

b) planets in earth signs in fire houses;

c) planets in air signs in water houses, and the reverse;

d) planets in water signs in air houses.

In placements of this sort, the specific nature of a planet (as far as the background is concerned) finds it hard to express itself freely. What happens when Mercury is in Taurus in the 9th house? Here Mercury is in a quiet, slow, reserved and somewhat passive sign, which inclines the individual to put everything on a firm basis and to reflect well before reacting. Thinking and communication are cautious and unpretentious, substantial and thorough, and are seldom flighty or exuberant. But, in the 9th house (a fire house) thinking and communication must express in an enthusiastic and opportunist terrain: a difficult matter for Mercury when it is in such a security-minded sign as Taurus, especially as the 9th house has as its point of departure a sense of adventure and material uncertainty. The material uncertainty comes in because, by not relying on material security, we find it easier to expand, to widen our horizons, to travel and to study. Thus Mercury is caught between two potential forms of expression, between security and insecurity. The individual is compelled to act as if he or she were brisker than he or she really is, and it pushed to enter an area in which, because of the Taurean background, he or she does not feel at home — even though, in itself, Mercury is thoroughly at home in the 9th house!

In this example we have a rather more serious conflict than that produced by the Sun in Aquarius in the 5th, which could still manage to express itself as an air factor in a fire house, that is to say, as a communicative ability in an intuitive house. There is no direct confrontation like that between wanting security and operating on a basis of insecurity as in the case of the earth/fire duality — which can obviously create acute problems over giving shape to the planetary factors concerned. So what do we see in practice in many instances? Either additional emphasis laid on the planet (Mercury in Taurus in the 9th can, for example, be very dogmatic or full of fads), *or* problems in developing the factor due to hesitancy (the individual with Mercury in Taurus in the 9th keeps his own counsel, but when he eventually sets to work he is unstoppable).

Air and water, too, present this kind of problem, for what happens when a strongly emotional planet has to express itself in a communicative and intellectual area of life? Say Mercury is posited in Cancer in the 11th house: these people will have difficulty in putting into words everything they feel rising up within. They need time for this. They understand their feelings perfectly, but simply cannot explain them. Therefore, when you question them, the answer is not likely to be on the tip of the tongue; they will probably give you some sort of answer, but the true response, or what they really intend to say, comes only later — perhaps not until some days later. Now when this factor seeks realization in such a communicative and intellectual terrain as that of the 11th house, the house of contact with friends and the public, we may anticipate that certain problems will arise. Mercury here makes these people want to have their say at every opportunity, and they will take part either by adopting a certain attitude or by playing a certain role (so typical of Cancer). But it may be that either they will not respond adequately to what is going on among friends, or they will create a false impression by a wrong attitude or by play-acting; and so they can become estranged from friends in a subtle way. They will be drawn to emotional friendships, but do not make particularly good impressions when talking and exchanging views with friends. So a dilemma is caused by a difference in the elemental qualities of sign and house.

People with this kind of chart can be advised of the duality and can have its difficult side pointed out, but should also be shown its good side. For example, people with Mercury in a water sign will usually be able to rely on feelings in communicative situations when they want to find out what is going on beneath the surface in their circle of friends. In fact there are a number of plus points in what is otherwise a very difficult placement.

3. THE FURTHER HOROSCOPE

Another nuance is the planet's relationship to the rest of the horoscope. Of course, we have to look at its position in the light of the elements and crosses but, when we have done that, we should examine other significant situations in the chart. To give an example, a person who has many planets in Gemini, and Mercury in Cancer will already have an air/water, or thinking/feeling, duality. But when all these planets are active in the 8th house, a water house, then Mercury in Cancer in the 8th will show to better advantage than the planets in Gemini will in that house, even if the Sun and Moon and the personal planets are all in Gemini. In other words, Gemini does not combine well with the 8th house, but Cancer does.

However, when the Sun and Moon are in Gemini, the element associated with consciousness (therefore the superior element) will be air, and planets in the element water will lie in the unconscious and so come to the fore involuntarily. In our example, this would mean that Mercury in the 8th has a compulsive aspect due not to its sign and house position taken on their own, but to its combined sign-and-house position as affected by the remainder of the horoscope. Once more we are reminded that we should never give blind credence to a stock interpretation taken out of a book. We must always look at the individual factors in the light of the whole, and then many refinements can be introduced.

And so, planetary factors in sign and house will show to better advantage when several others factors support them by pointing in the same direction. Hence the old astrological rule:

With one indication, there is a possibility;
with two, there is a probability;
with three or more, there is a virtual certainty.

Now, where we have three or more indications, they can influence each other even without mutual aspects, and can easily make themselves felt in other traits of character.

4. Dispositorships

One point we must not forget are the so-called dispositorships, of which there are two kinds: the dispositorship by a planet of a certain sign and the dispositorship by a planet of a certain house. The following points are important:

1. Sign dispositor or ruler: Each sign has a planet that naturally belongs to it. Mars is the ruler of Aries, Venus of Taurus, Mercury of Gemini, the Moon of Cancer, etc. We call this planet the dispositor of the sign. If there are other planets in the sign, the planet "rules" them. For example: when the Sun and Mercury are in Aries, the planet Mars is the dispositor of the Sun and Mercury because these two planets are in Mars' sign. It does not matter where Mars itself stands; if the Sun and Mercury are in Aries, then Mars rules them.

2. House dispositor or ruler: The cusp, or beginning, of each house stands in a certain sign. The house ruler is the planet belonging to the sign containing its cusp. For example, let's consider that the 3rd house starts in Sagittarius. Because Jupiter is lord of Sagittarius, it will also rule the 3rd house regardless of where it is placed in the chart. Each planet that stands in the 3rd house will come under Jupiter's rulership. But if the 3rd house starts in Pisces, its lord will be Neptune and any planets in the third house will be ruled by Neptune. So house rulerships are quite clear-cut.

As you will see from the following example, the sign and house ruler can be one and the same. If the 6th house starts in Aquarius, then Uranus rules the 6th. And if there is a planet in the 6th house in Aquarius, the planet Venus say, than Uranus rules Venus — not only as sign ruler, but also as house ruler — because Venus is in the 6th. Thus house and sign ruler can be one and the same, but are not always so. If Venus is posited in the 6th but in Pisces, then Uranus is house ruler of Venus but Neptune is its sign ruler, and, naturally, the effect is different.

It is important to pay attention to the rulers of the houses: the activities of any planets in a house will be amplified in an unmistakable manner by them. So much is involved in this subject that a separate volume will have to be devoted to it. But we can say in the meantime that a planet in a house makes a promise; but the lord (or ruler) of the house will decide, by its own placement and aspects, whether or not the promise is fulfilled and, if so, *how* it is fulfilled. This means that when we have a splendid planet standing in a splendid house, the prospects tend to look very bright; yet their promise will be fulfilled only by fits and starts when the house ruler is beset by difficulties in the chart.

5. SUMMARY

In summing up I would advise the reader to pay attention to the following points in the order given:

1. A horoscope is a unity: the houses are not a detached part of it but are closely connected with the rest of the chart.

2. Each individual house is linked in many different ways with other houses, quite apart from the question of aspects.

3. A planet in a house tells us something about which psychic energy manifests itself, or is deployed, in the area of life represented by that house. In other words, it tells us *what* we do or

which energy we use (which planet) in *what* circumstances or area of life (what house).

4. A planet stands not only in a house but also in a sign, so the background influence of the sign must be taken into consideration when making an interpretation. A planet in any sign functions in the manner indicated by that sign and therefore can do well in some houses and encounter problems in others. In other words, the activities of planets in houses are modified by the signs in which they stand.

5. A planet in a certain sign and house is not an independent entity, but is subject to the control of the ruler or rulers. What this planet does, by its sign and house position, is to promise various things; its promises need verification by reference to the sign ruler and house ruler, which usually occupy another sign and another house, and may have rather different aspects.

BIBLIOGRAPHY

Adler, G. Op verkenning in het onbewuste: Freud, Adler, Jung. Hilversum, 1934.

Arroyo, S. *Astrology, Psychology and the Four Elements.* Sebastopol, CA: CRCS, 1975.

Becker, E. *The Denial of Death.* New York: Free Press, Macmillan, 1985.

de Vore, N. *Encyclopedia of Astrology.* Totowa, NJ: Littlefield, Adams, 1976.

Duijker, H. C. J. *Encyclopedie van psychologie.* Amsterdam, Netherlands: 1976.

Greene, L. *Saturn: A New Look at an Old Devil.* York Beach, ME: Samuel Weiser, 1976.

Hall, M. P. *Astrological Keywords.* Totowa, NJ: Littlefield, Adams, 1975.

Hamaker-Zondag, K. M. *Aspects and Personality.* York Beach, ME: Samuel Weiser, 1990.

———. *Astro-Psychology.* London: Aquarian Press/HarperCollins, 1978. See *Psychological Astrology.*

———. *Handbook of Horary Astrology.* York Beach, ME: Samuel Weiser, 1993.

———. *Planetary Symbolism in the Horoscope.* Jungian Symbolism & Astrology, Vol. 2. York Beach, ME: Samuel Weiser, 1985.

———. *Psychological Astrology: A Synthesis of Jungian Psychology and Astrology.* York Beach, ME: Samuel Weiser, 1990; London: Aquarian Press, 1989. Previously published as *Astro-Psychology.*

———. *The Twelfth House.* York Beach, ME: Samuel Weiser, 1992.

———. Angstfactoren in de Horoscoop. In: Spica: Podium der Hendendaagse Astrologie, Jaargang 5 NR. 1, April, 1981.

Hand, R. *Planets in Youth.* West Chester, PA: Whitford Press, 1977.

Harding, M. E. *The "I" and the "Not-I".* Princeton, NJ: Princeton University Press, 1965.

———. *Psychic Energy*. Princeton, NJ: Princeton University Press, 1963.

Hone, M. E. *The Modern Textbook of Astrology*. London: L. N. Fowler & Co., 1970.

Jacobi, J. *Masks of the Soul*. London: Darton, Longman & Todd, 1977.

———. *The Psychology of C. G. Jung*. New Haven, CT: Yale University Press, 1973; and London: Routlege & Kegan Paul, 1942.

Jung, C. G. *The Archetypes and the Collective Unconscious*. Collected Works, Vol. 9, edited by G. Adler, et al. Princeton, NJ: Princeton University Press, 1968.

———. *The Collected Works of C. G. Jung*, trans. R. F. C. Hull, Bollingen Series XX. Vol. 8: *The Structure and Dynamics of the Psyche*, copyright © 1960, 1969 by Princeton University Press.

———. *The Development of Personality*. Collected Works, Vol, 17, edited by G. Adler, et al. Princeton, NJ: Princeton University Press, 1954.

———. Het ik en het onbewuste. Den Haag, Netherlands: 1965.

———. *Psychological Types*, Collected Works, Vol. 6, London: Routledge & Kegan Paul, 1977.

———. *The Structure and Dynamics of the Psyche*. Collected Works, Vol. 8, edited by G. Adler et al. Princeton, NJ: Princeton University Press, 1968; and London: Routledge & Kegan Paul, 1960.

Kant, Immanuel. Anthropologie, par. 5. Citation from Club Zurich: Die Kulturelle Bedeutung der Komplexen Psychologie. Festschrift zum 60. Geburtstag von C. G. Jung, Berlin, Germany: 1935. Teil I: Toni Wolff: Einfuhrung in die Grundlagen der Komplexen Psychologie, p. 52.

Kuhr, E. C. "Psychologische Horoskopdeutung." *Analyse und Synthese*. Band II, Wien, Austria: 1951.

Kündig, H. *Das Horoskop*. Die Berechnung, Darstellung und Erklärung. Zurich, Switzerland: Ansata Verlag, 1950.

Laplanche, J. *Life and Death in Psychoanalysis*. Translated by J. Mehlman. Baltimore, MD: Johns Hopkins University Press, 1985.

Meier, C. A. *Bewusstsein*. Lehrbuch der Komplexen Psychologie C. G. Jung. Band III, Olten, Switzerland: Walter Verlag, 1975.

Now available in English as *Consciousness,* The Psychology of C. G Jung, Vol. 3, trans. David Roscoe. Boston: Sigo Press 1989.

———. *Bewusstsein.* Erkenntnistheorie und Bewusstsein. bewusstwerdung bei C. G. Jung, Olten, Switzerland: Walter Verlag, 1975.

Meyer, M. R. *A Handbook for the Humanistic Astrologer.* New York: Doubleday, 1974.

Pelletier, R. *Planets in Houses.* West Chester, PA: Whitford Press, 1978.

Ring, T. *Astrologische Menschenkunde.* Band II, Frieburg, Germany: Hermann Bauer Verlag, 1969.

Rudhyar, D. *The Astrological Houses.* Sebastopol, CA: CRCS, 1986.

Sury, K. van. *Worterbuch der Psychologie und ihrer Grenzgebiete.* Olten, Switzerland: Walter Verlag, 1974.

Tyl, N. *Aspects and Houses in Astrology.* St. Paul, MN: Llewellyn, 1977.

———. *The Houses, Their Signs and Planets.* St. Paul, MN: Llewellyn, 1977.

von Franz, M.-L., & J. Hillman. *Lectures on Jung's Typology.* Zurich, Switzerland: Spring Verlag, 1971.

Whitmont, E. C. *The Symbolic Quest: Basic Concepts of Analytical Psychology.* Princeton, NJ: Princeton University Press, 1969.

Wickes, F. G. *The Inner World of Childhood.* Englewood Cliffs, NJ: Prentice Hall, 1976 and London, 1977.

———. *The Inner World of Choice.* Englewood Cliffs, NJ: Prentice Hall, 1963 and London, 1977.

Wolff, T. *Studien Zu C. G. Jungs Psychologie.* Zurich, Switzerland: Rhein Verlag, 1959.

INDEX

Karen Hamaker-Zondag is one of the leading members of the Astrological Foundation, *Arcturus*, in Holland. She is a graduate of the University of Amsterdam with doctoral degrees in social geography and environmental engineering. Her post-graduate study of psychology, astrology, and parapsychology has inspired a counseling practice where she combines Jungian concepts with astrological theory. She is the author of *Aspects and Personality, Handbook of Horary Astrology, Planetary Symbolism in the Horoscope, Psychological Astrology,* and *The Twelfth House,* all published by Weiser. She has lectured extensively in Holland, Belgium, Germany, England, the United States of America, Switzerland, Scandinavia, and Canada.